TABLE OF CONTENTS

INTRODUCTION FROM THE EDITOR

Thank you for purchasing XSI Illuminated: Foundation! We've put a lot of work into making this book as useful a resource as possible, and I'd like to go over some of the key features.

First of all, Foundation is written by instructors at Mesmer Animation Labs rather than programmers or demo artists, with comprehension and retention in mind. You'll find this material easy to read and understand, and theoretical and artistic discussion is included with the technical information. The tutorials are not specific recipes; they are flexible exercises that address "How?" and "Why?" instead of simply telling you what to do. The tutorials are also extensively tested for functionality and accuracy, which brings me to my next point...

Many 3D animation books are expensive, include a semi-functional CD, and are printed on a large scale, only once. Unfortunately, computer graphics software is not only written once; it changes very rapidly, resulting in a lot of out-of-date and inaccurate printed material. Our idea is to self-publish smaller books, in small print runs, and have our supplementary material, such as scene files and additional tutorials, available online (at www.mesmer.com/books/) instead of on a set-in-stone CD. That way, the books themselves are inexpensive and easily updated, the supplements can be updated and refined, and new content can be added any time. This also means that your feedback is welcome, and can actually be applied!

I hope you enjoy using XSI Illuminated: Foundation as much as we've enjoyed creating it. I am confident that you will find it to be an effective learning tool. If you do find it valuable, keep an eye out for XSI Illuminated: Special Effects and XSI Illuminated: Character Animation, as well as updates to Foundation as Softimage|XSI evolves. Have fun!

Brian Demong, Editor and Mesmer Production Manager

AUTHOR BIOS

ANTHONY ROSSANO is the Chief Executive Officer of Mesmer, Inc. After receiving his Bachelor of Arts in Psychology from the University of Washington, Rossano went to work for the Microsoft Corporation. In 1988, Anthony Rossano deserted his post at Microsoft to found Mesmer, Inc.

Technically proficient in a wide range of authoring and animation programs, Rossano's expertise lies in Softimage 3D|Extreme, Softimage|XSI, and Alias|Wavefront Maya Composer. Anthony has taught all over the world, and counts among his training clients PDI, LucasArts, Tippett Studios, Electronic Arts, Microsoft, Monolith, Psygnosis, Boeing, Lockheed, and Lear.

Anthony is a Level 2 certified Softimage Instructor, and has been working with XSI throughout its development and beta testing phases. Anthony is the author of Inside Softimage 3D, published by New Riders Publications, as well as numerous magazine articles and web tutorials.

SHINSAKU ARIMA is the Director of Mesmer Berkeley, where he is also a Softimage instructor. After receiving a Bachelor of Fine Arts from the University of Southern California, Arima worked as a fine artist for three years before putting his large-scale sculpting endeavor on hold and embarking on a 3D animation adventure.

After two and half years of working mainly with Softimage|3D and Alias|Wavefront Maya, Arima has taught 3D animation at numerous schools, including DeAnza College in Cupertino, Academy of Art College in San Francisco, Ex'Pression Center for New Media in Emeryville, and co-instructing at the San Francisco Art Institute with a Pixar artist. Primarily, he has been teaching at Mesmer Animation Labs in San Francisco, which recently relocated to Berkeley. Shinsaku is a Softimage|3D 201 certified instructor.

ACKNOWLEDGEMENTS

Anthony says:

"I'd like to thank the Softimage Educational team, Pierre Tousignant and Gino Vincelli, for giving me the opportunity to become involved with this incredible software tool, for taking the time to answer my questions and putting up with my incessant whining. Thanks also to my new Apple iBook, without whom this would not have been possible, and to the mental health professionals behind the bar in pubs and clubs around Seattle."

Shin says:

"Thanks to Anthony Rossano for giving me a great opportunity, Matt Ontiveros for teaching me my first Softimage class, Martin MacNamara for giving me my first 3D teaching job, and Nathan Vogel for letting me work on my first 3D production job. Thanks also to Jesse, Rachel, and Juan for being excellent company and fabulous party hosts, Serkan Salah for alpha testing, Guido Zimmerman for his great help on the illustrations, and to all my students, for teaching me how to teach. Above all, I would like to thank my mother and father, my wife Deirdre, and my two wonderful daughters Gabriela and Rachel for giving me endless joy in my life."

Brian says:

"I'd like to thank God, for everything; my father Charles Demong, Jr. for opening the door to computer animation for me; Karen Zinker, for her help on this project; my mother Paula Brody, my beautiful wife Sarah, Carol Demong, the Stewart family, Eb and Tandy, and The House of Many, for all their support."

CONTACT INFORMATION

Mesmer Inc. provides the content of the book as is, and makes no warranties regarding the accuracy or completeness of the material within it. That having been said, we welcome your feedback. Please tell us how we can make this book better and better!

Questions of a technical nature, for instance those regarding software installation or hardware configuration, will not be answered.

You may email us at: info@mesmer.com

You may write to us at:

> Mesmer Animation Labs
> 1116 NW 54th Street
> Seattle WA 98107

You may call us at: 206.782.8004

Please check out our other wonderful course offering, onsite classes, and distance learning at www.mesmer.com.

DIGITAL CONTENT FOR THIS BOOK

All the scene files, models, and other digital information used in this book may be downloaded free of charge from http://www.mesmer.com/books/

You may also use an ftp client to get the material. Direct your ftp software to ftp.mesmer.com/books/XSIfoundation then log in as anonymous with your email as the password. Within that directory is a zipped file named XSIFoundation.zip for PC based users, and a file named XSIFoundation.tar for Irix users.

HELP FOR TEACHERS

We have thoughfully provided free courseware building materials to make life easier for instructors who choose to use our book in class. If you are an educator, you may download the file XSIFoundTeacherResource.PDF which contains lesson plans, chapter outlines, sample tests and more useful material. You may obtain this material from the web at http://www.mesmer.com/books/ or from our ftp site at ftp.mesmer.com/books/XSIfoundation

XSI Hot Key Cheat Sheet*

1 (F1 in SI3D mode)	Model module
2 (F2 in SI3D mode)	Animate module
3 (F3 in SI3D mode)	Render module
4 (F4 in SI3D mode)	Simulate module
o	Orbit-mode (L = free, M = horizontal, R = vertical)
z	Zoom- and Pan-mode (L = pan, M = zoom in, R = zoom out)
s	Multi-mode view navigator (L = pan, M = dolly, R = orbit)
p	Dolly-mode (L = slow, M = medium, R = fast)
Shift-Space Bar	Multi-select (add objects to selection)
Space Bar	Selection mode (L = node, M = branch, R = tree)
f	Frame selection
a	Frame all
h	Hide or Unhide selection
Shift-h	Unhide all
Shift-Enter	Info selection
Enter	Open General property page for current selection
Alt-Enter	Open property page with all properties for current selection
c	Rotate object (L = X, M = Y, R = Z)
v	Translate object (L = X, M = Y, R = Z)
x	Scale object (L = X, M = Y, R = Z)
Shift-x	Scale object uniformly (L = slow, M = medium, R = fast)
Ctrl	Activate grid-snapping
t	Tag points (also enters Point Selection mode)
d	Duplication tool
Ctrl-d	Duplicate selected
m	Move point tool
w	Weight-map paint tool
Ctrl-w	Brush property page
Esc	End mode
k	Save keyframe on marked parameters
q	Render region tool (L = draw, M = toggle on/off, R = refresh)
Ctrl-x	Cut
Ctrl-c	Copy
Ctrl-v	Paste
Ctrl-z	Undo
Ctrl-y	Redo
Delete	Delete selection
Shift-Delete	Delete all (Careful! You can't Undo this)

* L, M, and R denote the left, middle, and right mouse buttons, respectively.

THE XSI INTERFACE AND BASIC CONCEPTS

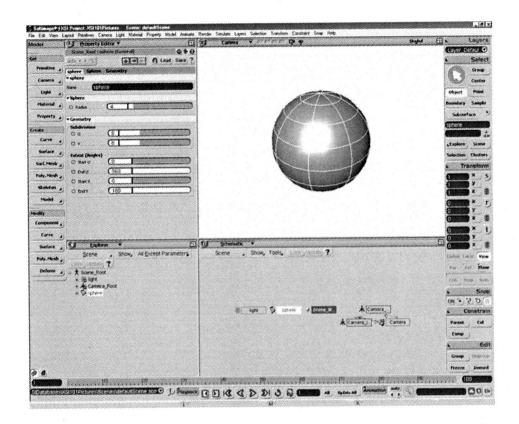

IN THIS CHAPTER YOU WILL LEARN ABOUT:

- Starting up the software
- The interface layout
- The four modules - Model, Animate, Render and Simulate
- The Main Command Panel
- Opening and saving Scenes
- Navigation Hotkeys
- Objects and Properties
- The Explorer and the Schematic View

INTRODUCTION

When the fine folks at Softimage released the first version of their new flagship animation and special effects package, XSI 1.0, earlier this year, Softimage users all over the world heaved a collective sigh of relief. Finally it was out the door. Years of waiting were over. Now came the question: was XSI 1.0 good enough to go head to head with all the best that Softimage's competitors had to offer? The answer, a qualified 'perhaps' was not terribly reassuring. XSI 1.0, while built on a fundamentally strong and impressive architecture, lacked some basic tools that would make life easier for production animators accustomed to long days and hard deadlines.

Now Softimage prepares to release a new version of the software, XSI 1.5. How does this version change the equation? Let's find out together.

In a nutshell, XSI 1.5 is all that 1.0 should have been upon its release. XSI 1.5 fills in the gaps, nails on a wealth of new tools and features, then polishes the surface to a high gleam with additional workflow enhancements.

XSI 1.5 is complete, it's coherent, it's faster and more stable, it has big new features and small workflow improvements.

XSI 1.5 maintains the same overall organization of the 1.0 release.

Drop menus along the top of the window replicate all the functions found in the graphical user interface (GUI) in case you should need something in one layout that is generally found in another.

In the interface, the major tools and functions are divided into 4 modules, Model, Animate, Simulate and Render. Each module is designed to present you with a set of tools that are all related to one part of the creative process. When you select a module by mouse or by keyboard, only those tools relevant to your current task show up in the left-hand stack of menu cells.

The Simulate module is new to XSI 1.5. Within Simulate users will find all the controls necessary for particle systems, cloth, softbody dynamics, and forces like gravity, vortex and wind.

In the middle of your monitor are the views, which can show you the 3D space in your scene, the view from a camera or a spotlight, or any number of other perspectives on your world. You can also dock the Animation Editor, the Dopesheet, the Explorer, a file browser, a Property Editor, the Render Tree, or even a web browser into these view windows.

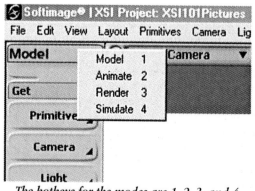

Right clicking in windows other than the 3D views will generally also bring up a context sensitive menu. This menu will show you options for use in that window, or if you are in the middle of modeling, it will show you various modeling operations you could perform at that point.

The hotkeys for the modes are 1, 2, 3, and 4 (F1, F2, F3 and F4 in SI3D mode)

On the right side of the screen lies the Main Command Panel, or MCP. The MCP is a consistent UI element, present in each module, containing buttons for those functions you might need at any time. The MCP houses the Scale, Rotate and Translate buttons, all the menus for selecting objects and object components, the controls for layering, grouping, and parenting, and the standard edit commands, including instances and duplicates.

STARTING SOFTIMAGE│XSI ON IRIX AND NT

Although XSI is identical in functionality on both SGI and Windows NT and 2000 platforms, launching the application is slightly different.

On Windows systems, go to the START menu on the main taskbar and then click on the 'Programs' option, then 'Softimage Products', then 'Softimage XSI'.

On IRIX systems, log in to the user account that has been configured for XSI, and get a shell window by choosing 'Desktop→Open Unix Shell' from the main menu. In that shell, type 'xsi' and hit enter to launch the program.

THE INTERFACE AND MODULES:

All the options and commands available within XSI are collected into the top menu bar in a series of cascading drop-down menus. Some of these menus are also found elsewhere in the interface in a graphical, easier to use form, but some options are found only in the top menu bar. Because all the options in the application are available in the top menu system, you can flexibly re-configure and customize the graphical user interface to suit your needs while still being sure that you can get to any command you might want.

File   Edit   View   Layout   Primitives   Camera   Light   Material   Property   Model   Animate   Render   Simulate   Layers   Selection   Transform   Constraint   Snap   Help

The top menu bar has all the menu options and features in the program

The menus that are not duplicated elsewhere in the interface are the File Menu, the View Menu, the Layout Menu, and the Help menu.

The File menu contains all the commands necessary to Open, Save, Import, Export, and Merge scenes and models, and the User Preferences and Keyboard hotkey mappings.

The View menu contains some options that seem redundant, but in fact operate in slightly different ways from the other areas of the interface where the commands are found.

View→Views has the commands to open the Animation Editor, the Animation Mixer, the Schematic, and other useful views into new windows of their own, rather than into one of the four view windows.

The View menu has the commands for customizing the interface, creating new toolbars and task bars, and it has a list of view filter options that apply to the entire session, rather than just one individual window. For instance, toggling View→Points on will show points in all the view windows, whereas toggling Show→Points from one window title bar will display points in only that view.

The Layout Menu

Softimage® | XSI Project: X

| File | Edit | View | Layout | Primitiv |

New Scene	Ctrl+N
Open...	Ctrl+O
Merge...	
Save	Ctrl+S
Save As...	

| New Project... | |
| Project Manager... | |

| Source Paths... | |

| Import | ▶ |
| Export | ▶ |

| User Preferences... | |
| Keyboard Mapping... | |

| Exit | Ctrl+Q |

The File Menu

The Layout menu is responsible for all the tasks related to creating and editing custom user interfaces. If you mess up your layout you can also restore the defaults here.

The Help menu has the access to the Windows-based help system, and to the Softimage web site.

The other menus are the same as the graphical versions, and will be explained later in this chapter.

WORKFLOW

The menus on the left side change for each of XSI's workflow modules: Model, Animate, Render and Simulate.

Proper workflow organizes to the process of animation. It creates a process with an achievable result. Workflow defines the most efficient manner of producing the result required. If you create a single object, then animate it, next apply color, then model it some more, add more color, create another object, and then follow the same meandering path again, it will be very difficult for you to complete your work. Segmenting the various duties of animation into workflow steps allows you to move through the process more efficiently, in an assembly line fashion.

THE FOUR MODULES OF XSI

Softimage | XSI is a completely integrated product that is then broken up into four different modules that correspond to different phases of the workflow process. Each of the modules replaces all of the menu cells on the left, while leaving the common menu commands and buttons in the Main Command Panel to the right side of the screen.

These modules are Model, Animate, Render and Simulate. You can enter these modules either by clicking on the Module name that is currently active (in the top left corner of the interface) and selecting a new Module from the list that cascades down, or by pressing the hotkeys that represent them: F1 for Model, F2 for Animate, F3 for Render and F4 for Simulate (or the numbers 1, 2, 3 and 4 depending on how you have your preferences set.)

MODEL

You start your workflow in the Model module, where you construct all your scene elements. Model's tools enable you to create objects from primitive shapes, draw curves, develop surfaces from those curves, and do all manner of editing of the models you make. Here you may also create Cameras, Lights, and new object Properties. The Model module contains all the tools for editing polygonal objects, for booleans, for blending and merging, and for working with Subdivision Surfaces.

ANIMATE

While regular animation keyframing and playback controls are always available at the bottom of the screen, the Animate module contains all the commands for adding different animation effects to your scene.

Here are the special menu commands for attaching objects to a path, for adding animateable deformations, and creating custom property pages.

The Animate module also contains the special tools for setting up virtual actors, assigning inverse kinematic skeletons, assigning skin, adjusting skeletal deformations, and weighting the skin to the IK skeletons.

Finally, the Animate module contains the Actions menu cells, which Store, Load and Save animation actions for use in the Non-Linear Animation Mixer.

RENDER

When your modeling, animation, and acting is complete, you move to the last steps: applying materials, shaders, and setting up the render.

Here in the Render Module, you can assign color and texture to the objects in your scene, create lights and Cameras, work with the Render Tree to build complex shader networks, and set up render passes and partitions.

Here also are the controls for the Render Region, the full frame preview, and the final render.

SIMULATE

The Simulate module (new with XSI 1.5) organizes all the dynamic simulations tools together into one workflow area. In the Simulate module you can create particle systems and physical forces like gravity, wind, and Vortices. You can create fluid simulations to imitate water flowing or splashing. You can create cloth simulations to drape material over a model. You can set up soft body collisions on objects so that collisions and gravity affect your characters, and you can create simple explosions.

ORGANIZATION WITHIN MODES

Inside each mode the menu commands on the left side are further organized to help you figure out where the tools you need are located. Within the Model Module, the stack is subdivided into three areas: Get, Create and Modify. The tools in the Get area help you bring new premade objects (like cameras, lights, or primitives), while those in the Create section help you make things from scratch. Finally, the Modify section contains tools you need to clean up models, modify the surface, move points, etc.

The Animate Module is divided into sections labeled Get, Create, Deform, Actions, and Tools.

The Render Module contains sections for Get, Modify, Render, Pass, and Tools.

The View Menu

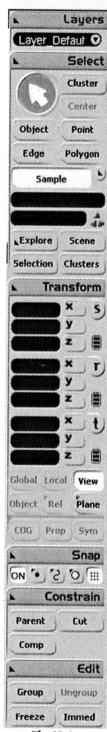

*The Main
Command Panel*

The Simulate Module contains sections for Get, Create, Modify and Tools.

When you read or speak the name of a command, it helps to say the section of the module it is in, like "Create a Curve with Sketch" which would correspond to the Create→Curve→Sketch command in the Model Module. Often by convention the name of the Module is left out, since you will quickly learn which module to be in for each kind of task.

RIGHT SIDE MAIN COMMAND PANEL

The Right side menu and button stack is called the Main Command Panel (MCP), and it contains all the functions that you are likely to use most often as you work in XSI. Using the MCP you can move, scale, and rotate objects, select objects and components of objects like points and knots, look at the animateable properties of objects, duplicate and delete objects and organize your scene into hierarchies, groups and layers. The MCP also has the controls for enabling the snapping options, which make precision modeling a lot easier.

TIMELINE

The timeline at the bottom of the scene shows you the duration of your scene, generally in frames. It has both a scrubber for you to manually set the current frame, and complete playback controls to play the animation in your scene forwards or backwards, rewind, or advance one frame at a time or one key at a time. The timeline also contains the basic keyframing tools, named the AutoKey, the Keyframe button, and the Animation Marking List.

FEEDBACK LINE

At the very bottom of the screen is the feedback (or status) line. This critical area can be a huge help to you as you learn and use XSI. Each time you activate a command the feedback line will show the name of the command on the left side, and a diagram of how each of the three mouse buttons will work with that command. For instance, if you decide to draw a curve with the Create→Curve→Draw CV NURBS command, the status line will tell you that the Left Mouse Button will add a point to the end of the curve, the Middle Mouse Button will add a point in the middle of the curve wherever you point the mouse, and the Right Mouse Button will add a point to the beginning of the curve.

Many commands require you to execute the command, then pick on one or more objects to complete the command. For instance, if you are lofting to create a skin over a series of ribs, you execute the Create→Surface→Loft command, and then you would look into the Feedback line to see that you must now pick with the Left Mouse Button on each rib in turn, and finally complete the command by clicking the Right Mouse Button, which is labeled "End Picking" in the feedback line at the bottom of the screen.

It is almost always a good idea to turn off or complete a command when you are done with it, to avoid accidentally using it again in a way you do not intend. Often you can exit from a command by clicking the Right Mouse Button, but you can always exit a command by tapping the Escape key on your keyboard. Tapping Escape before a command is completed will cancel that command, while hitting Escape after a command is completed will return you to the 'Nil' tool, which means that you won't accidentally do anything you don't want to do.

Whenever you have a question about how to proceed, check the Feedback line.

XSI USER INTERFACE CONVENTIONS

TRIANGLES MEAN DROP MENUS
Whenever you see a small triangle anywhere in the interface, it indicates either that it is a drop menu, or that you can use it to expand or collapse a group of options. For instance, most of the menu cells in the left hand stack have a diagonal triangle in the bottom-right corner, indicating that if you click on them a list of options will pop out. In the same way, the Camera View has a triangle indicating that if you click it you can change the camera view into some other view. The Snap buttons in the MCP have little triangles pointing up and left, which means that if you click the Right Mouse Button on them you will be rewarded with a context sensitive menu offering up further options.

Property pages have a different kind of triangle. It is either pointing down, indicating that the list of properties under that section is fully expanded, or it points right, indicating that the section is collapsed and no properties in that section are showing. You can click on the triangle to toggle it back and forth.

UNDO
XSI has a potentially unlimited undo stack, although by default it is limited to 50 undoes. Every single thing you do during a session can be undone, in the order that you performed the operations. This is called the "undo stack" because new operations are added to the top of the stack, removed from the top when you Undo, and placed back on the stack when you Redo.

The XSI Undo uses the standard Apple/Windows control keys: CTRL-Z to Undo, and CTRL-Y to Redo.

You can view the most recent command on the top of the stack in the feedback line at the bottom left of the screen, and the most recent 25 commands by clicking on the triangle next to it.

You can change the default number of default operations that are undoable by going to the File→User Preferences menu at the top of the screen which will pop up a preferences dialog. In the first tab, labeled "General" you can set the "Number of Undo Levels".

SELECT, SHIFT AND CTRL
To Select objects in XSI, you hold the space bar to enter the standard selection mode. While the spacebar is held down you can draw a rectangle that touches some part of the object you want selected. When you release the mouse that object will become selected, and show highlighted in white in your 3D views.

The timeline controls

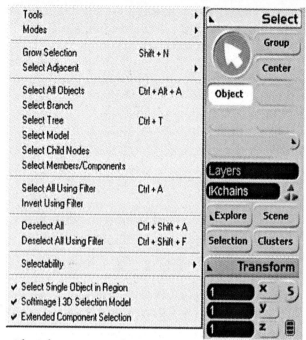

The Selection Menu showing the correct settings for the SI3D selection model

NOTE: Please make certain that your selection options are set correctly: In the Select menu of the MCP on the right side, verify that all three menu items at the bottom are checked on: "Select Single Object in Region", "Softimage 3D Selection Model", and "Extended Component Selection."

When you want to select more than one object, parameter, or property in XSI at a time, you will use the standard Shift and CTRL keys to extend, shrink, or toggle the selection. For instance, if you had three spheres and one was selected, you could hold Shift and then select the others to add them.

Since holding the space bar, Shift and CTRL while accurately clicking requires the manual dexterity of a concert pianist, you can also use just the space bar and the CTRL key while clicking on objects to toggle them between selected and unselected.

CONTEXT-SENSITIVE MENUS

In some places other than the regular geometry view menus, clicking with your Right Mouse Button will pop up a context-sensitive menu with special commands that are active only there and on the object you were over. For example, in the Explorer and Schematic views you can inspect, change names, and much more by right-clicking on the name of an object. In the Mixer, the Right Mouse Button pops up clip and track options. In the Animation Editor, the Right Mouse Button has curve options. When in doubt, try right-clicking.

STICKINESS

One method used by Softimage | XSI to enhance your workflow is the concept of stickiness. When you choose a menu command that might possibly be executed many times in a row, Softimage executes the command on the first object you specified and stays in that command mode until you hit the Right Mouse Button or choose another menu command. This makes it easy for you to group your tasks into processes and apply a command to many objects in a sequence.

If you have completed modeling a large number of objects individually and now need to group them into hierarchies, for example, you would click on the Parent button. XSI then remains in the Parent mode as long as you need it, allowing you to construct many elaborate hierarchies without choosing the Parent command over and over again. When you are done with a command, make a habit of pressing the Esc key to put the command away, which avoids unintentional use of that tool next time you click an object. Not all tools in Softimage work like this — just the ones that can be executed without calling up a dialog box.

THE SI3D SELECTION MODEL

Hotkeys can also be "sticky" (if you have turned this option on in File →User Preferences). When you tap the space bar lightly, for example, XSI stays in selection mode. When you tap the "O" key, XSI stays in orbit mode. (Note: Turning on the Sticky key option in the User Prefs is a bad idea. If you become very fast and proficient with XSI, the time delay that defines 'tapping' a key will begin to become ambiguous, and hotkeys will start acting sticky when you don't want them to. It's a good idea to leave Enable Sticky Keys off. This option is located in the File→User Preferences area, under the Interaction tab.)

The stickiness and Shift-CTRL selection methods just described can become slow and confusing when you are working fast with multiple objects. The old method used in Softimage 3D | Extreme has been preserved, and it accelerates working with selections, node/branch/tree selection, selecting tags, and working with selection and other tools at the same time. To use the SI3D model (recommended strongly), go to the File→User Preferences dialog and in the Interaction tab turn off 'Enable Sticky Keys' and set the Default tool to 'Nil'. Close the dialog with OK and then in the Selection menu in the top right of the MCP, make sure that the three bottom options are all on: 'Select Single Object in Region', 'SI3D Selection model', and 'Extended Component Selection'. Now to select objects you hold the space bar down and pick at or draw a rectangle over objects, branches, and trees. Also, now the tag selection tool (hotkey T) works to add, subtract, and toggle tagged selections. You can still use Shift to make multiple selections, much like using Multi mode in the old Softimage 3D application.

VIEW WINDOWS

The majority of the screen is given over to the View Windows. The View Windows provide you a glimpse into your scene in a number of different ways: in a 2D orthographic view, as a 3D perspective corrected view, as a linear list of components, and as a schematic diagram of interconnected models. You can also use these View Windows to browse what's on your hard drive, and to work in other interfaces within XSI, like the Animation Editor and the Animation Mixer. You can arrange your interface to have as many or as few View Windows as you like, but the default configuration is to show four of these views into your scene.

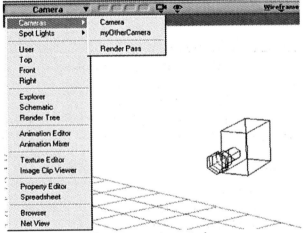

The Camera view window

At the top of each view window is the title bar. At the left of the title bar is a letter identifying that view, and then a drop menu showing what type of view it is. You can click directly on that title, which has a small triangle next to it (indicating that it is a drop menu), to select a different view. The Cameras option lists all the Cameras in your scene, and will change the view to look through whichever you choose. You can look through a spotlight using the Spot Lights option. The User option is a perspective view that does not correspond to any defined camera, which is useful when you want to work in your scene without disturbing the placement and settings of the Cameras. The Top, Front and Right views are orthographic views, meaning that they look into the scene as if it were in two dimensions, without perspective.

Note: If you want a 3D orthographic view, you can create a new camera and set its Projection to be orthographic in the Camera Property page.

CARTESIAN SPACE AND THE VIEW WINDOWS

Softimage|XSI sets up a virtual 3D world for you that is almost infinitely big but completely empty. This 3D space is organized according to the Cartesian coordinate system. This means that any point in the Softimage virtual world can be located precisely with three values: the point's location along the X-axis, the point's location along the Y-axis, and the point's location along the Z-axis.

Each of these three axes - X, Y, and Z - is an invisible straight line (a vector) stretching infinitely far in both directions. Each axis (X, Y, and Z) runs at a right angle (90 degrees) to each of the other axes. In other words, each axis is perpendicular to the other two axes.

If you are sitting in front of your computer looking in Softimage|XSI's Front View window, the X-axis is usually visualized as running from left to right, directly in front of you, like a horizon line. The Y-axis is the "up" axis and is usually visualized as running from the bottom to the top of your screen. The Z-axis is invisible to you because you are looking at the exact end of the line, running in and through your screen.

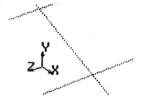

The X, Y, and Z axes

Each of these axes runs through a point in the exact center of the virtual 3D world called the global origin. All the axes meet as they pass through it. As they proceed on through the global origin, they extend in both the positive or negative directions.

Every point along an axis has a value, expressed in Softimage units. You can determine what a Softimage unit corresponds to in the real world by setting the units in the File→User Preferences box under the Unit Settings tab.

Because every position on the individual axes can be measured, you can define a point in space by choosing one point on each axis. Any point in space can then be located in a Cartesian coordinate system by specifying the values of the three axes, as in X=7, Y=41, Z=30, or, in shorthand, XYZ = 7,41,30.

Softimage|XSI has the job of converting the 3D virtual space I just described into a 2D virtual space that it can draw on a flat computer monitor for you to see and work with. The program does this by projecting each point in the virtual 3D space onto a 2D plane (called the projection plane) and drawing it to a View window.

Each of Softimage|XSI's View windows can display the projection plane from a different perspective, called the view plane. By default, the windows use the Top, Front, Right, and Camera view planes. Each view plane comes with a small icon showing you the orientation of the three axes in that view, so you can orient yourself in 3D space. Because each plane is really only a two-dimensional construct, it can show you only two out of the total three axes in the 3D space. The Top view shows the X- and Z-axes, which make up the XZ plane, the Front view shows the XY plane, and the Right view shows the ZY plane. Each of these views is orthographic, which means that all parallel lines are projected to the screen as actually parallel. In this way, you see a view that acts as a flat view port into the 3D world.

The last window is the Perspective View window. In Softimage|XSI, the Perspective View window is by default the first camera window. This is the view that your camera sees when you render your animation. You may add in other Camera later to view the scene from other angles. This window doesn't have to stay parallel to two of the major axes, although it's still a 2D view plane. In other words, you can move the camera freely throughout the 3D virtual space and look at the scene from any angle, not just the top, front, and right sides. This View window is not orthographic, but perspective, which means that Softimage performs perspective-correction projection when it draws the 2D view plane.

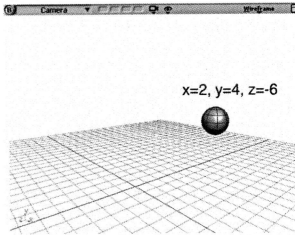

The global origin at the axes' intersection and a point defined by the values on each axis

In this way, Softimage can show you a 2D simulation of 3D space that provides you with a simulation of depth: parallel lines converge into the distance and objects seem to grow smaller as they move farther away. The severity of these effects changes depending on the width of the camera view angle used, so that you can easily simulate a fish-eye lens or a telephoto lens.

MOVING AROUND WITH THE HOTKEYS

Hotkeys are keyboard shortcuts essential to working with Softimage|XSI. Refer to the Common Hotkeys chart in the front of this book for quick reference.

To move around in the Top, Front, and Right View windows, position your mouse anywhere inside of one View window, hold down the Z key on your keyboard and the Left Mouse Button, and drag your mouse around. The Z key is the Zoom hotkey.

Now try using the Z hotkey with the Middle Mouse Button. This zooms into the View window. Try the Right Mouse Button to zoom out of the View window. Now hold down the Z hotkey and look at the Status Bar at the bottom of the screen. The Status Bar shows you the result of the hotkey for each of the three mouse buttons.

If you use the Z hotkey to Zoom in and out of the Camera window, you aren't just scaling the view, you're increasing or decreasing the field of view of the camera lens, which affects how distorted your Camera view gets. It is a good idea to use the P hotkey instead of the Z hotkey in the Camera window whenever possible. The P hotkey is the Dolly hotkey, which actually moves the camera back and forth to see more or less instead of changing the view angle of the camera. Try it out in the Camera window.

The P hotkey has another feature that is common to many functions in Softimage|XSI. When you hold down P, each of the mouse buttons does the same thing but in varying amounts. For instance, the Left Mouse Button dollies slowly, the middle button dollies at a medium rate, and the Right Mouse Button dollies rapidly. This way you can get the exact amount of control you need for big moves or for small precise ones.

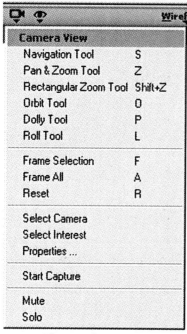

The Nav drop menu

Another crucial hotkey that works in the Perspective Window is the Orbit (O) hotkey. The Orbit hotkey allows you to change the view plane of the camera, by orbiting it around the camera interest (the point in space where the camera is aimed). Try it out in the Camera window (it doesn't work in the Top, Front, or Right views). The Orbit key allows you to see your work from any angle. As you orbit, watch how Softimage|XSI uses perspective correction to make the part of the grid that's farther away seem smaller. This effect is the basis of simulating a 3D space with a 2D image plane.

The last hotkey does the job of all the previous keys. It's Zoom, Pan and Orbit all rolled into one key, named the S hotkey. Hold down the S key and drag with the left, middle and Right Mouse Button to control the view plane.

Some other hotkeys are useful to know as well. The F hotkey frames the selected element, showing you the entire element in the active View window. This is often faster than zooming around until you can see the whole object. The A hotkey frames all the objects in the scene. You may also zoom into a rectangular selection onscreen by simultaneously holding down the Shift key and the Z hotkey and dragging a rectangle onscreen with your Left Mouse Button. Doing the same with your Right Mouse Button zooms out of a rectangular section area of the screen. Take a few moments to try these hotkeys.

REARRANGING THE VIEW WINDOWS

You can customize the view that you see while working with Softimage|XSI. Although you can have more than four View windows onscreen at any one time, you will generally work with four or fewer. You can arrange the windows as well by changing their orientation, the plane they show, and their relative sizes.

First, note that the views are all marked with a letter to designate them: A, B, C, and D. Each view can show you an orthographic view, like the Front view or the Top view; it can show you the view from a camera you have placed into the scene, or even the view from a spotlight in the scene.

RESIZING THE VIEWS

On the top corner opposite from the letter is a small Resize box. Clicking a View window Resize box with the Left Mouse Button expands the window to fill the entire screen, removing the other windows from view. Clicking the Resize box with the Middle Mouse Button causes that window to grow horizontally, replacing the window to the right or left of it, but leaving the other windows to the top or bottom. Clicking again with the Middle Mouse Button causes it to regain its former size. Clicking the Resize box with the Right Mouse Button gives you a drop menu with other options.

The different display modes

You can also click and drag the dividing line between windows to resize them to any size. Try it out!

To restore the windows to occupy even quadrants of the screen click exactly on the middle where the dividing lines between the panes come together with the Middle Mouse Button.

THE NAV DROP MENU

Next to the View Window drop menu lies the Camera drop menu (identified with a small Camera shaped Icon). The Camera menu primarily contains the menu equivalents for the navigation hotkeys like Pan, Zoom, Orbit, Frame, and Reset. However, it contains two other useful features: the ability to immediately select the Camera or Interest for that view, and the Capture options. Capture starts a playback but records the contents of the chosen View as a series of frames to disk, then pops up the Flipbook window which contains the controls for playing back the frames to review your work.

THE SHOW MENU

The Show Menu immediately to the right of the Nav menu in the View title bar toggles the visibility of different kinds of information that you could view in the window. Since XSI can show you so much information about each object in the scene, it is necessary to filter that information, showing only what is most useful for the stage of the project that you are currently in.

You can turn on and off cameras, 3D geometry, curves, lights, nulls, chains, and texture controls for each view independently. You can also show components like points, knots, centers and normals differently in each view.

The toggles in the Show menu are generally the same as the toggles in the View menu at the top of the screen, but they apply only to that window.

The Show drop menu

DISPLAY METHOD

When you are viewing the scene through either an orthographic or perspective view you have some options for how the view is displayed.

In the top right corner of each View menubar is the menu for the view display style. It will have the name of the currently active method, which will be one of the following: Bounding Box, Wireframe, Hidden Line Removal, Shaded, Textured, or Rotoscope.

Load a scene from the project data for this book using File→Open so you will have something to look at.

Load the 'stonehenge_done' scene.

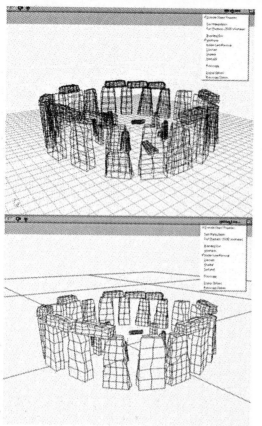

A scene in Wireframe and hidden line view styles

If you do not have the content for this book installed, you may download it from http://www.mesmer.com/books/. Click on the link for XSIFoundation15.zip to download the project files, then unzip them with WinZip (get a free version at http://www.winzip.com/) and save them to your folder on your computer.

WIREFRAME AND HIDDEN LINE

The first option, Wireframe, is the view that you have used up to this point. Wireframe view mode doesn't actually show the surfaces of objects, just the curves that make up the surfaces. Each object is transparent, so you can also see the curves on the back of each object and those objects that are behind it. This can become confusing. The Hidden Line Removal view style directly below the Wireframe draws only those curves on the surface that face towards the camera, hiding the back facing portions of each surface. Hidden Line also sorts the objects by order of distance from the camera, so that closer objects obscure further ones. This view method is quite fast and provides a better sense of depth in the scene.

SHADED AND TEXTURED

Shaded view uses the OpenGL graphics hardware in your workstation to display the surface of each model in your scene, using a simple shading method. It can show light and color, but not transparency, bump, or most special effects (Softimage|XSI creates a default infinite light for you automatically, in case you don't have your own yet).

The Shaded view can give you a better visual representation of where things are in your scene and what they will look like in the final render, but it can be quite slow if the complexity of the scene exceeds the capabilities of your OpenGL hardware. You can customize your shaded view to suit your needs by adjusting options in the Shaded→Display Options menu. Try out these options by toggling on the 'Mixed Viewing Mode', 'Wireframe On Top' and 'XRay Shading' options in the Property page that pops up. Each View camera can have different view mode settings. Next, in the same property page (Shaded →Display Options), change some settings so that the selected object will be shaded, but the other objects will be displayed in hidden line, by setting the Static and Interaction modes in the Unselected Objects column to 'Hidden Line'.

The textured view mode adds any surface 2D image textures on top of each shaded object so you can see texture placement. The Textured view relies on the OpenGL graphics hardware of your computer to draw the textures. If your card has insufficient texture memory this can be very slow. In addition, XSI only shows the last applied texture, so multiple layered textures will not be shown very accurately. Procedural textures and shaders won't show at all.

ROTOSCOPE VIEW MODE

The Rotoscope view mode is a tool that allows you to bring in a sequence of frames as a background image and then see the images behind your work in Softimage. This rotoscoping technique is often used in film work where real-life film contents ("practicals") are integrated with computer graphic imagery (CGI).

For example, if you are adding an animated character to a scene in which a group of computer-generated characters sit down for dinner in a real-life restaurant, you could shoot film of the table in the restaurant, with waiters wandering by and real people dining in the background. The film would be developed, scanned into a computer, and provided to you as digital frames. You could then bring these background plates into Softimage so that you can verify the correct placement of the computer-graphic characters you are animating.

When you toggle on Rotoscope, The Camera Rotoscopy property page is opened and you can choose an image or sequence of images to view behind your work. Try loading the landscape.pic file by clicking on the Image Name drop box, and navigating to the Pictures directory of the XSIFoundation project.

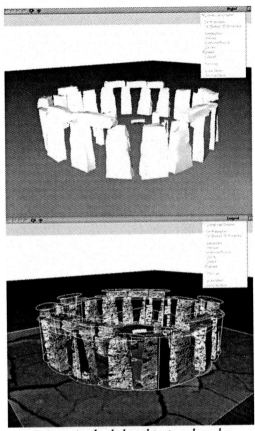

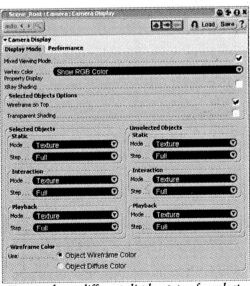

A scene in shaded and textured modes

Otherwise you may use the New button to import another image from your own collection.

OPENING, SAVING, AND PROJECTS

XSI uses totally new Open and Save dialogs that are a synthesis of both NT and Irix file browsers. As a result, they look a little different and have some new features.

On the left side of the dialog is the list of folders under the current place in the file system (hard drive or servers). Only folders are shown here, not files. Where you see a plus sign next to a folder, that folder has something in it, and you can click on the plus to reveal the contents. When you have clicked on a plus, the list cascades out, and the plus turns into a minus. You can click on the minus to collapse the folder.

You can have different display types for selected, unselected, near, and far objects

The Rotoscope mode places your scene on top of a background image

If you click directly on the name of a folder, the contents of that folder (both folders and files) will be shown in the larger right panel of the open or save dialog.

BROWSING THE PATH

The 'path' is your current location in the file system. The path starts with a '/' on Irix, which means 'the root', and 'c:/' on Windows, which means 'the top of drive C'. After that is a list of each folder you traversed down into to get to this point on the disk. For instance, '/disk2/people/bobby' translates into English as 'in the bobby folder, which is in the people folder, which is on disk 2, which is at the root of the file system.'

You can type directly into the path line and then hit enter to go there, or you can browse by clicking the 'up' button to go up the path, getting closer to the root, or by double clicking on folders in the right side to descend down into them.

All the contents of the folder at the end of the path are shown in the larger right side area.

NOTE On Irix you can only save into folders that your user has permissions for (a smart security precaution). Unfortunately, XSI defaults to the installation path, which should never be the path to your user account. You will want to use the 'X' icon immediately to set the default path to your own user account so you can save and open files without browsing the path.

The contents of the right side can be shown as either text listings or as thumbnails by clicking on the 'Clapper' and 'List' icons in the upper right corner. The large 'X' icon will mark this location as the current location to return to automatically, next time you use the browser. Other useful icons are the Paths button and the 'Star Folder' icon on the left side. Each allows you to rapidly jump to a favorite location on the disk, much like adding a bookmark in a web browser allows you to jump to a saved location on the web. You can set up your own favorite locations, first navigating to the location you want to mark, and then clicking the top-left 'Star folder' and choosing the 'Add to Favorites' option.

The bottom of the window shows the OK and Cancel buttons. If you are in the Save Scene dialog box you can pick an existing scene and then hit OK to save over it, replacing it, or you can enter a new filename in the File Name line and then hit OK to create a new scene file.

PROJECT MANAGEMENT

XSI has a sophisticated project management system that is designed to make it easy for you to manage multiple jobs at once, and keep revisions within each job organized. This is accomplished with the Project Manager dialog box, located in the File menu (File→Project Manager).

The major container for all your work in XSI is called a Project. You may have as many Projects as you wish on your machine, and you can also share Projects that are located on a central server. You might wish to create a new Project for each new client you take on, or each new project that you undertake.

Each Project is really just a folder system, containing sub-folders that organize the different parts of the work that you create.

Those folders are: Actions, Audio, Backup, DS Presets, Expressions, Fcurves, Models, Pictures, Queries, Render_Pictures, Scenes, Scripts, Shaders and Simulation.

Your scenes are mainly saved into the Scenes folder, but you can also choose to save Models externally into the Models folder. Your rendered frames will end up in the Render_Pictures folder, and the Pictures folder is a good place to put texture maps. Audio clips used for sync should be placed in the Audio folder.

Within each Project you may have as many different scenes as you wish. A scene file binds up all the models, lights, cameras, textures, shaders, and everything else into one file. To completely save all your work during a session you use the command File'Save or File'Save As, which writes a new scene into your current Project.

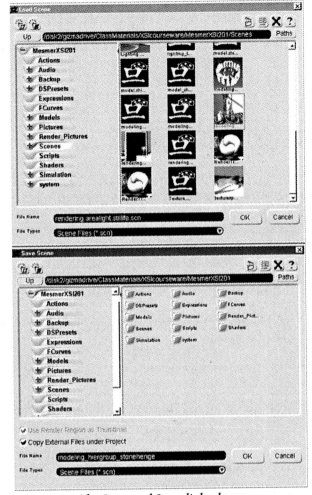

The Open and Save dialog boxes

It's a good idea to name your scenes with a descriptive name and a version number so you can always get back to your previous work if you decide to go back a few steps. For example, if you were working on a character animation for the PuffyStuff company, you might name the scene 'puffystuffCharacter1'. XSI will append the file extension '.scn' to your name for you automatically.

You can also save an image thumbnail of the scene along with the file, to help you see which one was which at a later date. To do this, draw a render region on screen somewhere in the Camera view. Then when you choose File'Save, check the button marked 'Use Render Region As Thumbnail'.

EXAMINING AND SWITCHING PROJECTS

You can see what project you are currently working in, switch to a different one, or even create a new project with the Project Manager. To see the Project Manager, click on File'Project Manager.

The list of Projects is found on the left-hand side of the Project Manager dialog box. The scenes contained within that Project are listed on the right-hand side. You can pick items from either side. You can also use this dialog box to delete entire Projects or Scenes. Be very careful of these options, and only use them if you really want to throw away all your hard work.

You can create new Projects here in the Project Manager, or you can use the File'New Project menu item. Remember that you can save new Project folders only to areas of the file system that you have privileges to. If you try to save a Project to an area you do not have permissions to change you will see an alert saying "the disk is write protected". Either save somewhere else, contact your SysAdmin, or change the permissions yourself.

MOVING SCENES FROM ONE PROJECT TO ANOTHER

You can move scenes from one project into a new one by simply opening the scene, then switching Projects in the Project Manager and doing a Save. Or, by using Save As and navigating to the location of the new Project in the path and saving the scene into the Scenes folder. When you do that, be sure to also check on the box in the Save dialog that is marked Copy External Files Under Project. This will automatically look into your scene and copy any textures, shaders, or other files used in your scene to the new Project.

THE OBJECT-ORIENTED PARADIGM AND PROPERTY PAGES

XSI is deeply object-oriented, and each object in it exists in a structure of objects, each with their own attributes, called properties. Since everything in XSI is an object with distinct properties, all objects can be treated in similar ways. Each can be selected, moved around in space, or in the list of all objects, called the Explorer, be copied, pasted, and so forth. Each can also be inspected in a standard interface box called a Property Page, or Property Editor.

The Property Editor is the single most ubiquitous interface element in XSI - each object has myriad different property pages showing options for things like location in space, visibility options, material attributes, and much, much more. To explore properties, get a primitive NURBS Sphere with Get'Primitive'Surface'Sphere. Now change your lower right view to be a Schematic view by clicking on the name of that view (it probably says "Right") and pull down the drop list to "Schematic".

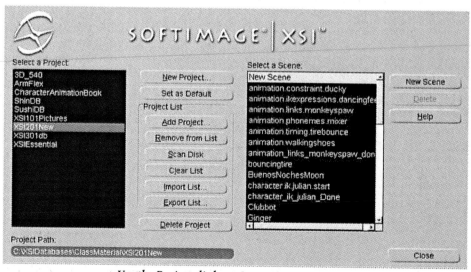

Use the Project dialog to organize your scenes

There are several different ways to inspect the properties of an object. One method is to locate the object of interest in either the Schematic view or the Explorer view, and click just once with the Left Mouse Button on the colored icon to the left of the object name (zoom in closer if you do not see the icon). This causes the general property page for that object to pop up. If the object was a Sphere, you will be able to edit the radius of the sphere, it's name, and the number of U and V isolines in

the Sphere. If the object was a light, you will be able to change those properties that are specific to the light, such as the color, the falloff, the spread, and whether or not it casts shadows. Each object has different properties, and you can even add properties to them as you work within Softimage | XSI.

Real-world objects and their properties

PROPERTY GROUPS

Properties in similar areas are grouped into tabs within the general property page. These tabs have a title (like Geometry, or Phong) to identify them within a horizontal Grey bar in the interface, along with a small triangle. The triangle can collapse or expand that tab to limit which properties you see in the general property page.

There is a shortcut to the General Property page for any object. You can simply select the object and hit the Enter key. Using the combination Alt-Enter will inspect all the object's properties in one long property page. You can also use the Edit menu in the MCP (right side, Edit→Properties) to look at the General Properties, the Modeling Properties, the Animation Properties, the Rendering Properties, the Viewing Properties, or any Custom Properties that you have added.

Properties can be organized into sets that you look at together:

General Properties include the name of the object.

Modeling Properties include how the object was made, its surface UV detail, and any geometry or deformation operators that have been applied.

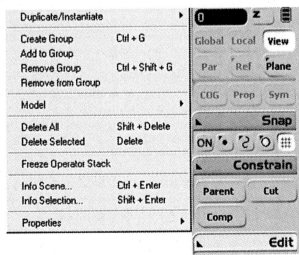

You can get the property page you want from the Edit menu

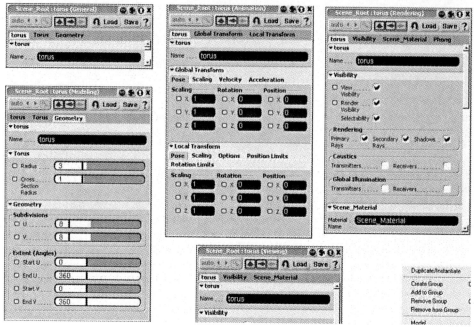

Examples of property pages

Animation Properties include the object's current Scale, Rotation, and Translation, as well as Velocity, Acceleration, and any Positional or Rotational limits that have been applied.

Rendering Properties include the object material and shaders, the geometry approximation for the object, the object visibility to the camera and in reflections and refractions, as well as links to the ambient light in the scene.

Viewing Properties control specifically whether or not, with what level of detail, and in what draw style, the object is rendered to the screen.

LOCKING AND RECYCLING PROPERTIES

Many views, like the Property Editor or the Animation Mixer, will show you whatever object is currently selected. Sometimes you will want to keep a specific object open for editing while going on to select other objects. Generally you do this by locking the window or property page. To lock a window view, click on the "Lock" button in the title bar of the window. To lock a property page, click on the small lock icon in the top-right corner of the page. This will keep the property page open for that object and that property. If you inspect a different property, it will pop up in a new property page. When you are done with that locked property you can either close the property page with the small X in the top-left corner, or turn the page back to recycle by clicking on the three-sided swirling recycle icon in the top-left corner of the property page.

Each Property page also has buttons to Load and to Save the object or property. These are the small L and S

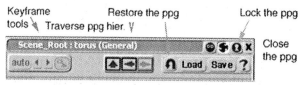

Each property page has the same buttons in the header

buttons in the top of the page directly below the Lock and Recycle buttons. If you have a Render Region defined, it will be added to the saved Property page as a thumbnail. These saved Property pages are called Presets.

DOCKING THE PROPERTY PAGE

Because you will use properties so frequently, they can often clutter the screen and obscure the interface or parts of the scene that you would rather see.

It's a good idea to allocate one of your View windows to show all the property pages that pop up. You can do this by clicking on the View title (Top, Right, camera, etc) and selecting the 'Property Editor' option near the bottom of the list. Now all new properties will be drawn into that window, and if they are too long they will scroll.

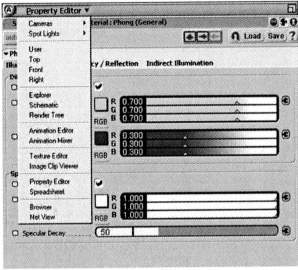

THE TRANSIENT SELECTION EXPLORER

You can show property pages in a window

Since each object might have a great many properties, there is a way to pop up a property page that doesn't show everything, but just has the information you want to work with. That's the Selection button, and is located on the right side of the screen in the Main Command Panel (MCP), directly below the text entry boxes. When you click on the Selection button, a drop box appears showing all the properties of the currently selected object as a series of cascading icons and names. Simply click on the property you want to edit, and a property page showing just that info will pop up.

Seeing only the properties you are interested in will help your understanding and workflow a lot. Get used to using the Selection button whenever you want to work with the properties of the selected item.

ORGANIZING OBJECTS AND PROPERTIES WITH THE EXPLORER

Because there are so many new objects and properties, organizing them to find what you need is an important consideration. The Explorer view is another way to organize all the objects in your scene.

In the Explorer view, all objects in the scene can be listed, or the list can be filtered to show only objects in the current layer, partition, render pass, group, or selection. This complete view of everything in your scene can be useful, but more often the quantity of information available there makes it hard to find what you want. If you find yourself overwhelmed by the explorer, stick with using the Selection button to find properties.

To enter the Explorer view, click on the light green view title drop menu in an existing view window and select the Explorer option.

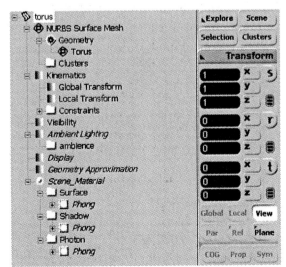

The Transient selection explorer shows you just the properties on the currently selected item

The Explorer can show a lot of information

THE SCHEMATIC VIEW

The Schematic view can be used to arrange your scene, select models, view the relationships between objects in a hierarchy, see constraints between objects, and work with materials and textures.

The Schematic view window is a pretty important window in XSI, and it can quickly get cluttered. Feel free to move the items in the schematic window around as much as you like, by simply pointing at an object, clicking with the Left Mouse Button, and dragging it around. You can also hold down the Shift key, and drag a selection rectangle to select multiple objects at once.

It's a good idea to lay out the items in some sort of order that makes sense to you in relation to the model you are building. For example, if you are building a human figure, you would place the body in the middle of the schematic, with the head on top, the hands out to the sides and the feet below. That way you can easily choose whichever body part you want to work on, without struggling to find it in the scene.

You can also turn on or off different types of information in the Schematic view. If you are working on adding Materials you might want to use the Show menu to display Materials as well as Models. You can also choose to see constraints, expressions, operators, and simulation links as colored lines connecting models in the Schematic. If the number of links showing in the Schematic gets overwhelming, look in the Show menu from the Schematic titlebar and toggle on the option to Show "Links on Selected Nodes Only".

The Schematic menu has a very useful context-sensitive menu that you can show at any time by right-clicking in the Schematic window. If you click over empty space you will get a menu offering to frame, rearrange, select, pan, or zoom. If you click over an object you can inspect properties, rename the object, delete it, duplicate it ,and create instances of it.

You can show and hide objects in the Schematic view by selecting the object and tapping the H hotkey (for 'Hide') on your keyboard. Hidden objects still appear in the Schematic, but have an outline form to differentiate them. To unhide the object again, press the H hotkey.

You can collapse hierarchies to save space in the Schematic view by clicking on the parent object with the Right Mouse Button and choosing Collapse Node.

Search entry ➞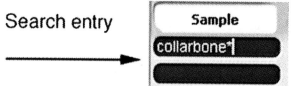

SEARCHING FOR OBJECTS

XSI also supports the use of searching, complete with expressions and wildcard characters for finding and selecting scene objects.

You can read the name of the selected element, and enter a name to search for

You can search for and select objects by entering a string to match in the text entry box near the top of the Main Command Panel.

For instance, if you have a cylinder named 'my.cylinder' and a sphere named 'my.sphere' you could select either one by entering its name into the top text box in the MCP.

You can also use wildcards to select more than one object. You could, for instance, type 'my*' in the text selection box, and XSI would select both

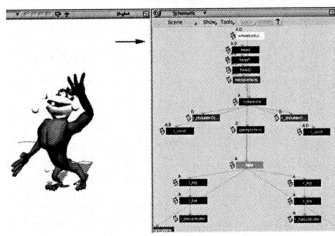

The Schematic view is useful for visualizing what's in your scene

the objects 'my.sphere' and, 'my.cylinder'. Entering '*cyl*' would select the cylinder, or all the cylinders if more existed in the scene.

You can also use this feature to select a branch (an object and all its children), by adding a plus sign after the name of the object. If you have a hand named 'my.right.hand' that is the parent of five fingers, you could enter 'my.right.hand+' to select the whole hand branch.

CONCLUSION

Whew! That was a long chapter about a great deal of important, but sometimes dry, information. It's important because you will use the tools for finding, organizing, and selecting objects constantly as you work within XSI. You should consider reflecting back on this chapter a few months later, after you have had a chance to work in the software. You will likely find quite a few useful tidbits that escaped your notice the first time through.

QUIZ

Please take a few moments to test your knowledge of the topics covered in this chapter.

1. HOW MANY MODULES ARE THERE IN XSI?
    a. Four
    b. Five
    c. Three

2. WHAT DO THE LETTERS "MCP" STAND FOR?
    a. Master Control Program
    b. Main Command Panel
    c. Menu Control Properties

3. THE HOTKEY FOR TUMBLING YOUR CAMERA IS:
    a. O
    b. P
    c. M

4. WHAT'S THE BEST WAY TO INSPECT AN OBJECT'S PROPERTIES?
    a. Shift-ALT-CTRL-F6
    b. Use the Selection button in the MCP.
    c. Dig through the Explorer window.

5. THE X-, Y-, AND Z-AXES ARE _____ TO EACH OTHER.
    a. perpendicular
    b. parallel
    c. at 45-degree angles

6. WHAT'S A PROPERTY?
    a. real estate
    b. any attribute stored on an object by object basis
    c. an animateable parameter

7. TYPING "MY*FOOT+" IN THE SELECTION BOX WOULD SELECT WHICH OBJECTS?
    a. my.left.foot
    b. my.left.foot, my.right.foot and their children
    c. my.left.foot, my.left.arm, and all their children

8. WHICH VIEW MODE SHOWS THE COLOR OF THE SURFACE MATERIAL AND THE LIGHTS ON IT?
    a. Rotoscope view
    b. Texture view
    c. Shaded view

9. WHICH MODULE DO YOU FIND THE PREVIEW BUTTON IN?
    a. Model
    b. Animate
    c. Render

10. WHICH ORGANIZATIONAL VIEW ALLOWS TO YOU MOVE OBJECTS AROUND IN A 2D WINDOW?
    a. Explorer
    b. Schematic
    c. Perspective

2 BASIC TERMINOLOGY AND MODELING

IN THIS CHAPTER YOU WILL LEARN ABOUT:

- How to start a fresh scene
- All the basic names for objects and components
- How to create models from primitive shapes
- All about polygons
- All about NURBS (Non-Uniform Rational B-Splines)
- How to move, scale and rotate objects
- How to efficiently select objects, hierarchies, and components
- How to model organically by pushing and pulling points

INTRODUCTION

In this chapter you will learn a lot more about the terminology used in XSI (and most other 3D applications) to describe the objects you will work with in the software. You will learn about objects and centers, control points and vertices, knots and boundaries.

You will soon have a chance to put together a simple scene and view your work.

STARTING FROM SCRATCH

When you want to get rid of everything on the screen without saving changes, or if you simply want to load a fresh scene to work on, use the File→New menu command to clear the scene. This command removes all objects from use, clears the undo stack, and cleans up memory. Now with a new scene you have the computer equivalent of a blank sheet of paper to start work on.

BASIC NOMENCLATURE: POINTS, CURVES, POLYGONS, SURFACES

Before you can get started using the tools in Softimage|XSI to make models and scenes, you'll need to learn the body of terminology used throughout this book and the Softimage|XSI product. Most of these terms are used in ways that are standard to the 3D animation world, but some are not. If you take the time to understand the terminology now, even when it becomes technical, you have an easier time using Softimage|XSI to create good work.

Point = Zero Dimensions

Line = One Dimension

Triangle = Two Dimensions

Square = 2 or 3 Dimensions

A point, a line, a plane, and a cube are 0-, 1-, 2-, and 3-dimensional objects, respectively

Almost everything in Softimage|XSI is constructed by placing points in 3D space. A point is simply a zero-dimensional location in 3D space, usually given by the X, Y, and Z coordinate system. Two points connected together can define a straight line. If something is linear, it is composed of straight line segments, each with a point at either end. Each linear segment is a one-dimensional object, because two end points define a one-dimensional vector. In fact, a straight line is the definition of one-dimensional. If two segments are joined together, they become a two-dimensional object, because they now have three points. A two-dimensional plane is easiest thought of as a triangle floating in space. If three segments are joined together so that each segment is perpendicular to the other two, then they become a three-dimensional object, like the sides of a cube, or the 3D axis on each viewport in XSI.

SPLINES, CURVES, NURBS

A spline is a line shape that is defined by two or more points plotted in space. A synonym for spline is curve. Softimage|XSI uses both terms interchangeably. There can be linear curves, even though the names seem to be exclusive of one another. Softimage|XSI uses only one kind of spline curve, called NURBS.

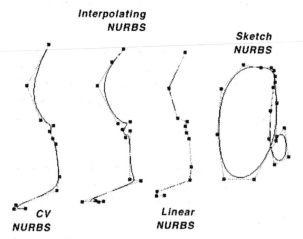

These are all different kinds of spline curves. All are also NURBS

NURBS (Non-Uniform Rational B-Spline) curves are the most complex, and the most useful, found in any 3D program.

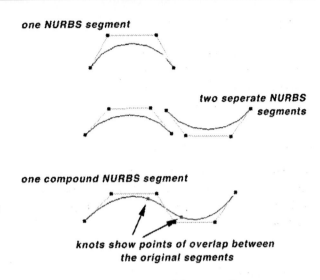

All NURBS are actually composed of a number of segments, although you as the user perceive an unbroken curve. The segments are joined together at invisible intersections called knots. The knots usually do not lie at the same place as the control points that you see when you create a curve, because the NURBS curve finds a best fit through the control points that you lay down when you plot out the curve. For a basic Cubic NURB, four control points are required to create the smallest segment.

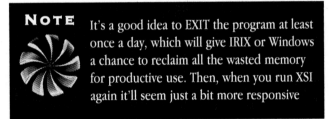

knots show points of overlap between the original segments

Each NURBS curve is created from smaller pieces, connected together at knots

Being composed of a series of knots makes a curve "piecewise", which emphasizes that the curve is actually a compound made up of lots of smaller pieces that are joined together at the ends. NURBS curve segments can be of various orders and of different parameterization, which is to say that the knots connecting the segments can be spaced in different ways.

NOTE It's a good idea to EXIT the program at least once a day, which will give IRIX or Windows a chance to reclaim all the wasted memory for productive use. Then, when you run XSI again it'll seem just a bit more responsive

CURVE ORDER

The mathematical formula that describes each line segment between knots can be of varying complexity. A first-order curve has a linear equation, a quadratic equation is used for second-order curves, and a cubic equation is used for third-order curves. Third and higher order curves maintain positional and tangential continuity as one segment joins another. This creates very smooth curves that seem to be one unbroken filament.

The order of the curve segment defines how smoothly it transitions into a neighboring segment. In a linear curve, the segments share a knot and a point, but they are not tangent to each other at that knot, so you see a sharp edge there. Two segments that are not tangent to each other seem to break into a sharp angle at the point at which they intersect. Second order curves are perfectly tangent to each other where they join, transitioning smoothly from one to the next, so that without the control points showing, you wouldn't know where one segment ends and the next begins.

The NURBS curve has several benefits. The points can be unequally weighted, so that one point attracts the curve more closely than the others. This is what makes the curve rational. This allows for the creation of corners in an otherwise smooth curve. It may also be trimmed to any length, because the knots defining the ends of segments can be placed at any point along the curve.

If a spline is closed, that means that the end of the last segment of the curve is co-located with the start of the first segment, creating an unbroken path. By themselves, splines are invisible to the rendering engine, because they have no real surface.

CENTERS

Each object is located in Cartesian space. The coordinates of the object are given by the position of the object center relative to the global center (also called the origin). This means that every object in Softimage|XSI has an object center, called a local center.

The local center is the point from which the object scales, so if the local center of a ruler is in the geometric center of the ruler, it grows equally outwards from the middle when you scale it. If you move the center to the bottom of the ruler and scale it, the ruler grows up from the bottom edge.

Similarly, the object rotates around the local center. Put another way, the local center is the axis of rotation for that object. To make a door object swing open appropriately, you would need to move the local center to the hinge edge of the door. Then the door rotates around the edge of the door instead of the middle.

This local center is fundamental to the behavior of every object in the XSI 3D environment.

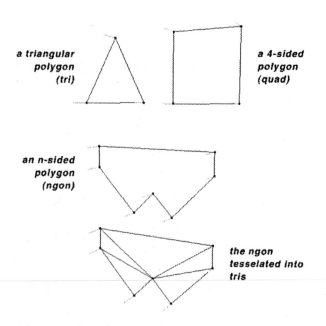

a triangular polygon (tri)

a 4-sided polygon (quad)

an n-sided polygon (ngon)

the ngon tesselated into tris

The parts of a Polygon: vertices, edges, normals, and polygons of different types

POLYGONS

The polygon is another basic building block in the Softimage|XSI object system. A polygon is a shape defined by three or more points, called vertices (plural) arranged in space. Each vertex (singular) is connected to at least two neighboring vertices with straight line segments called edges. This method of linking points in space by edges creates the geometric shapes called polygons.

There are several kinds of polygons. The most basic polygon has only three sides and is called a triangle. The next size up from a triangle is a square, also called a quad, which has four vertices and four sides. From there on up, polygons are called n-sided.

POLYGON MESHES

An object can be composed of a single polygon or a group of polygons. An object composed of many polygons is called a polygon mesh. A polygon mesh object is composed of one or more polygons that share vertices and edges.

If two polygons share two or more vertices, they also share an edge between those vertices. Polygons like this remain connected at the edge like conjoined twins connected at the hip: move one polygon and the other has to stretch to stay joined at the edge. Polygons that share edges can be broken up so that they no longer share edges.

Because each vertex contains a value for the X position, the Y position, and the Z position, polygon datasets can be quite large.

NORMALS

Both polygons and NURBS have another important component called the normal. The normal is a vector line segment emanating from the each polygon or NURBS patch that indicates which way the object is facing. That is to say, "which side of the polygon is the front side and which is the back". Imagine getting on your socks this morning - the first thing you checked before you put one on was whether it was inside-out or right-side-out. Surfaces in XSI can be just like the sock - either side could be showing. Swapping sides (turning an object inside-out) is called inverting the surface. For polygonal meshes it becomes very important that all parts of the mesh have coherent normals that all point out in the same direction. Imagine if part of your sock was inside out but another part was not.

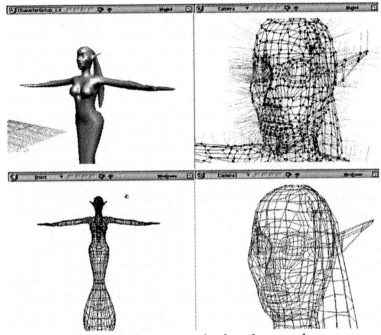

A simple character made of a polygon mesh

Softimage|XSI uses this information in several important ways. First, it determines at render time which surface is facing the camera and renders only that part, to save render time. Second, XSI uses the normals during the render to smooth the shading on edges between polygons, helping to reduce the typical jagged, faceted look of polygonal models.

The normals can be shown or hidden differently in each view window of Softimage|XSI. When shown, they look like thin, blue hairs sprouting from the surface of your models.

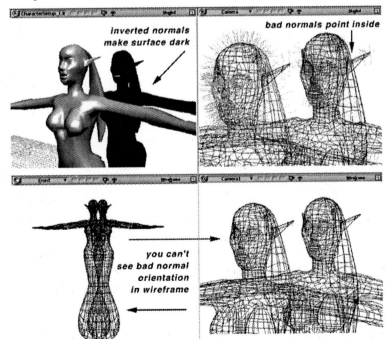

Normals help in shading, and also show which way the surface is facing

NURBS PATCHES, BOUNDARIES, U AND V

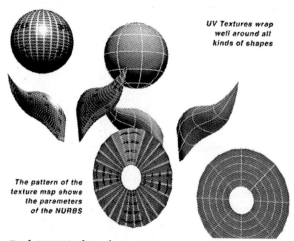

UV Textures wrap well around all kinds of shapes

The pattern of the texture map shows the parameters of the NURBS

Each NURBS object has a UV parameter space that follows the contours of the object

So far we've talked about NURBS curves, but we can also make NURBS surfaces. NURBS surfaces are a patchwork of smaller rectangular patches. The patch can be thought of as a network of spline curves, with the intersections between the curves connected by a web of geometry, creating a surface.

The edges of a patch are often called the boundary curves because they define the boundaries of the patch. One boundary runs in the U direction and one boundary runs in the V direction. U and V are just like latitude and longitude on the Earth - they always run perpendicular to one another.

When the patch is more or less rectangular, the boundary curves look like they are the edges, but when the patch looks more like a sphere, the boundary curves look more like the poles of a planet.

To see this in XSI, get a primitive sphere and a primitive grid, then show the boundaries in the Camera view by toggling on the Boundaries option in the Show menu (Show looks like an icon of an eye, located in the menubar of the Camera view). The U boundary shows in Red, the V boundary shows in Green.

Each location in UV space exactly describes a location on the patch surface, just as every longitude and latitude combination describes a unique location on the Earth. This precise capability to locate positions in the UV parameter space is one of the main advantages that NURBS patches have over polygon objects.

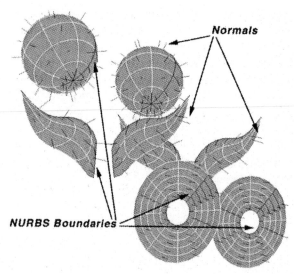

Normals

NURBS Boundaries

The boundaries are the open edges in U and V

Patches can, like splines, be closed or open. In an open patch, the two U edges, or the two V edges, are connected. A patch with one edge (or parameter) closed looks like an unbroken ribbon. A patch with both parameters closed looks like a solid object where the U and V parameters stretch completely around in an unbroken surface, like a sphere or a torus. It's very useful to remember that, no matter what the shape, NURBS patches are always made up of small rectangles.

APPROXIMATION AND TESSELLATION

Because XSI renders only triangles, a patch is really only an approximation of a surface made of lots of very small triangles. How closely the polygonal surface approximates the mathematical precision of the patch determines how smooth and accurate the final surface is. The process of approximating the surface by breaking it down into a number of triangles is called tessellation.

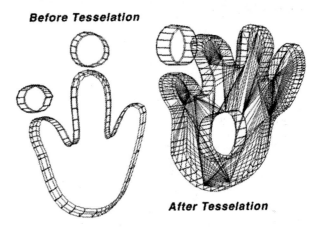

Before Tesselation

After Tesselation

As a general rule, the more triangles that are used to approximate the patch, the better it looks. The degree of approximation used to tessellate the patch down into triangles at render time can be controlled precisely in

Tessellation is when the NURBS surface is reduced to many small triangles for rendering or display

Softimage | XSI. You can set the Step parameter (in the Geometry Approximation property page under Surface U and V step), or you can allow the mental ray to choose the proper Step for you by enabling the Length/Distance/Angle option in the same property page. The Step is the number of times each UV patch section is divided into smaller sections before it is finally divided into two triangles. This capability to easily trade off between surface smoothness and the number of triangles is another key advantage of using patches over polygons in your modeling tasks.

SPECIAL FEATURES OF NURBS PATCHES

Because the knot of a NURBS curve can be located at any point along its length, a NURBS curve can be trimmed to any length. Similarly, a NURBS patch can be trimmed to any shape by projecting another NURBS curve onto the first surface, in the same way that you trim a cookie out of a sheet of dough with a cookie cutter. The trim curve can just be projected onto the surface for later use, it can define a hole in the surface, or it can become the outer boundary of the surface, causing everything outside the curve to go away. (Note: Trims are not yet supported in XSI 1.5.)

NURBS Goblets all look the same

Because of the more flexible parameterization of NURBS patches, it is also possible to connect two separate NURBS patches into one contiguous surface by merging the two original surfaces. Another method of achieving a similar result is to create a third surface that blends evenly between two original surfaces to create a joint between them, much like using putty to fill in the crack between sections of drywall when building a house.

The Goblets after tesselation with 2 steps, 4 steps, and 6 steps per Isoparm

This object has been tessellated with different U and V steps to make different levels of detail

Points on NURBS patches can also be weighted, just like points on NURBS curves, so that NURBS surfaces can have combinations of smooth curves and sharp angles.

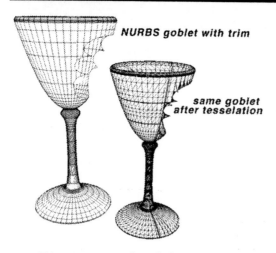

NURBS goblet with trim

same goblet
after tesselation

Trimming can make a hole in a NURBS

NURBS currently represent the most sophisticated way of creating complex surface geometry in surface modelers, such as Softimage|XSI. Although using NURBS is more complex than using regular patches or polygons, the additional features and flexibility of NURBS make them the only way to go for many types of surfaces, including organic shapes and complex precision surfaces.

SELECTING OBJECTS

When you want to do something with an object, first you need to select it.

The simplest way to do this is to use the selection hotkey: the space bar. Whenever you have the spacebar held down, you are telling XSI that you will now point at an object and select it. You can click directly on an object, or you can drag a box around an object, touching at least one part of it to select the object.

To select more than one object, you must hold down the Shift button along with the space bar and click or drag with a mouse button.

Which mouse button you use also is important. If you want to select a single object (a "node") you click with the Left Mouse Button. To select a branch, meaning any object and all the objects below it in its hierarchy, use the Middle Mouse Button. To select an entire tree (everything in the hierarchy), use the Right Mouse Button. In XSI, the Right Mouse Button is also used to select the entire Model, which is a tree hierarchy that has been defined as a special kind of tree. Models can have their own name space, and can be saved separately from the scene file to facilitate importing and exporting, sharing, and collaborative workflow. We'll discuss the hierarchy in a later chapter – for now just use the space bar with the Left Mouse Button.

NOTE To make things confusing, there are two different selection models in XSI: the XSI selection model and the SI3D selection model. The author highly recommends the SI3D selection model. To use this, first check the Selection menu in the top of the MCP and check on SI3D Selection Model and Extended Component Selection. Then, also turn off Sticky Keys in the File➔User Preferences Menu under the Interaction tab.

XSI introduces another selection method called the Lasso Tool, which is like a lasso selection tool on a Macintosh. Using this you can draw an irregular shape and select objects that are either inside the lasso or are touched by the line you draw. The hotkey for Lasso is F8, but you can also activate the Lasso tool from the Select menu at the top of the MCP.

The last new selection method in XSI is called 'Freeform'. When freeform is on (hotkey F9), you draw a scribble line on-screen and whatever objects are touched by the line will be selected.

THE SELECTION MENU

The Selection menu in the MCP has each of these selection methods, and you can turn them on and off here when you forget the hotkeys.

The Selection Menu also has the useful options Select All, which means select all objects, and Select All Using Filter, which selects components using the filter currently chosen in the Filter menu (directly above the Object Name box in the MCP).

Perhaps the most useful option is the Invert Using Filter option, which works like the Invert Selection command in Adobe PhotoShop. Sometimes it's easier to select the stuff you don't want, and then toggle everything, than to select all the stuff you do want.

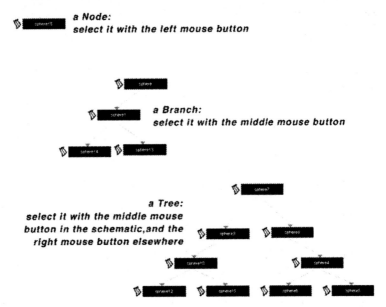

a Node:
select it with the left mouse button

a Branch:
select it with the middle mouse button

a Tree:
select it with the middle mouse button in the schematic, and the right mouse button elsewhere

Use a different mouse button depending on how much, or how little, of a hierarchy you want to select

GET PRIMITIVES

Softimage|XSI includes a variety of pre-made primitive shapes that are useful in basic modeling. These primitives include both splines and surface shapes, and can generally be made as either polygonal meshes or NURBS surfaces. These are often a good starting place in your modeling tasks. There are seven categories of primitives in XSI. Each has a property page where you can interactively customize the primitive to fit your needs.

1. Null: a null object, used for organizing hierarchies.

2. Curve: default arcs, circles, spirals, and squares.

3. Polygon Meshes: cones, cubes, cylinders, discs, grids, spheres, and toruses.

4. Surface: NURBS discs, grids, spheres, and toruses.

5. Implicit: Implicit objects are the base primitives used to make the polygon and NURBS models.

6. Control Objects: Physical forces used in simulations: waves, attractors, gravity, vortices, wind.

7. Lattice: a deformation cage that you can control manually.

To try this out, choose Get→Primitive→Surface→Torus.

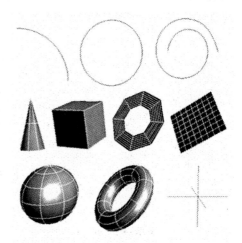

The Primitives menu is where you can choose a building block to start with

The property page that pops up when you create a primitive (the General property page) is there for you to customize the primitive to your needs. Start by changing the name from "Torus" to "MyTorus". Then click on the Torus tab of the property page to see the variables that are specific to the torus: radius and cross section. Change these to your liking. Finally, click on the Geometry tab of the property page. Increasing the subdivisions will make the objects appear smoother when they are rendered.

Starting with a primitive shape and then cutting, transforming, or deforming that shape into something else is the most basic form of modeling, and it's a quick way to get things done. Experiment with the primitives in the Get➔Primitive menu to see what's there.

NULL OBJECTS AND A FEW OF THEIR USES

In the Get➔Primitive menu, you will find a command that seems a little obscure at first, called Get➔Primitive➔Null, which brings a special kind of object into being. A null is an object that has no geometry at all. No lines, no points, no polygons, no surface at all. It is really just an object that consists of only a local center. The tremendous utility of the null comes from the fact that when objects are linked in a hierarchy, each parent node adds transformations to all the child nodes. This means that a null object can be used as a parent in a hierarchy when you just want all the children objects to be linked together at the same level. The whole null grouping can then be scaled, translated or rotated together, by selecting the top of the hierarchy as a branch. That null can also be animated, and the animation on the null will cascade down into the child nodes connected to it.

Nulls are also a critical part of inverse kinematic (IK) skeletons in XSI, and they can help out tremendously in constraint-based animations.

TRANSFORMATIONS: SCALE, ROTATION, TRANSLATION

The transformation cells in the Main Command Panel (MCP)

The three basic operations for all objects are the transformations: scale, rotation, and translation. You will use these commands to move objects around your scene, make them bigger or smaller, and spin them into the desired position. When you begin animating you will most likely spend the majority of your time setting keyframes on scale, translation, and rotation, and mixing up animations based on these changes. Together, scale, rotate, and translate are called by the shorter term "transformation".

The interface buttons for scale, rotate, and translate are located on the right edge of the interface in the Main Command Panel, under the menu heading "Transform". To transform an object, first select it with the space bar, and then click on one of the transformation button with the letter corresponding to the type of transformation you want: S for scale, R for rotation and T for translate. Finally, click and drag the mouse in your scene with the Left Mouse Button to make the change interactively.

There are hotkey keyboard shortcuts for the transformations. Tapping (or holding) the X key will activate the Scale menu cells, hitting the C hotkey fires up the Rotate cells, and hitting the V key will activate the Translate cells. A mnemonic device to remember which goes with which is "XCV = SRT", where the order of the letters matches up.

When you have one transformation active (say, scale), each of the three mouse buttons acts differently: the Left Mouse Button scales in X, the middle in Y and the right in Z. The status line will remind you which is which, but again the keys go in order of the mnemonic "XYZ = LMR" so that XYZ matches which finger you use - left, middle, right - when you click the mouse.

Each of these functions can be performed relative to one axis, two axes, or three axes at a time. For instance, you can rotate an object around the X-axis, the Y-axis, or the Z-axis. Rotating all three at the same time will cause an object to tumble.

MANIPULATORS

To help you remember which axis is which, and to make it easier to use the local axes when the object is all out of whack with the global axes, XSI has a type of user feedback called a Manipulator. The Manipulator is slightly mis-named, since you don't actually grab it with your hand (or your mouse) but it does show you which axis is which and provide you with clues about what the Transforms will do.

When you activate the Translation menu cells, a manipulator shaped like three arrows color coded Red, Green and Blue to match the colors of the local axes, pops up at the center of the object. These arrows point in the direction that the object will move when you drag the mouse with either the Left, Middle or Right Mouse Button.

When you activate the rotate menu cells, a manipulator pops up showing three gimbals, again color coded Red, Green and Blue and indicating which way the object will rotate with different mouse buttons. When you do drag with a mouse button, the manipulator shows how far you have rotated the object.

When you activate the scale menu cells the Manipulator is a set of color coded axes with small cubes at the ends to show you how you might scale the object.

When you scale an object in all axes at the same time, the object grows or shrinks while retaining its proportions; but if you scale in only one axis it will grow or shrink along that axis.

To transform an object in just one axis, you can also choose to click only on that part of the transformation in the Main Command Panel. In other words, you can click only on the X button in the S area of the transformation cells. To get back to activating all the axes, click on the icon with the three black bars below the S, R, or T buttons.

For instance, if you wanted to scale a cube into a rectangular tabletop, you could click in the Y button in the Scale part of the MCP panel then drag the Left Mouse Button down to make the cube less tall. To scale the tabletop uniformly again, click back on the uniform icon (three black bars) below the S icon.

When you have one axis of a transformation active (say, scale just in Y), each of the three mouse buttons does the same thing, but in different amounts: the Left Mouse Button goes slowly, the Middle Mouse Button goes more rapidly, and the right performs the action at the fastest rate. By using each mouse button you can get exactly the level of control that you need: left to right, slowest to fastest. Look to the status area at the bottom of the screen to see a description of each mouse button's function within the menu cell.

If you click directly into the area of a transformation button where the decimal number reads out, you can enter a value directly into that box. Hitting the Enter key, or selecting another cell, causes the change to take place.

You can also use another slick method of interactive feedback. Try clicking into a text entry box and dragging with the Left Mouse Button either left and right, or in a circular motion, to dial up or down the number in the box. The scene will update when you slow down your motion, or let up on the mouse button. This also works in property pages.

When you need to scale, rotate or translate an object uniformly, hold down the Shift button while you drag. This causes the object to scale uniformly along all axes, to rotate in discreet 15 degree increments, and to translate in perfect one-unit increments along whatever axis you are using .

NOTE You can also enter simple formulas into the transformation cells. If you type "5+" into the Translate Y cell, your object will go 5 units higher. If you type "R(1,9)" your object will pick a random height between 1 and 9. This also works on multiple selections: try making 10 spheres, and with them all selected, entering L(1,20) in the Translate X cell to make a linear adjustment to their translation in Y from 1 to 20 over the range of spheres.

STONEHENGE: AT A GLANCE

TOPICS COVERED

In this tutorial you will get a chance to practice moving blocks around in 3D space.

You'll learn how to:

- Create primitive objects
- Move objects in space
- Scale, Rotate and shape objects
- Pan, Zoom and Orbit to look around in your scene

MATERIALS REQUIRED

The tutorial uses the 'stonehenge_start.scn' scene from the courseware you may download from the internet. Point your web browser to http://www.mesmer.com/books/ and download the XSIIlluminated.zip file for PCs or the XSIIlluminated.tar.gzip file for Irix machines. You may use WinZip to unzip the PC version, and use the commands

```
gunzip XSIIlluminated.tar.gzip
```

```
tar -xf XSIIlluminated.tar
```

to extract the Irix version.

TUTORIAL: STONEHENGE

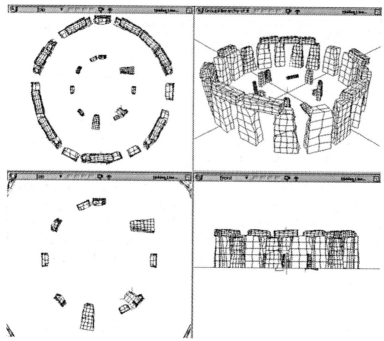

Let's try this out by creating a simple scene constructed only of primitive cube objects of varying sizes and proportions, and placed in space so to simulate the collection of obelisks found at Stonehenge, in Wiltshire, England.

Of course, it was their idea first, and creativity counts for a lot in this world whether you're a druid or an animator. What do you suppose was on the other side of those portals?

A layout diagram of Stonehenge

STEP 1. OPEN THE STONEHENGE SCENE

The Stonehenge_start scene has all the component posts, lintels, altars and other small stones you will need to build Stonehenge. All you will need to do is arrange them into the right shape. Before we start moving posts and lintels, let's mark out the plan for the area so we know where things go.

Look at the overhead view, the top view (the XZ plane) and click the A hotkey with your mouse somewhere in that view to frame all objects.

STEP 2. MAKE SOME GUIDES AND A GROUNDPLANE

Now create a primitive circle with the Get→Primitive→Curve→Circle command.

We'll use this circle as a guide when we place the stones, but since it was created in the XY plane, and we want it in the XZ plane, we'll have to rotate it first. With the circle selected, click directly into the numeric area of the Rotate X menu cell with your Middle Mouse Button and enter the value 90, which means ninety degrees. Hit the enter key to execute the command. In the top view you should now see the circle.

In the circle property page, check the radius - it should be 4 units. This will be the inner circle of smaller stones.

Make another circle out of the first by duplicating it with the CTRL-D hotkey combination.

Change the new circle's Radius to about 11 units. This will be the guide for the larger ring of bigger stones.

Name the smaller circle 'innercircle' and the bigger one 'outercircle' using the general property pages.

Start by building a ground plane with a simple grid object. Use the Get→Primitive→Surface→Grid command to bring a grid into existence. If you have the preference for Auto-popup of Property Editors on, the general Property Editor for the grid will pop up instantly. If it doesn't, click on the Selection button in the MCP to browse the properties of the Grid, locate the Geometry property, and click directly on the small icon to the left of the word Geometry to view the grid's properties.

Now that you are looking at the Grid property page, leave the U and V length alone, but increase the Subdivision in both U and V to 15.

A grid is created, but it isn't large enough to cover the area in front of us in the scene, so we'll need to enlarge it. Use the Scale area of the MCP to make the grid bigger in X and Z, to form a base for our monuments. Now the grid stretches to the horizon, but it's awfully flat looking.

Let's bump the grid up in a random rolling fashion by using a randomize command on the grid. In the Model module, choose Deform→Randomize (with the grid still selected), open the Randomize Operator property page from the transient selection explorer (the Selection button in the MCP), and change the displacement Y multiplier to .8, and experiment with the other sliders to get the look you want. The Randomize effect will randomly move the location of each control point in the grid a little bit, creating a rolling hillside. Look at it in shaded view.

STEP 3. ARRANGE THE STONES
Open a schematic view and zoom out in it to see all the objects there. The stones are organized into groups according to type. Start placing the smaller stones onto the inner circle by translating them in both top and front views.

Refer to the images here of the Stonehenge layout for assistance. Place the post on the circle and flush with the ground plane, with the translation menu cells. Then, in the View translation mode, click with your mouse in the top view to drag the post to the circle. Use the front view to adjust the position in Y.

Remember to also rotate the stones around Y so that they all face the middle. Some stones may be laid down on the ground, as if they toppled during the intervening 20 centuries.

Next, place the larger upright stones around the outer circle.

Hint: The stones are easy to move into position in the top view.

Hint: The stones might not be at the right ground height. Move one to the right elevation and look at the Translate Y edit box in the MCP to see how high it is. Select all the other stones and type that number into the same edit box to make them all the same height.

STEP 4. MOVE A LINTEL
The lintel is the flat, broad piece of stone that caps the two posts. Use the translate and rotate menu cells to place each lintel roughly on top of and resting on the two posts.

STEP 5. MAKE THE OTHER DOORWAYS
Copy the stones you've built and place them in groups to match the layout of Stonehenge in the figures here, or if you wish, construct your own mystical portals and lay them out as your spirit dictates. Because we haven't yet learned how to group objects, you will have to scale and rotate the giant stone blocks one at a time.

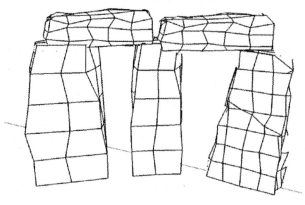

Two posts and a lintel

STEP 6. EXAMINE YOUR WORK

Place your camera wherever you wish in the scene by using the O, P, and Z supra keys within the perspective window.

View your work in shaded mode by selecting Shaded from the view style drop menu at the top of the Camera view.

When you are done, save your work with File➔Save As and examine the finished scene by loading Stonehenge_done for comparison.

The Stonehenge exercise helped you pull together a scene into a cohesive, visible work of art.

Seeing the collection of shapes come together into a scene is the most rewarding part of the animation process (outside of seeing your name in the credits at the end of the show).

You may have noticed that if you selected multiple objects (with the Shift key held down during selection) and then scaled them, or rotated them, each object was transformed relative to it's own local center. For instance, if you selected two posts and a lintel and tried to rotate them in Y so that you could align them with the circle, each part would spin on it's own, losing contact with the other pieces. Similarly, if you wanted to scale a portal smaller, using the Shift-Select method simply makes all the parts smaller, and then you have to reassemble the pieces. That's not too hard when the model is made of three cubes, but for more complex models it would be unforgivable. There is a better way.

When objects are in a hierarchy, they can be transformed relative to their parent's local center, instead of their own. And, if the hierarchy has several levels to it, each level can be a different local center for the transformations. That means that if the portal was in a hierarchy, just for example with the lintel the parent of both posts, selecting the whole hierarchy with the Right Mouse Button and the spacebar would allow you to move, scale and rotate the portal as you wish, and its parts would always remain in the correct proportions and orientation. In addition, most animation can be performed on hierarchies, at the node, branch, and tree levels. This is a concept of great importance in Softimage, because without it you can never build and animate anything with more than one piece. Hierarchies are covered in the next chapter.

Extra Credit for those who know about hierarchies already:

One way to organize your work is to create a parent-child hierarchy. Try this out by creating a Null object (Get➔Primitive➔Null) and making it the parent of all the smaller posts around the inner circle.

Use the Escape key when you are done to avoid accidental parenting (if only it was this easy in real life...)

Now make each lintel the parent of the stones below it.

SELECTING AND TRANSFORMING CENTERS, POINTS AND CLUSTERS

All objects are made up of smaller things called components. Examples of components are points, lines, polygons, isolines, boundaries, and knots.

Sometimes you will want to select and move just a Component of an object, not the whole object itself. For example, the local center of the object is a component, and you will often wish to change the position of the local center when modeling and animating. Each individual point is a component, and can be moved separately. A saved group of points is called a cluster, and clusters can be transformed as well. On surfaces, each isoline can be selected and translated, and the boundary edges can be selected and transformed. There are many more components that respond to the transform menu cells, and you can see a complete list by clicking on the Component Filter button, in the Selection panel of the MCP, which is the top part, directly under the big arrow symbols, in the tiny diagonal triangle drop menu.

This component filter works in two ways. First, your selection tools will only work to select whatever kind of item is active in that list. The active item is the item that is printed on the menu button itself when you let go of the menu.

Secondly, when you have a component selected in the filter, the transformation cells will only operate on components of that type.

Some components are so commonly transformed that they have their own buttons and hotkeys.

OBJECT MODE

Object means that whole objects and hierarchies can be translated, rotated and scaled. Object is the most common mode; you used it to move, scale and rotate objects for the Stonehenge scene. When in Object mode, the transformation keys work on all the vertices of the current object equally. There is an Object button in the Selection panel of the MCP, and you can use this to switch back to Object mode after using one of the other component filters.

The Component menu allows you to pick just what you want

CENTER MODE

When Center mode is selected, then the transformation keys operate only on the local center of an object. The object vertices remain located in global space where they were. Moving the center of an object allows you to change the axis of rotation, determine where the object scales from, and from where the object's position in space will be measured.

POINT MODE

When you enter Point mode by tapping or holding the M hotkey, you can point at and transform individual points, one at a time. You can also define groups of vertices or points, which is called tagging.

Tagging is so commonly used in XSI that there is a hotkey for it: T. Whenever you hold down the T hotkey you can select and deselect points to add to the current tagged group for that object. Then, when points are tagged, you are automatically placed in Point filter mode, and the transformation menu cells to work only on that tagged group. Try it out by tagging points on a sphere with the T hotkey and then translating them to make a pear. Check the status bar when you have the T hotkey held down to see how the three mouse buttons will operate differently. If you are using the XSI selection model (not recommended for this) you have to use Shift and CTRL in addition to the Left Mouse Button to add and remove tagged points to and from the selection. If you use the SI3D selection model (much better for this), then the Left Mouse Button adds to the group, the middle removes from the group and the right toggles tagged points back and forth. You can check your selection model by looking at the bottom of the Selection menu in the MCP.

CLUSTERS MODE

Normally, when you are done manipulating tagged points, you move on and do something else, and the tagged group that you had selected is lost. You can save that group if you want, by turning it into a Cluster, with the Cluster button in the lower portion of the MCP under the Edit menu.

Now that cluster can always be selected again, using the big Plus (+) button at the top of the MCP, in conjunction with Point filter mode, by selecting the object in Object filter mode and clicking on the Cluster Explorer button in the MCP at the bottom of the Selection area.

SELECTING POLYGON COMPONENTS WITH THE FILTER

Polygonal meshes are made up of polygons, and polygons are made up of vertices and edges.

Each component of a polymesh (polygon, edge, and vertex) can be selected so that you can work with it. You can select just one at a time or groups of components. You cannot, however, select some edges AND vertices at the same time; it's one component type at a time. This one at a time selection method is called a Filter. With the Polygon selection filter active you can only select polygons, with the Edge filter on, you just select Edges, and so on.

The Selection Filter is located in the MCP near the top. Since Point, Edge and Polygon are so common, buttons for just those filters appear automatically in the MCP whenever you have a Polygon object selected. They do not show when you have a NURBS object selected.

When you click on the Point button, you can select points using the standard selection tools, by holding the space bar and clicking on vertices or dragging a rectangle around them. Similarly, if you click the Edge button at the top left of the MCP you can select groups of Edges. The Polygon button filters the selection tool so that it only works on Polygons.

SETTING SELECTION PREFERENCES

There are two selection methods in XSI - the standard Windows method, which uses Shift and CTRL to extend selections, and the Softimage 3D Selection model. We'll refer only to the Softimage 3D Selection model in this book.

NOTE You need a good three button mouse for polygon modeling, because you need to use one finger per button. The kind with a wheel in the middle just won't do, because your middle finger doesn't stay there easily. If you have a wheel mouse, use your middle finger on whoever can get you a new one.

COMPONENT SELECTION HOTKEYS

While there are buttons in the MCP which activate the component filters, using them would be very slow. You would have to take your eyes off the object you are working on, move the mouse cursor up to the MCP, make a change, then go back to the object, hold the space bar and make the selection. Since you'll be doing this thousands of times each day as you sculpt, that method just won't do. The faster way is to use the hotkeys for component selection.

SELECTING VERTICES

If you hold down the T key with your left hand you can select, deselect and toggle vertices with the three mouse buttons. With the T hotkey down, drag a rectangle selection around some of the vertices on your Sphere. Note that the vertices become tagged in red (Hotkey T for Tagged). Note that the Point filter is automatically enabled.

If you want to add to the group of selected points, just hold T again and drag a rectangle around those points, and they will be added to the others already tagged in red. If some points became selected that you didn't want, drag a rectangle around those with your Middle Mouse Button and note that they are removed from the tagged group. Try dragging a rectangle around the whole Sphere with the Right Mouse Button, and see that the tagged group is inverted: those that were not tagged now are, and those that were are no longer. This convention, where the Left Mouse Button adds to the group, the middle removes, and the right toggles is called the Extended Component Selection model, and works for all components.

SELECTING EDGES

If you hold down the E key with your left hand (Hotkey E for Edge), you can select, deselect and toggle edges with the three mouse buttons. The Left Mouse Button adds Edges to the selection, the middle deselects edges, and the right toggles edges. Selected edges show in red, deselected edges show in amber. Drawing a selection rectangle will select all edges that are within the rectangle or touch the rectangle, on both sides of the object.

SELECTING POLYGONS

Polygons are special - they have two different component selection hotkeys. The Y hot hey selects polygons in the same way that you select edges and vertices, by dragging a rectangle that selects all the polygons that are entirely within the selection rectangle.

The selected polygons will show in translucent red. The problem is that while you are working in shaded view, you might be selecting polygons on the back of the object without knowing it, and messing up your model. To solve this problem, the U hotkey was pressed into service. When you hold the U key, you can click over the middle of a polygon, and only the polygon facing out of the model towards you will be selected. This is called Raycasting, and it is very useful. You can also hold U while dragging a stroke across the model to paint in a selection. As usual, the extended component selection model means that the Left Mouse Button adds to the selection, the middle removes polygons from the selection, and the Right Mouse Button toggles polygons.

Remember that the hotkeys are crucial to fast, efficient workflow. Practice with them until they are second nature. Hotkey E works on edges, T selects vertices, Y selects polygons by rectangle, and U selects polygons by raycasting.

For the truly adventurous, each of these can also be modified with the other selection tools, freeform and lasso, although this requires the manual gymnastics waggishly called "Finger Olympics".

SELECTING AND TRANSFORMING TEXTURE SUPPORTS

When your object has one or more texture maps on it, you will often need to move those maps around, rotating and scaling them to the exact placement you want. This is done by selecting the Texture Support in the 3D view window, or in the Explorer, and using the transformation cells in the MCP just as you would on any other object. If you have Created a Texture support, it will show up in the 3D view as a green Wireframe object.

SELECTING AND TRANSFORMING NURBS COMPONENTS

If you have a NURBS object selected, you can choose NURBS-specific options from the Selection filter list.

Isopoint selects a location anywhere on the surface of the model, and reads back to you the location in U and V of that point.

Knot filter allows you to select surface knots, although these cannot (in XSI v1.5) be transformed.

U and V knot curves select an entire knot line in the surface.

U and V isolines selects an isoline on the surface and reads back its position.

Boundary selects only U and V edges in the surface.

TRANSFORMATION OPTIONS

When you have one or more of the transformation menu cells activated, some new buttons will become active below the SRT area, just above the Constraint menu. These buttons control what the transformation is performed relative to. For instance, you might wish to translate the object relative to the global center (Global mode) or you might prefer to translate it relative to the objects own local center (Local mode).

If you want the object to move relative to the axes of its parent (the object above it in the hierarchy) you may use Parent mode (Par on the button).

When you are in View mode, the object moves relative to the view mode that your mouse is over when you drag. This is like the DRG mode of Softimage 3D 3.9. View mode is the most useful mode unless you need to make precise adjustments.

Scale can be relative to either the object's local center or a parent reference object.

Rotation can happen relative to the Global or Local axes.

UNIFORM TRANSFORMATIONS

When you are transforming objects after modeling them, and you want them to scale up evenly in each axis, one way to do it is simply hold down each of the three mouse buttons at the same time while you drag. The problem with this method is that you may not get each mouse button depressed at exactly the same instant, which would cause the model to become distorted slightly as it scales up. If you hold down the Shift modifier while dragging with the Scale cells active, you will be assured that the model will scale uniformly. As an added bonus, the Left Mouse Button will grow the object slowly, the Middle Mouse Button will grow the object at a medium rate, and the Right Mouse Button will make the object grow most rapidly.

FREEZING, RESETTING TRANSFORMS, AND ALIGNING OBJECTS

Once you have an object transformed, you may wish to un-transform it. You can easily return it to the position where it was created (or the position in which it was frozen) by choosing the Reset All Transforms option from the Transformation menu. This returns Scale to 1,1,1, rotation to 0,0,0 and places the object back at the global center. The hotkey combo is CTRL-Shift-R. Resetting transforms actually changes the shape of the object, removing the effects of the scale, rotation and translation on the vertices.

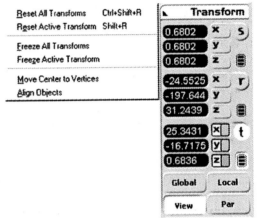

The transformation menu

Sometimes you will want to set all the transformations back to the starting point without changing the shape of the object. This is called freezing the object. Each vertex is held precisely where it is, but the Center of the object is returned to 0,0,0 and scaled to 1,1,1 without any rotations. Freezing is less important in XSI than it was in Softimage 3D 3.9.

XSI includes a very handy Align feature, also in the Transform menu. Any number of selected objects can be aligned in space (translated) to either the middle point of the group, or the highest point or lowest point in the group, or aligned with the first object that was selected.

XSI can also return a center to the geometric middle of an object (or to any other place you require) with the Transform➔Move Center to Vertices tool. To use it, tag some points (or all points) on the object, and execute that menu command. The center will move to the middle of those tagged points. If you do not tag any points the center will go to the middle of the object bounding box.

ORGANIZING THE SCHEMATIC VIEW

The schematic view window is a pretty important window in Softimage, and it can quickly get cluttered. Feel free to move the items in the schematic window around as much as you like, just as you would move objects around the scene: with the translate menu cells.

There are also automatic commands to clean up and organize the schematic view, located in the menu bar at the top of the schematic view window. The Tools→Rearrange tool will spread out all the items in the Schematic view. The Tile command is better - it spreads out the hierarchies in the Schematic view without changing the position of the child nodes, so that if you have a hierarchy that you have carefully arranged it won't be completely messed up when you organize the Schematic view.

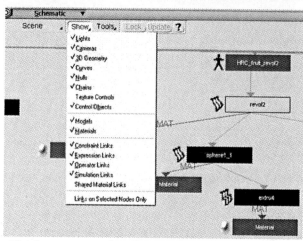

The drop menu in the schematic has tools to reorganize things for you

ORGANIC MODELING: AT A GLANCE

TOPICS COVERED

In this tutorial you will practice what you have learned by creating some primitive objects and making a bowl of fruit out of them. You will create them by changing their geometry properties in a property page, and by pushing and pulling points and groups of tagged points on the surface.

You'll learn how to:

- Create primitive objects
- Modify object properties
- Sculpt shapes with the transformations

TUTORIAL: MAKING A BOWL OF FRUIT

Very often, pushing and pulling points is a good way to quickly create simple shapes. Smooth, organic shapes are the easiest to create in this manner. In this tutorial you will quickly create a bowl of simple fruit shapes by moving points and by tagging and transforming the tagged group of points

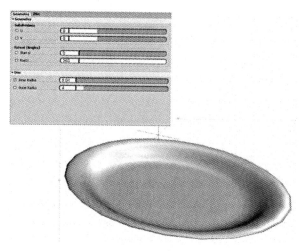

The bowl is just a disc

STEP 1. MAKE A BOWL

Get a primitive surface disc. In the general property page, change the Disc/Inner Radius to zero, so that there is no longer a hole in the middle of the disc.

Tag the outermost three points that sit close to the last row (V) around the outside of the disc. Use the T hotkey and the three mouse buttons to add and subtract points from the tagged group until you have the ones you want selected. You are automatically in Point filter mode because you used the T hotkey.

Translate those points up in Global Y to form the lip of the fruit plate.

STEP 2. MAKE A PEAR

Get a primitive surface sphere, and in the Geometry tab of the general property page, add more rows in V (V subdivision) so you have some more points to tag when making the shape of the pear. Eleven or twelve rows in V should be fine. In the Sphere tab of the property page, change the name of the object to 'pear'.

In the front view, frame the pear and tag the rows of points at the top pole and the next row down. Translate them up in positive Y to make a neck for the pear.

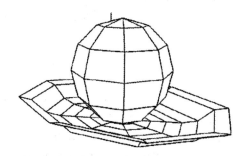

The pear begins life as a sphere

Untag those points, and tag the next two rows down. We want to make these thinner, scaling them down in X and Z. To do this, activate all the scale cells and hold down both your left and Right Mouse Buttons, and drag to make the neck of the pear smaller.

Make the rows at the base flatter and fuller. Sculpt the base of the pear to your liking using the same method: selecting rows of points and scaling and translating them. Keep a your pear framed in the perspective view so you can see how it looks as you work.

Rough up the pear with the M hotkey. In the perspective view, show the points on the surface by pulling down the Show menu and toggling on the Points option. Now you can see each point even when they are not tagged. Hold down the M hotkey and click and hold the Left Mouse Button over a point, then drag the mouse to move just that point in space a bit. Do this repeatedly on different points to make the pear less uniform. Orbit the pear with the O hotkey as needed while moving points.

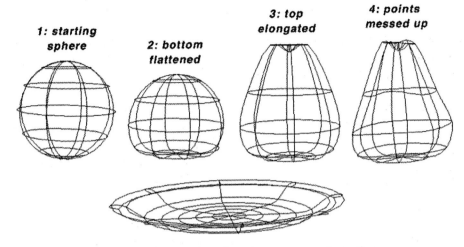

1: starting sphere
2: bottom flattened
3: top elongated
4: points messed up

With some points tagged on the sphere, you can shape the pear

Place the pear in the dish. Scale and translate the pear as needed to fit it onto the dish you made. Rotate it a bit so it doesn't look so stiff. Duplicate the pear and transform the second pear so it is a different size, in a different place on the dish, leaning against the first pear.

STEP 3. MAKE MORE FRUIT

Make some other fruit as desired, using the same methodology of tagging and moving points. Try an apple, a plum, or an orange. Extra credit for a banana.

CONCLUSION

Now you have had some good basic experience creating objects, moving them around, selecting components and doing basic organic modeling. In addition, you should have a firm grasp of NURBS and Polygon terminology and differences.

You should also understand the rather fully featured selection tools in XSI, and be able to limit your selection to the objects or components that you want to work with.

NOTE Each move you make results in a move operator, which you can see by clicking on the Selection button in the MCP. These illustrate that you can undo any one of these moves at any time. When you are done, it's a good idea to flatten all these move operators. Click the freeze button at the bottom of the MCP to flatten the operator stack and cook all the moves down into a final shape for the pear. You can still undo them all with Command Z.

QUIZ

1. WHICH OBJECT TYPE USES CURVED LINE SEGMENTS?
    a. NURBS
    b. Polygons
    c. Both

2. WHICH COMPONENT WILL YOU NOT FIND ON A NURBS SURFACE?
    a. knot
    b. isopoint
    c. vertex

3. WHAT COMPONENT WILL YOU NOT FIND ON A POLYGON?
    a. isoline
    b. edge
    c. normal

4. WHICH OBJECTS HAVE A CENTER?
    a. sphere
    b. polygon mesh
    c. all objects

5. DO POLYGONS HAVE U AND V COORDINATES?
    a. yes
    b. no

6. "DIVIDING UP A MATHEMATICALLY DERIVED SURFACE INTO MANY SMALL TRIANGLES" DESCRIBES WHAT TERM?
    a. Trimming
    b. Weighting
    c. Tessellation

7. WHEN SCALING AN OBJECT, HOLDING THE SHIFT BUTTON WILL:
    a. add to the selection
    b. make it bigger
    c. scale uniformly

8. WHICH MENU IS THE ALIGN TOOL IN?
    a. Model / Modify
    b. Transform
    c. Constraint

9. THE TRANSFORMATIONS ARE:
    a. Scale, Size, and Thickness
    b. Scale, Rotation, and Translation
    c. Motion and Animation

10. WHEN AN OBJECT ROTATES IN LOCAL MODE, IT'S ROTATING AROUND:
    a. The middle of the screen
    b. global 0,0,0
    c. It's own axis

11. WHEN A CAMERA ORBITS, IT IS ROTATING AROUND:
    a. the middle of the screen
    b. its own axis
    c. the camera interest

3 ORGANIZATION, HIERARCHY, AND GROUPS

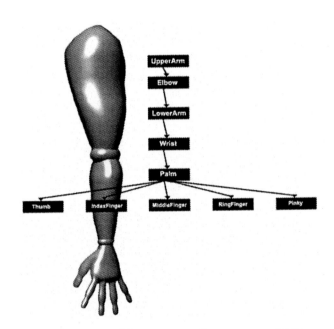

IN THIS CHAPTER YOU WILL LEARN ABOUT:

- What are hierarchies, parents, children, trees, models, groups, and inherited transformations?
- Why are hierarchies useful in animation?
- How to use and organize the Schematic View
- The difference between selecting by node and selecting by branch
- How to use and organize the Explorer

INTRODUCTION

In this chapter, we will discuss how to create a relationship between objects called a hierarchy. We will discuss terminology and metaphors to understand the concept. We also learn how to use the Schematic view and Explorer to build a hierarchy by parenting and cutting objects. At the end of the lesson we will create an arm out of multiple objects, all connected by a hierarchical relationship.

HIERARCHY

As your scene grows with more objects, lights and other elements, you have to find a way to organize your scene in some way. Without clear organization, picking an element can become a very tedious job and your eyes will be very sore and red at the end of the day. A hierarchy is one way to organize scene elements to create an understandable structure.

Imagine you modeled an entire arm with its palm attached to the arm, and fingers attached to the palm; it looks just like the arm of a normal human being. Any element with another element attached to it is called a parent. In this arm metaphor, the arm is the parent of the palm and fingers. In turn, the palm is also the parent of fingers, since the palm is higher up in the hierarchy compared to the fingers. Any element under a parent is called a child. The fingers are children of the palm and the palm is a child of the arm.

This whole hierarchical structure (the whole arm) is called the tree.

Consequently, the top of hierarchy is called the root. Any sub-hierarchies under the root are called branches. So the arm is the root of this particular hierarchy and the connections between the palm and fingers are branches. If nothing is attached to or is below the element, you can simply call it a node. However, a node can refer to any single object as long as you can see it in Explorer, even a parent or a root.

You can imagine an uprooted and upside-down tree as a hierarchy with its root up in the air and branches and leaves pointing down.

A model is a way to merge different hierarchies into one hierarchy. By using a model node, you can combine groups of hierarchies, sections of a hierarchy, and/or any nodes under one null to create a super-hierarchy. A model node is non-rendering since they are nulls. You could make a yo-yo and group it in the same model hierarchy as an arm. It's one extra way to create more control over your hierarchy.

Group is another way to organize objects. You must be screaming, "Why do we have so many ways to create organization?" However, a group works a bit differently than normal parent/child relationships. Any operations applied - such as deformation tools, shaders, materials, and textures - are mutually shared by objects in the group. Of course, you can create groups within groups to create parent/child relationships as well. Groups override previously applied textures, materials, etc, but pre-grouped values are saved separately. We will explore how to apply groups later.

INHERITED TRANSFORMATIONS

Hierarchy is not just there to organize and to help you select objects efficiently. Another function of hierarchy is that by selecting an entire hierarchy or at any branches, transformations such as scaling, rotation, and translation applied to a parent can be passed on to children. This is called inherited transformation. This is very useful, because by just transforming a parent, you can apply relative transformation of a parent to all children, even if you have thousands of objects. Let's say, for example, that you want to transport a huge pine tree to Times Square for a Christmas display. You won't bring all tens of thousands of pine needles, hundreds of branches, and a trunk individually to Times Square and attach them there. You will simply cut the tree at the base and move everything intact. That's the power of hierarchy.

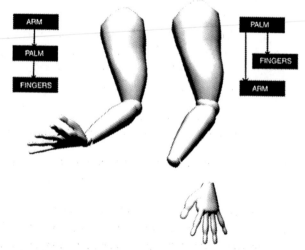

Different parenting methods create different results

There are many ways to create this parent-child relationship. You really have to think about what is the best way to create a hierarchy, so each element will interact properly.

For example, if the palm mistakenly becomes a parent of the arm, when the arm is moved, the palm and fingers will remain at the same place. Transformation of the arm is not inherited by the palm and fingers, because they are not children of the arm.

USING THE SCHEMATIC VIEW

The Schematic view is used to analytically view hierarchical and other relationships between elements. You can change a viewport to Schematic view by opening the change view menu located on top left of each viewport. Left-click on change view menu to get a pull-down menu and select the Schematic view. If you just started a new scene you will see default Scene_Material, a light, and a camera, with two constraints and two nulls.

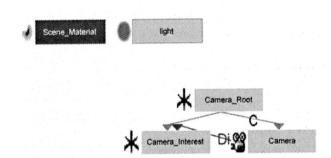

The default schematic in an "empty" scene

The boxes represent elements. Connections, such as hierarchy and constraints, are shown as a line between boxes.

You can create a hierarchy in the orthographic or perspective viewport too, but to see the tree-like hierarchy structure, schematic offers the best way to display it. You can't really see a relationship clearly in orthogonal or perspective view.

You can use the normal orthographic view mode hotkeys to move around in schematic view. For example, you can pan and zoom with the Z key, and frame selected object with the F key.

HOW TO CREATE A HIERARCHY

You can quickly create a hierarchy by using the Parent button, which is located on the right of the Main Command Panel, just below transformation cells. Select an object and then click the Parent button, which puts you in Parenting mode. While in Parent mode, left-clicking an object will make it the child of the object you have selected, middle-clicking an object will make it the parent of the object (or objects) you have selected, and right-clicking (or clicking the Parent button again) will end Parent mode.

You can now see lines connecting the objects in the schematic view. Which mouse button you use to when selecting objects will make a big difference when selecting objects in a hierarchy.

Left-clicking will choose any node as a single object. Selected objects will be highlighted in white, and if you hold the Left Mouse Button, you can move the selected objects around.

Middle-clicking on a parent will select the branch that belongs to the parent. For example, if you middle-click on Camera_Root, you will select the entire camera branch, including the actual Camera and the Camera_Interest. This is called Branch Selection. Notice if you select a branch, you can move the entire hierarchy by holding and dragging with the left or Middle Mouse Button. This is very important!

Right-click in the empty space or on a node, and a window will pop up, giving you a wide range of options. You can, for instance, rearrange a hierarchy to vertical or horizontal, delete a node or a branch, duplicate, and show properties of selected elements.

You may collapse and expand the hierarchy. This is very useful if you have many hierarchies in your scene. When a branch is collapsed, the parent will have a plus (+) mark on the left side of it, so you won't lose it.

To collapse or expand a hierarchy, Right-Click over it and choose either Collapse or Expand from the context sensitive drop menu.

Again, hierarchy creation can be done using other views as well, but the Schematic view gives you very efficient viewing and selecting options for hierarchy.

CUTTING HIERARCHY

Oops, you didn't mean to make that connection, did you? When you make a mistake or you want to rearrange hierarchy, you need to cut the connection between parent and child. You can do this by using the Cut button, which is located just to the right of the Parent button. Simply select the object you want to detach from the hierarchy, and click the Cut button. Now the connection line between the objects is gone.

USING THE EXPLORER TO EDIT HIERARCHY

Alternately, you can use Explorer to view and edit hierarchy. The Explorer can be opened by changing the view menu. You can also open a floating Explorer window by choosing View →Views→Explorer from the top menu bar.

The Explorer will display hierarchical structure a little differently than the Schematic view. The Explorer shows hierarchy branching out from left to right; the farther right you go, the lower you are on the hierarchy. Connections are displayed with vertical lines. If a line has a + or - sign, the element contains a hierarchy tree underneath. Clicking + expands the tree, and clicking - collapses the tree. You can hide any unnecessary hierarchy this way, to create a clutter-free display. You can also navigate through elements by using the arrow keys. The up- and down-arrow will move up and down the node in the hierarchy. The right-arrow will expand hierarchies, and the left-arrow will collapse them. Also, cutting and moving hierarchies can be much faster with Explorer: you simply hold the Left Mouse Button on the node, and drag it on top of the parent-to-be. If you want to cut the relationship, just drag the node to the Scene_Root node. Renaming nodes is also very easy: just right-click on the node and select Rename from the list that pops up.

"So why do we even bother with Schematic view?", you might ask. The great advantage of the Schematic view is that it is much more graphical, and you can arrange your hierarchies in any shape you like. For example, if you create a very complex human skin and skeleton setup, you can arrange the hierarchy to resemble a human, to speed up your selection process. If you are a visual thinker, graphic representation might be easier to understand in the beginning. Also, the Schematic view is based on Softimage 3D's Schematic view. If you are moving up to XSI from Soft 3D, it will be much more familiar to you than the Explorer view.

HOW TO GROUP OBJECTS TOGETHER

If you want to apply only operations and shared textures to objects, you can use group instead of hierarchy. You can create groups by selecting any number of objects and clicking the Group button, located in the Edit panel. If you want to add more objects to the group, first select a group you want to add objects to, then Shift-select the objects you want to add, and choose Edit→Add to Group from the Edit panel. Edit→Remove from Group will take selected objects out of a group. You can free every object from a group and erase the group node by selecting a group and clicking the Ungroup button.

Let's practice what we have learned so far with the following tutorial.

ROBOTIC ARM: AT A GLANCE

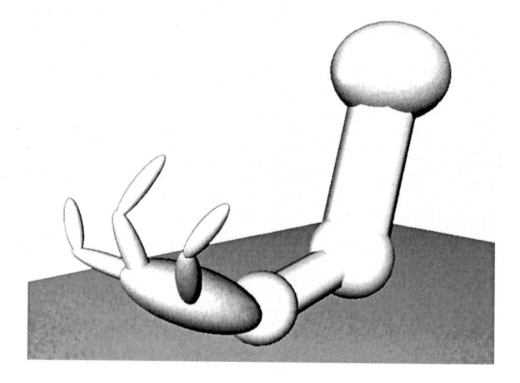

TOPICS COVERED

Previously, the structure of an arm was used to explain the concept of hierarchy. In this tutorial we'll continue that example by constructing an arm out of primitive objects and assembling a hierarchy.

You'll learn how to:

- Create hierarchy by using the Parent button.
- Use the Schematic view to edit hierarchy.
- Use hierarchy to take advantage of inherited transformation.

TUTORIAL: ROBOTIC ARM

STEP 1. CREATE THE ARM

Use Get→Primitive→Surface→Sphere. Change the sphere's name to "shoulder" in the General property page. Set its radius to 2 by dragging the bar next to the Radius property. You can also type "2" directly where number is displayed.

Get→Primitive→Polygon Mesh→Cylinder to obtain a polygon cylinder for the upper arm. Change its name to "upperArm" and Height to 7.

Let's move upperArm down a bit, so its top end is in the center of the shoulder. In the Front of Right view, with upperArm selected, press the V key to activate the translate menu, and drag it down (-Y) into position.

Change the Right view to Schematic view. You can see shoulder and upperArm, but they don't have a connection yet.

STEP 2. ASSEMBLE THE HIERARCHY

Now we will make our first hierarchy: the shoulder will be a parent of the upperArm. Select the shoulder sphere, then click on the Parent button, located at the right side of the window just below the Translation menu cell. If you look at the status line at the bottom of the screen, you will see that you have three choices. Since we are picking upperArm as a child, the Left Mouse Button is the one we want. Simply left-click on upperArm in any window, including schematic view. Now, upperArm is highlighted also, but slightly gray. As

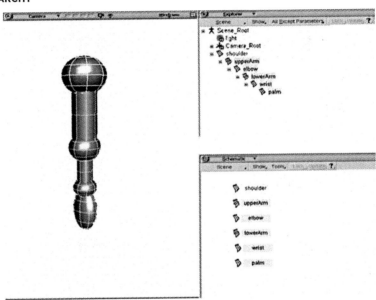

This is the hierarchy of an arm

this color scheme suggests, these two objects are branch selected, and the bright white sphere is the parent of grayish cylinder underneath. You can now see the hierarchical structure in schematic view: there is a line between shoulder and upperArm. Be sure to right-click (anywhere) to end Parent mode, so nothing is added to the hierarchy accidentally.

Let's duplicate the entire hierarchy to create the elbow joint and the lower arm. Make sure shoulder and upperArm are branch selected. In the Schematic view, right-click on shoulder, and choose Duplicate from the menu that pops up. Now you have a new hierarchy, called shoulder1 and upperArm1.

We should rename these new objects to avoid confusion. Right-click on shoulder1 and open the property editor by hitting Enter key, then change its name to "elbow". Using the same method, change upperArm1 to "lowerArm".

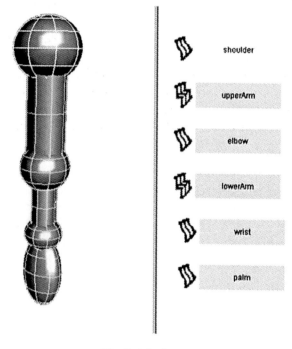

shoulder

upperArm

elbow

lowerArm

wrist

palm

The finished arm

The elbow and lowerArm were duplicated right on top of the shoulder and upperArm. To move them into position, branch select them by middle-button-selecting elbow (which should result in both elbow and lowerArm being highlighted), and in the Front or Right view, translate them in -Y, so that the bottom of upperArm is in the middle of the elbow.

Let's connect these two hierarchies. Select upperArm by itself (node select), click the Parent button, and then click on elbow. Now there is a one long string of hierarchy from shoulder to lowerArm. Right-click to end Parenting mode.

Add a palm to the arm. Create a NURBS surface sphere by choosing Get→Primitive→Surface→Sphere, then change its name to "palm" and radius to 1, and close the property page. Scale the palm on the X-axis in Front view and Z-axis in Right view, so you have a thinner and flatter palm. Place the palm at the tip of lowerArm by translating it on the Y-axis.

Previously, we have selected the intended parent, clicked the Parent button, and then picked the child. Let's use a slightly different method for the palm. With the palm selected, click the Parent button. Look at the Status line at the bottom of the screen; it says middle-click to select a parent. So, middle-click on lowerArm to make it the parent of the palm.

STEP 3. MOVE THE ARM: INHERITED TRANSFORMATION
You are all done! To move this arm, you can simply branch select from the shoulder or elbow joint and rotate in any direction you desire. Try this: middle-click on the elbow in schematic view. Make sure the elbow is highlighted in white and lowerArm and the palm have turned gray. Rotate the elbow to flex some muscle. LowerArm and palm should follow elbow's rotation since they are children of the elbow. Meanwhile, the shoulder and upperArm remain at the same place, because they are higher up in the hierarchy. Do the same thing for the shoulder: rotate and translate to see how every part of the arm follows the transformation relative to the shoulder's transformation.

Inherited transformation is an extremely useful tool. Schematic view is also very helpful when selecting objects and hierarchies, since you can see the entire structure, and you don't need to be in a selection mode to select objects. 3D animation is very time-consuming, so the speed and efficiency these tools give you is very important for you to become a successful artist. And your eyes are saved too.

CONCLUSION

You learned how to create hierarchies and what they are used for. You will use these techniques repeatedly to organize your work. You also learned some new terminology. "Parent" and "child" refer to relationship of objects within a hierarchy. An entire hierarchy is called a "tree" and top of the hierarchy is called the "root". Inherited transformation helps you transform and animate many objects at once. Model and Group are two additional ways to organize objects. We also learned how to use the Schematic and Explorer views to create and edit hierarchy. By now, you should be comfortable with the concept and use of hierarchy; use it to your advantage.

QUIZ

True or False?

1. INHERITED TRANSFORMATION IS VERY USEFUL FOR TRANSFORMING MULTIPLE OBJECTS.
    a. True
    b. False
2. GROUP OVERRIDES HIERARCHY RELATIONSHIP.
    a. True
    b. False
3. THE MINUS (-) SIGN IN THE EXPLORER WILL EXPAND A HIERARCHY.
    a. True
    b. False
4. A "CHILD" IS THE TOP OF A HIERARCHY.
    a. True
    b. False
5. BRANCH SELECTION LETS YOU SELECT MULTIPLE OBJECTS THAT BELONG TO SAME BRANCH.
    a. True
    b. False
6. THE CUT BUTTON REMOVES AN ELEMENT FROM ITS PARENT ABOVE.
    a. True
    b. False
7. A "ROOT" IS A BOTTOM END OF A HIERARCHY.
    a. True
    b. False
8. NODE REPRESENTS THE END OF HIERARCHY.
    a. True
    b. False
9. A "PARENT" ALWAYS HAS OTHER ELEMENTS UNDERNEATH IT IN A HIERARCHY.
    a. True
    b. False
10. "TREE" IS ANOTHER WORD FOR AN ENTIRE HIERARCHY STRUCTURE.
    a. True
    b. False
11. THE EXPLORER IS AN ALTERNATE WAY TO EDIT THE HIERARCHY GRAPHICALLY.
    a. True
    b. False

4 SIMPLE POLYGON MODELING

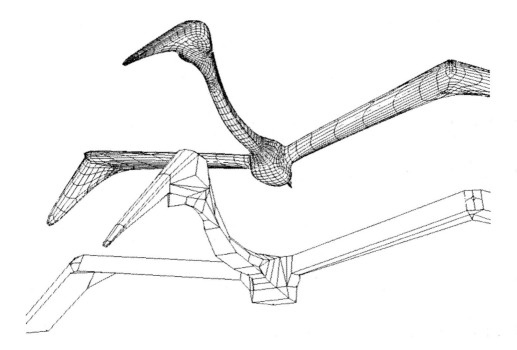

IN THIS CHAPTER YOU WILL LEARN ABOUT:

- How to choose whether to work on polygons or NURBS
- All about polygon terminology
- How to use the polygon building tools
- How to create objects starting with a polygon primitive
- The process of sculpting and gradual refinement
- What Subdivision Surfaces are, and how they work in XSI
- Sub-D Surface technique

INTRODUCTION

XSI uses two main surface types for building objects: NURBS and Polygons. Each has distinct advantages and disadvantages, and so each one is better for some tasks than for others. NURBS are mathematically defined curving surfaces that are infinitely smooth, while polygonal surfaces are made up of many straight line segments. This means that it is easier to make (and edit) a really smooth NURBS surface than a really smooth polygonal surface. However, NURBS are always rectangular patches, and are very hard to connect together into more complex shapes. Using polygon modeling tools and techniques, an artist can easily make shapes of whatever topology he wishes (not just rectangular), and separate polygon objects are easy to merge together into one object, and won't show seams.

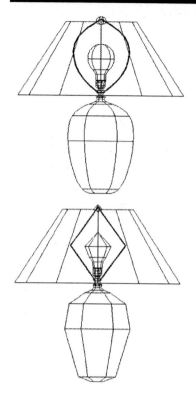

NURBS can be converted into polygons

POLYGON MODELING TOOLS

In a Surface modeler, objects have no density, no material inside their shapes. Objects are just infinitely thin shells surrounding nothingness. Those shells tended to be built of many small line segments, connecting the dots to form a surface Mesh. In surface meshes, the simplest way to connect the dots is with straight lines. An object created from a series of dots connected by straight lines is called a polygon mesh.

POLYGONS IN GAME ENGINES

One of the big advantages of polygons is that they are simple to display on-screen. All a computer has to do is transpose the straight lines onto a view plane, fill in the shape either with a solid color, a shade, or a texture map, and move on to the next polygon. As a result, where computers need to draw to the screen rapidly, polygons have been often used. Games are just such an occasion. In order for you to wander the 3D environment of your favorite game, the game engine has to draw the entire world from your point of view many times a second. The faster it can draw the world to the screen, the smoother the motion seems and the better your gaming experience.

How many times each second the game can draw the screen is largely dependent on how many polygons are in the scene. More polygons are going to take more time to draw. As a result, early game systems had very limited polygon 'budgets', and were able to display only 2,000 to 5,000 polygons per frame while drawing 30 frames per second.

More modern machines like the Dreamcast and Playstation2 have increased in power to the extent that they can easily draw more polygons per frame than there are pixels on screen, resulting in near perfect resolution, very crisp images and few visible polygon artifacts. Certainly the next step will be to use the ever-increasing computational power to draw more complex curved surfaces, but for now games still rely heavily on polygonal modeling.

Surfaces in XSI are hollow

POLYGON GUIDES FOR NURBS MODELING

Even when your character will really need to be created with multiple NURBS patches and stitched together, it is often easiest to build a low resolution polygonal model of the character first to use for prototyping. You can make quick and easy adjustments to shape and proportion, and then trace that polygon mesh with NURBS curves to build the final NURBS surface patches. XSI has great tools for you to draw perfect curves right on polygonal characters, making it much easier to build the patches you need.

POLYGON TERMINOLOGY

Polygons are simple, but there is some terminology to learn first, before we begin exploring the polygon tools in XSI. First, lets change the feedback that XSI gives us so that we can see the parts of the polygon that we are talking about.

In the Camera view, go to the Show menu, which is located under the Eye shaped icon at the center of the View title bar and make sure that Points, Normals, and Boundaries are checked on, so they will show up in the Camera view.

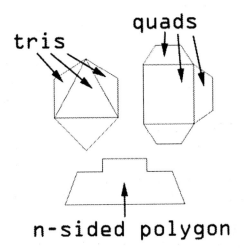

The Show Menu is where you toggle on different feedback options

Now get a Primitive→Polygon Mesh→Sphere and examine it in the Camera view.

Each polygonal mesh is made up of many smaller individual polygons. A polygon is a geometric shape with at least three sides. Three-sided polygons are called triangles, four sided polygons are called quads, and polygons with more than four sides are called n-sided polygons. A polygon can generally have as many as 255 sides, but it's a much better idea to keep them simple. A complex polygon with many sides can always be broken up into more polygons each with fewer sides.

EDGES

The side of a polygon is called an edge. When an edge of one polygon abuts the neighboring polygon, we say that the edge is shared, or closed. When the edge is on the outside of the shape, or abutting a hole, we say that the edge is open.

Polygons can have anywhere from 3 to 255 sides

VERTEX, VERTICES

The points in space that connect the edges are called Vertices. A single point is called a vertex. Vertices are located in Cartesian space with values for the X, Y and Z axis, so we might say that a vertex is at -3,5,8 which would mean that it is 3 units in the negative direction in X, 5 units up in Y, and 8 units forward in Z, relative to the global center.

NORMALS

Each polygonal mesh, being an infinitely thin shell of a surface, has an inside and an outside. Since the render can render just the inside, just the outside, or both, it's important to know which way the surface is facing.

If you built an object that was inside-out (and this happens a lot) then it might not shade or render correctly. The best way to check the direction of the surface is to examine the Normals. Normals are the thin blue lines radiating from each vertex like spiky blue hair. Normals extend in the outside direction of the surface. Technically, they are perpendicular to the surface, but sometimes we just call that "normal to the surface". If the normals are pointing inside your object, it's inside-out and needs to be inverted.

Try using the Modify→Surface→Inverse Normals command on your sphere to see what that would look like.

It is very important that all the polygons in a mesh have normals facing the same direction. Imagine that if some of the polygons faced out in your sphere and some faced in, it would be really hard to figure out how to render it correctly. If you were developing the model for use in a real time renderer, it would show strange holes and artifacts in the object that would look bad. As a result, you should pay attention to the Normal direction as you build polygon objects. Generally, XSI tries to not let you create such mixed polygon surfaces, but should you accidentally create one, you can select just one polygon (covered next) and invert just that selected polygon with Modify→Poly Mesh→Invert Polygons.

So, to repeat our terminology, polygonal meshes are made up of polygons, and polygons are made up of vertices and edges. Polygons, vertices, and edges are called Components. You will work with each type of component using that component mode from the filter selection at the top-right of the Main Command Panel (MCP.)

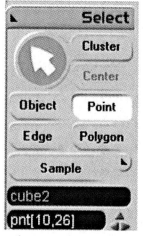

The components: Edges, Vertices, and Normals

THE POLYGON COMPONENTS FILTER

Each component type (polygon, edge, and vertex) can be selected so that you can work with it. You can select just one at a time or groups of components. You cannot, however, select some edges and vertices at the same time; it's one component type at a time. This one-at-a-time selection method is called a Filter. With the Polygon selection filter active, you can only select polygons; with the Edge filter on, you just select Edges, and so on.

The Selection Filter is located in the MCP near the top. Since Point, Edge and Polygon are so common, buttons for just those filters appear automatically in the MCP whenever you have a Polygon object selected. They do not show when you have a NURBS object selected.

SELECTING COMPONENTS

While there are buttons in the MCP which activate the component filters, using them would be very slow. You would have to take your eyes off the object you are working on, move the mouse cursor up to the MCP, make a change, then go back to the object, hold the space bar and make the selection. Since you'll be doing this thousands of times each day as you sculpt, that method just won't do. The faster way is to use the hotkeys for component selection.

SELECTING VERTICES

If you hold down the T key with your left hand you can select, deselect, and toggle vertices with the three mouse buttons, respectively. With the T hotkey down, drag a rectangle selection around some of the vertices on your Sphere. Note that the vertices become tagged in red (Hotkey T for Tagged). Also note that the Point filter is automatically enabled.

If you want to add to the group of selected points, just hold T again and drag a rectangle around those points using the Left Mouse Button, and they will be added to the others already tagged in red. If some points became selected that you didn't want, drag a rectangle around those with your Middle Mouse Button and note that they are removed from the tagged group. Try dragging a rectangle around the whole Sphere with the Right Mouse Button, and see that the tagged group is inverted: those that were not tagged now are, and those that were are no longer. This convention, where the Left Mouse Button adds to the group, the middle removes, and the right toggles is called the Extended Component Selection model, and works for all components.

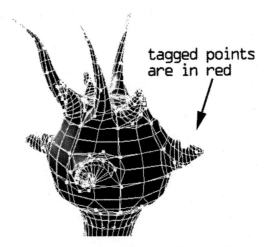

Tag, Untag, and Toggle verts with T and the Left, Middle, and Right mouse buttons

SELECTING EDGES

If you hold down the E key with your left hand (hotkey E for Edge) you can select, deselect, and toggle edges with the three mouse buttons. The Left Mouse Button adds edges to the selection, the middle deselects edges, and the right toggles edges. Selected edges show in red, deselected edges show in amber. Drawing a selection rectangle will select all edges that are within the rectangle or touch the rectangle, on both sides of the object.

SELECTING POLYGONS

Polygons are special - they have two different component selection hotkeys. The Y hotkey selects polygons in the same way that you select edges and vertices, by dragging a rectangle that selects all the polygons that are entirely within the selection rectangle.

The selected polygons will show in translucent red. The problem is that while you are working in shaded view, you might be selecting polygons on the back of the object without knowing it, and messing up your model. To solve this problem, the U hotkey was pressed into service. When you hold the U

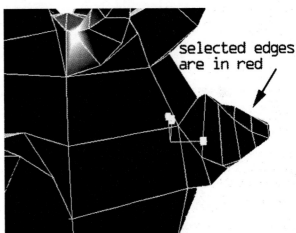

Select, Unselect, and Toggle edges with E and the Left, Middle, and Right mouse buttons

key, you can click over the middle of a polygon, and only the polygon facing out of the model towards you will be selected. This is called Raycasting, and it is very useful. You can also hold U while dragging a stroke across the model to paint in a selection. As usual, the extended component selection model means that the Left Mouse Button adds to the selection, the middle removes polygons from the selection, and the Right Mouse Button toggles polygons.

TRANSFORMING EDGES, VERTICES AND POLYGONS

Once you have a component or a group of components selected, you can sculpt the shape of the polygon object by transforming them. Polygons, vertices and edges can be scaled, rotated and translated to change the shape of the object.

You may also move individual vertices by holding the M (for Move points) hotkey, click-and-holding with your mouse at an individual vertex, and dragging to translate it.

When you have a component or group of components selected and you plan to transform them, the big question is always, "transform them relative to what?"

You can change the way that the components are transformed by clicking on the mode buttons in the MCP, right below the Transform cells, Global, Local and View.

raycast polies in red

Select, Unselect, and Toggle polygons with U and the Left, Middle, and Right mouse buttons

Generally the most useful method when working with components is the Local mode. When you translate a single component in the local mode, that component moves relative to its local axis. When translating a polygon, for instance, local Y is always normal to the surface (out from the surface) no matter how the polygon is facing in global space.

When you have more than one component selected in a contiguous block (that means that they are touching) then there is only one local axis for all the touching components together. That axis is the average of all the individual axes. Keep in mind that when the components are not touching, each has its own axis.

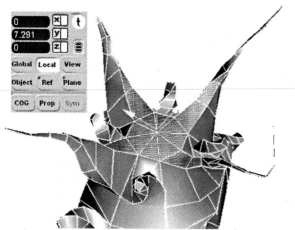

Local, Object, and Global are useful in different circumstances

Now try out transforming the components:

1. Try selecting every other polygon in a ring around the equator of your sphere (use U to raycast polygons), and in local mode carefully translate them in each axis to see the effect.

2. Try selecting all the edges around the middle of the sphere with the E hotkey, and scale them uniformly. See the effect that shortening them will have on the circumference of the sphere.

3. Try selecting a group of vertices near the top of the sphere with T, then extend that selection to include the similar points around the bottom again with T and the right button. Translate, scale and rotate these vertices to see the effect.

DRAWING POLYGONS FROM SCRATCH AND ALIGNING EDGES

You may also draw polygons one at a time by plotting points in space for the vertices, either starting from scratch or by sharing an edge with an existing polygon.

The important thing to understand when manually drawing polygons is that the polygons you draw must be kept facing the same direction as those around them. In other words, you want the normals of the new polygons you are drawing to match the direction of the normals all around them. If you drew one polygon with normals facing the wrong way, that might show up as a hole, or create problems later in modeling.

The direction that you draw the vertices of the polygon (either clockwise or anti-clockwise) determines which direction the normals will face. XSI will also warn you when you create a bad polygon by highlighting the edge between the good and bad polygons in green, as long as you have turned on Show Boundaries ion the Show menu at the top of the view window you are using.

To draw a polygon from scratch, choose the Add/Edit Polygon tool from the Polygon Mesh menu in the Model Module, and click with the Left Mouse Button to drop the first vertex in space wherever your mouse cursor is pointing. Move your cursor and click again to drop the next vertex. A line will connect the two, showing where the edge will be, with an arrow showing the correct direction of the polygon. Click a third time to drop the next vertex, and complete the most basic polygon, a triangle. You may continue to click if you wish to create a polygon with more edges. If you click with the Middle Mouse Button you will start a new polygon. The Add Polygon tool wants to connect the new polygon you are drawing to the existing polygons that you have drawn already whenever possible. If you click on a vertex of the selected polygon while in the Add Polygon tool, that vertex will be used and shared, and any edges that can be drawn in will also be added and shared. This intelligence ensures that your polygon geometry is as accurate as possible, that it shares vertices and edges whenever possible, and that the normals all point in a consistent direction.

When you are done with that tool, tap the Escape key on your keyboard to escape the tool and stop dropping vertices. Try to use the Hotkey for Add Polygon, which is N instead of the menu command.

SERIOUS POLY MODELING

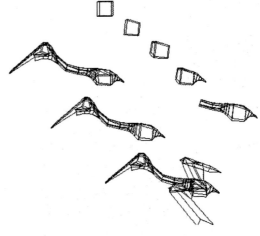

Often the most productive manner of polygon modeling is to start with a primitive object, and then refine that shape gradually to get the shape that you want. When you use this method, there is no right or wrong command to use at any given time, no set sequence of steps that must be followed, and no clear point at which you are done. You just look at what you have, imagine how you could make it better, and gradually refine the model. By turning it in the Camera view you examine the form of the model, and make decisions about how you could move polygons around, where you could add more edges to increase detail, and where you could translate vertices to make a more perfect shape.

The evolution from a cube to a Quetzacoatl

You may choose a primitive object that is similar in some way to the shape of the object you are modeling. Most people start with either a cube (easiest), a cylinder, or a sphere.

As you create more detail on the object by adding edges and duplicating polygons, the model takes on the shape you want.

Since this is a process of refinement, it makes sense to approach the task with more of an artistic, sculptural approach than the technical engineering approach required of NURBS modeling.

THE OPERATOR STACK, IMMEDIATE MODE AND FREEZE

When you execute a command on the polygon primitive object, it becomes an operator in the operator stack. Each and every move - each added vertex, each added edge, and each transformation of a component - is logged. In many ways, the model is actually still a primitive, and XSI rebuilds it constantly, repeating each command you have ever made. Since you'll make hundreds or thousands of changes to the model while sculpting it into a new shape, this method is overkill, and will slow down your productivity. There are two options to resolve this problem.

FREEZE

When you use the Freeze Operator Stack command from the Edit menu in the MCP, or click the Freeze button near the bottom of the MCP which does the same thing, all the changes that have been preserved in order in the operator stack will be combined and cooked down into the final shape of the mesh, then discarded. After a Freeze operator stack command you will be left with a simple polygon mesh in the same shape it was before, but with no operators. While you cannot now edit those operators, you could always Undo (command-Z) to restore the operator stack.

IMMEDIATE MODE

It seems like a hassle to first create a big operator stack then freeze it to remove the stack, so the Immediate mode was invented. When the Immediate mode is toggled on with the Immed button at the bottom of the MCP, operations are frozen as soon as they are completed, so that no giant operator stack is created. This does not mean that Undo won't work - it still remembers the last 20 things you've done so you can recover from mistakes.

If the operator is something that never requires you to see a Property Editor, like moving a point with the M hotkey, the operation will just be done and frozen without any further intervention on your part. If the operator requires a Property Editor to take input, like the CTRL-D Extrude command, the Property Editor will open as a modal dialog box with OK and Cancel buttons. You can make changes and when you click OK the command will execute and the operation will be frozen.

Immediate mode is the most convenient way to work when polygon modeling.

ADD EDGE

Many times a fantastic way to add more detail is to split one polygon into two. XSI has a fantastic tool for dividing polygons exactly how you want them, called Add Edge. Using Add Edge, you can either create just a new edge stretching from two existing vertices on the same polygon, or you can add a new vertex along the edge of a polygon and connect it to an existing vertex, or create another new vertex to join it to with a new edge. The tool provides excellent feedback as you work, and will not let you create bad edges.

To use Add Edge, first select the polygon object , then click on the Polygon Mesh→Add edge command and move your mouse over the mesh. Note that as you move over vertices and edges they are highlighted in Red, to indicate which you are about to split. Click to approve a starting vertex or edge, and then move your mouse to the opposite vertex of the same polygon, and click to select it. A new edge will be created connecting the two vertices. The tool cannot connect vertices that are not part of the same polygon. Tap the Escape key on your keyboard to complete the tool so you can start over fresh.

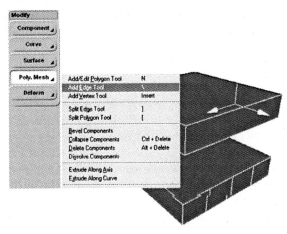

Adding an edge subdivides a single polygon into two polygons

Try it again - this time start with an edge, and rather than clicking, click and hold your Left Mouse Button to keep the command active, and slide the point back and forth along the edge by dragging the mouse left and right. When you have the spot you want, let off the mouse button. Wave your mouse over another edge of the same polygon (Add Edge cannot work across multiple polygons in one shot) and click again to split the polygon in two. Note that this time new vertices were also created, in addition to the edge.

You can use the Add Edge tool to chain together edges, each one starting where the last left off. On your sphere, start in the middle of an edge, and click in the middle of the next edge over. Then immediately click with the Left Mouse Button again on the next edge along the sphere to continue the edge, and keep going around the sphere. When done, you can click the Right Mouse Button to stay in the tool but choose a new starting position for a new edge. You can stay in the tool as long as you have edges to create, then tap the escape key on your keyboard to quit the tool.

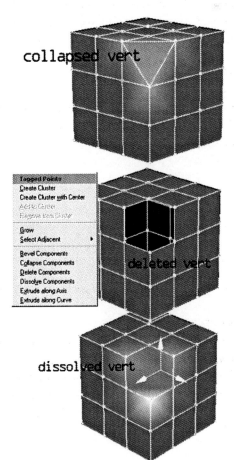

DELETING POLYGONS, VERTICES AND EDGES

Just as you can add more Polygons, vertices and edges, you can also delete them. When you select a polygon or group of polygons with the hotkey U, you can delete the polygons with the Delete key on your keyboard, or the Edit→Delete menu command from the MCP(FACT), leaving holes in the model. This tool is great for creating windows, doors and other openings in polygonal models.

Delete, Dissolve, and Collapse all remove vertices with different results

However, if you select either a vertex or an edge and use the Delete button or the Edit➜Delete command, that component is removed, and XSI tries to patch the space by creating a bigger polygon surrounding it. This method of removing polygons is called Dissolving.

COLLAPSING POLYGONS, EDGES AND VERTICES

When you collapse a component, something entirely different happens. Collapsing a polygon or an edge generally means to shrink that component down to a single point in space, and then replace it with a vertex. This keeps your surface whole and unbroken, which is generally a good thing.

However, when you select a Vertex and use the Poly Mesh➜Collapse Component tool, it removes that vertex and all the edges that were connecting it, then creates a new polygon to patch the hole.

DISSOLVING EDGES, VERTICES AND POLYGONS

Dissolving a component is like deleting a component, but then the resulting hole is filled in with a new polygon so that the surface is still complete and unbroken.

FROM NURBS TO POLYGONS

Both polygonal surfaces and NURBS have unique advantages and downsides. The key is to use the right tool for the right job, and sometimes that means swapping from NURBS to Polygons and vice versa. XSI has some wonderful tools to do just that.

GOING FROM NURBS TO POLYGONS

Getting from NURBS to polygons is easy, since all NURBS are eventually broken down (tessellated) into a polygon mesh anyway. XSI has a neat operator called NURBS to Mesh that will tessellate for you, while giving you control over the level of detail in the resulting polygon mesh. This level of detail is even animateable (until you freeze the operator stack.) Simply select a NURBS model and choose the NURBS to Mesh command in the Create➜Poly Mesh➜ menu. A new object is created, with an operator in its operator stack. If you open that operator into a Property Editor, you can adjust the Step in U and Step in V sliders to gain more or less detail in the resulting mesh.

POLYGON REDUCTION TOOLS IN SOFTIMAGE|3D 3.X

While the detail you get from the NURBS to Mesh tool in XSI is regular and depends entirely on the detail built into the original NURBS model, Softimage 3D|Extreme 3.x has other polygon reduction tools that will reduce detail in models non-uniformly, preserving edges and areas where the surface changes, while getting rid of more detail in the smooth low contrast areas of the model. These tools, Effect➜GC_Polygon Reduction and Effects➜Polygon Reduction are more appropriate for a really low-polygon level of detail work.

CONCLUSION

The polygon toolset in XSI is fantastic, and brings both a new level of sophistication and a standardized ease of use to both beginning and sophisticated polygon modelers. XSI's ability to work with Vertices, Edges and Polygons all in the same way certainly makes life much easier and more productive.

JELLYFISH: AT A GLANCE

In this tutorial you will learn:

- All about basic Polygon modeling
- How to select polygons, edges, and vertices
- How to sculpt shapes by transforming components
- How to duplicate and extrude polygons and vertices
- How to Extrude polygons along a curve
- How to smooth polygonal objects

TUTORIAL: JELLYFISH

Our goal in this tutorial is to use the most basic polygon modeling tools in XSI to create a beautiful, elegant and simple model, starting from a basic polygonal primitive.

We'll duplicate polygons, edges, and vertices, we'll move polygons and components around singly and in groups, we'll add edges and vertices, and we'll extrude polygons along a curve. Starting from a polygon mesh sphere we'll quickly create a very cool jellyfish that we can animate in an interesting way later on.

We'll focus on sculpting the general shape of the jellyfish, creating tentacles and contours, without worrying too much about the finished surface. When we are done we can adjust the smoothness of the polygon mesh to put the finishing touches on the jellyfish.

Remember - polygon modeling is a creative endeavor. There is no one correct way to do it. If you have ideas of your own that you want to try, please do experiment and improvise.

If you want to be able to get back to where you were before an experiment, duplicate your object periodically as you go so you can always go back to a previous version.

STEP 1. START WITH A SIMPLE OBJECT AND THEN REFINE IT.

Get a polygonal mesh sphere and open the geometry property page (immediate mode must be OFF at this point). We need to have enough detail around the equator of our jellyfish to pull out little bumps and nodules, but the sphere currently only has 8 polygons around the middle, which is not enough.

We want a pattern of bumps around our jellyfish like this: little bump, twisted tendril, little bump.

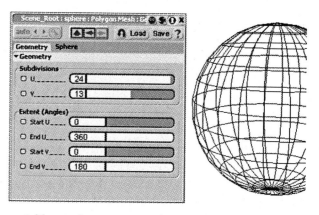

Add enough rows in U and V to make sculpting easy

This pattern will repeat 8 times around the jellyfish and there are three bumps and tendrils per pattern, so we'll need 8* 3 or 24 subdivisions around the middle of the sphere. Set U to 24 in the Geometry Property Editor (PE).

Set the V subdivisions to 13 so we have enough detail in the sphere, from top to bottom, to work with. The odd number (13) of subdivisions ensures that one row of polygons will go perfectly around the equator.

STEP 2. FREEZE THE OPERATOR STACK BEFORE CONTINUING.

Now with the basic Sphere ready to go, we no longer need to have an operator stack recording each and every move we make. So, freeze the sphere with the Freeze button and then turn on the Immediate mode toggle button near the bottom of the MCP. When Immediate mode is on, each move and tool will be frozen after it is completed, which will make our job faster and simpler. We can always turn Immediate mode back off at any time.

STEP 3. MAKE THE BELL SHAPE OF THE JELLYFISH.

Select three rows of polygons at the equator of the sphere using the polygon Select By Rectangle hotkey, which is Y. Now scale the three rows in Global Y to make them half as tall as they were. These will become the lip of the Jellyfish, and we want more fine detail here so we made the rows smaller.

Deselect the rows using the Y hotkey and the Middle Mouse Button so that you don't accidentally transform these polygons by mistake later on.

Now, tag all the points in the lower half of the jellyfish (not including the points around the very middle) and scale them in Object mode Y to completely invert the lower half inside the upper half. Object mode means that the points will scale relative to the center of the sphere object.

Gently scale these same points in X and Z (hold down the left and Right Mouse Buttons at the same time) to make the inside membrane slightly smaller inside the outer shell. Stop when the top row of tagged points is even with the bottom of the equator and untag just that top row, and then keep going. Untag all the points (T and the Middle Mouse Button) when you are done turning the sphere inside out to form the jellyfish.Step 4. Add some detail to the top of the jellyfish.

STEP 4. ADD DETAIL TO THE TOP OF THE JELLYFISH

The top of a jellyfish has areas that are thicker, arranged in a star shape radiating from the center. On our Jellyfish we can do the same thing by selecting some polygons in a pattern and duplicating them, then raising them up and out just a little bit. Using the polygon Select by Raycast hotkey U, select a stripe of four polygons, starting with the second from the top and extending down almost to the equator.

Make up your own patterns if you wish

Our jellyfish will have six of these bumps, so repeat this pattern every fourth column. Refer to the figures to get some ideas about neat patterns for this, and experiment with your own.

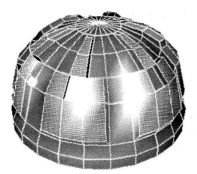

With these patterned polygons around the top half of the jellyfish bell selected, extrude them with the Extrude Polygon on Axis hotkey, which is CTRL-D. This created new polygons, which lay exactly on top of the other ones.

We need to move these new polygons a little bit. Activate the transform area of the MCP, and make sure that you are in Local transformation mode. When in local mode, each group of polygons will move according to its own axes, which is often useful.

Now, translate the selected polygons only in Y, which will move the polygons up and out from the center just a little ways. You may also scale these polygons down in X and Z slightly, also in local mode.

We've just created contours like a topographical map. Don't worry about how blocky it looks now, this will become smooth later. Deselect all the polygons since we are done with them now.

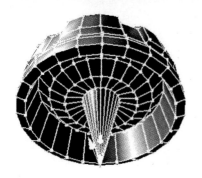

The center drops down

STEP 5. PULL OUT THE UNDERSIDE OF THE JELLYFISH.

Using your best artistic judgement, select some polygons in the middle of the underside of the jellyfish and translate them in global Y to add more mass to the middle of the jellyfish.

Deselect those polygons, and then tag the point in the absolute middle of the bottom of the jellyfish. Translate the tagged point down in global Y just a bit. We want the middle of the bottom of the Jellyfish to drop down a ways more but we need more detail. When you extrude a tagged point, new edges and polygons are created which would give us more detail.

Extrude the tagged point with the CTRL-D hotkey. Now move the selected center point down a little more, repeat the CTRL-D again, and move it down some more. Untag that point when done.

STEP 6. ADD SOME MORE SHAPE TO THE BOTTOM.

We could add more detail to the polygons surrounding the bottom point we just pulled out to create some ridges that would look interesting. Look at the edges just connected to the center point that we pulled in the step above, and select every fourth one with the Select Edge By Raycast tool, hotkey I.

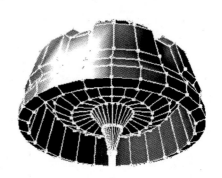

Extruding the center vertex adds more polygons

When all six edges are selected, extrude these edges just like we extruded the points and the polygons, with CTRL-D. New edges, new points and new polygons will be created. Translate these new edges in local Y to make them move out from the center just a little ways.

STEP 7. ADD SOME SMALL BUMPS AND TENDRILS.

On the underside of the rim of the jellyfish, there are 24 polygons. We can use these to create small bumps and tendrils in the pattern bump-bump-tendril repeating around the rim.

Select every third polygon and extrude it with CTRL-D, then translate it in local Y a little ways from the lip and scale it down a bit in local X and Z. This will make a small bump there when finally smoothed.

Deselect these polygons, and select every third polygon next over along the rim. Repeat the extruding and scaling process, but make these bumps a different length and size.

The Immediate
Mode Button

Immediate mode is easier to work in

Deselect those polygons, and select the remaining 8 polygons of the lip. These we will extrude in a different way to make more interesting tendrils.

We want to adjust the properties of the tendrils after we execute the command, which would not be possible in Immediate mode, so turn off Immediate mode. This means that when we do our extrusion we'll get a Property page for it where we can make changes (or even animate them).

With Immediate mode off, execute the PolyMesh→Extrude Along Axis command in the Modify→Poly Mesh menu. You can also get this command by holding down the Alt key (or CTRL-ALT on Irix) on your keyboard and left clicking. Left-click over one of the selected polygons.

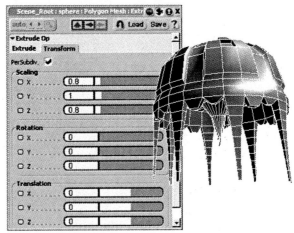

The polygons will be extruded slightly, but we want to do much more. Select the jelly-fish as an object (with the spacebar) and search in the Selection button of the MCP to find the Extrude Op. Open it by clicking on the icon. In the Extrusion Op Property Editor (PE), make sure that the Frame toggle is on,

The longer fringe parts

which will transform each polygon relative to its own local axis and be easier to control and more interesting.

Next, adjust the extrusion Length slider to about 4, and increase the number of subdivisions to 7 to make the tendril more detailed. In the Transform tab of the PE, you can adjust how each subdivision of the extrusion is scaled, translated or rotated. Adjust the Rotate in Y to about 15 degrees, and make the scale in X and Z about .80, which means that each new segment in the extrusion will be 80% as big as the prior one. As you make these changes you can see the tendril grow and change.

Make sure you close the PE and deselect the polygons at the ends of the tendrils before you move on. Now we have nice bumps and tendrils around the rim of the jellyfish.

STEP 8. MAKE FOUR LARGER TENTACLES.

Our jellyfish needs four larger, longer tentacles that will trail behind, contracting and expanding as the creature swims. These need to be animated eventually. The clever way to do this is to extrude some polygons from the base of the creature along a curve. Then the extrusion itself can be animated and the curve shape can be animated.

Examine the underside of your Jellyfish (is it a boy or a girl?), and select four polygons (every sixth in a circle) somewhere near the middle of the underside.

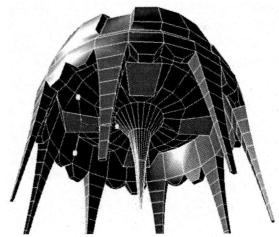

Here come the tendrils

We want these polygons to be quite flat in the XZ plane, so they extrude straight down. Make them flat by scaling them in OBJECT Y, then scale them slightly larger using Local X and Z, and translate them down a ways so they become good foundations for the tentacles.

Using the CV NURBS Curve tool, draw a serpentine curve in the Front view, starting at the global center with about 6 control points. This will become the shape of the tentacles.

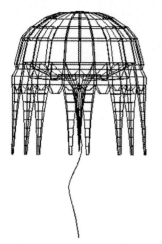

Select the jellyfish again with the spacebar, and activate the selected polygons by tapping the U hotkey or by clicking on the Polygon filter button in the MCP.

Choose the Poly Mesh➔Extrude Along Curve tool, and then pick on the curve to finish the command. Again, select the jellyfish as an object or enter Object mode, open the Extrude PE (there will be two now - we want the top one) and check that Autorotate is off and Perpendicular is on.

Increase the number of subdivisions to 12, to make for a smoother tentacle, and again adjust the scale of each subdivision in the transform tab to perhaps 0.9 in Scale X and Scale Z, with a small rotation in Y for additional interest.

This NURBS curve will shape the tentacles

Try out the End slider to see that this makes the tentacles extend and contract. You could animate this later as the creature swims.

OK - we are done with the polygon modeling!

STEP 9. SMOOTHING THE SURFACE

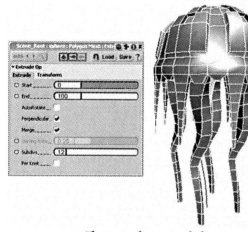

The tentacles, extruded

Select the jellyfish as an object, and in the Selection button find the Geometry Approximation PE and open it up. By default, the Geo approximation property is shared with all objects and we want one specifically for the Jellyfish, so in the dialog choose to create a local copy.

In the Polygon Mesh tab, increase the Mesh Subdivision to 2 and then examine your jellyfish in the shaded view and the render region.

Looks good! Apply a cool translucent material, then save the Jellyfish so we can animate it later.

The completed jellyfish

QUIZ

1. THE SUBDIVISION SURFACE TOOLS WORK ON NURBS
   a. True
   b. False

2. WHICH IS NOT A PART OF A POLYGON?.
   a. Edge
   b. Control Point
   c. Vertex

3. WHICH DO YOU FIND ON A POLYGON?:
   a. Boundary
   b. Knot Curve
   c. Normal

4. IN XSI POLYGON MODELING, WHAT CAN YOU EXTRUDE?
   a. NURBS curves
   b. Normals
   c. Edges, Vertices and Polygons

5. WHAT IS THE HOTKEY FOR SELECT POLYGON BY RAYCAST?:
   a. R
   b. P
   c. U

6. WHICH ONE OF THE OPTIONS BELOW DOES NOT MAP TO A MOUSE BUTTON WHEN YOU HAVE THE E HOTKEY HELD DOWN (IN THE SOFTIMAGE 3D SELECTION MODEL, EXTENDED COMPONENT SELECTION)
   a. LMB: Add to selection
   b. MMB: Start Over
   c. RMB: Toggle Selection

7. THE OPERATOR STACK ALWAYS STORES EVERY CHANGE YOU MAKE TO A POLYGON OBJECT:
   a. True
   b. False
   c. False if Immediate mode is on

8. HOW DO YOU FLATTEN THE OPERATOR STACK TO SIMPLIFY MODELS
   a. Immediate Mode
   b. Freeze
   c. Delete the operators

9. SUBDIVISION SURFACES
   a. Rule
   b. Suck
   c. What's Sub-D?

10. WHICH IS NOT A BOOLEAN MODELING OPTION
   a. Intersection
   b. Condition
   c. Difference

BASIC ANIMATION AND KEYFRAMING

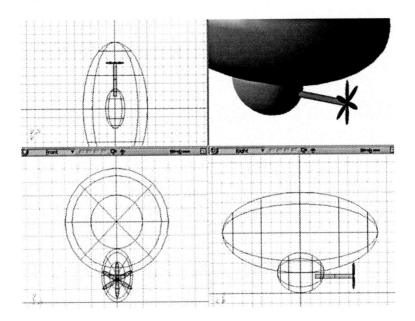

IN THIS CHAPTER YOU WILL LEARN ABOUT:

- Fundamental animation concepts and terminology
- How to start making animation by keyframing
- How to use the animation panel, the timeline, and the playback control
- How to use the property editor to add and erase keyframes
- How to use the marking widget to selectively keyframe properties
- Animation techniques to enhance your animation

INTRODUCTION

Softimage|XSI excels in animation functionality. Animation can be a very complex endeavor, but by learning XSI's sophisticated animation tools, we can achieve any desired motion. In this chapter we will learn basic keyframe animation concepts which are derived from traditional 2D animation. We will also cover how to apply these keyframing techniques to 3D animation, by utilizing XSI's many animation tools to create and preview animation. Softimage|XSI allows you to animate almost all parameters in the property page, which puts you in the director's chair giving you total control to move, pulsate, and morph anything you want.

WHAT IS ANIMATION?

There are many variations of animation that have been made in the past 200 years. It is very hard to clearly define what animation is. If animation is defined in a very technical manner, its definition could be the process of creating moving images by making and recording a sequence of images and then displaying them at a very fast rate. Our eyes get fooled into believing those chattering mouths of anime characters are real, since images are played in rapid fire. The sequences of images are called frames; a frame is the shortest unit of time in animation. The actual length of a frame is dependant on which media you are creating animation for. To create North American NTSC video format, you need 30 of these frames to represent one second's worth of animation. In other words, one frame is about one thirtieth of second. European PAL format, on the other hand, displays 25 frames per second. Film requires 24 frames for a second. In reality, only about 8 images are made for a second in typical TV cartoons, because it costs too much for a typical TV production budget to create 30 images to represent 1 second. Well, now you know the secret of those chattering mouths.

Our second definition comes from the fact that word animate means "to give life to" and "make alive". This definition of animation would be that it is the technique of giving the illusion of life to something inanimate, such as a computer-generated image. It's easily said, but it's hard to do, especially if you want to stir your audience's emotion with the acting in your animation. We will discuss basic animation techniques later in this chapter.

BASIC TERMINOLOGY

There are many ways to create animation, notably hand-drawn (cel) animation, Stop-motion (such as Wallace and Gromit(tm) claymation), and 3D computer animation. In hand-drawn animation, an animator creates key poses, or "keyframes", to establish an important frame, by drawing the extreme poses. The frames between these key poses are later filled with "in-between" drawings. Imagine Karate Kid (KK for short) practicing his high kick on the pole. An animator would create keyframe drawings by drawing KK with great concentration, just before he launches himself to kick. Then he or she will draw KK finishing his smooth kick. Later, another artist will fill the gaps between the two keyframes by drawing in-betweens. 3D computer animation is basically the same process, with two big differences: you set keyframes of KK's move, but instead of hiring some poor souls to do in-betweens for you, the computer churns out in-betweens by a process called "interpolation". Filling the blank space between two keyframes is now done by a machine, which doesn't usually complain about endless, tedious tasks.

The other big difference is that 3D computer animation can create 3D sets and characters which enable an animator to light and compose the scene any way he or she desires, and change it at any time.

Now you know the basic theory of animation. You will learn more about animation techniques later. Let's learn how to keyframe in XSI and start cranking out the animation!

KEYFRAME ANIMATION WITH XSI

To create animation in XSI, you need to set at least two keyframes (since the program needs at least two points to interpolate between).

To set simple keyframes on the scale, rotation or translation of a selected object, just activate the transformation you want to key by clicking on s, r or t in the MCP, drag the timeslider to the point in time where you want to save a key, and click on the Key icon in the Animation panel below the timeline.

The hotkey shortcut for that button in K.

For more complex animation tasks, use the features of the Animation Panel.

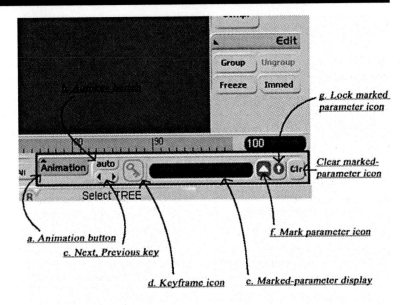

The Animation panel

These are the functions of each button from left to right:

a. The Animation button at the far left of the animation panel opens a drop window with many common animation commands, such as Set Key, Remove Key, and Copy Animation.

b. The auto button toggles the AutoKey function on and off. This function automatically sets a keyframe when you change any parameter on an object. It can be a very good timesaving device when you have to keyframe a lot objects many times, just be sure to set a keyframe for the starting position manually.

c. The two arrows below the AutoKey button will skip to the next and previous keyframe for the selected object.

d. The large button with a key icon is called the keyframe (or simply key) button, and is used for adding a keyframe at the current frame. The key button won't be available until you select an element's animateable parameter. The key button can be four different colors, depending on the situation. If the keyframe button is gray, then there are no keyframes for the selected parameter at all. If it is green, there are keyframes for the selected parameter, but not at the current frame. If the key button is red, the current frame is a keyframe. If it is yellow, a change has been made to the selected parameter, but it has not yet been keyed. Simply click the key button to set a keyframe (it will turn red). Clicking the key button on an existing keyframe (where the button is already red) will remove the keyframe.

e. The dark gray bar next to the key button is called the marked parameter display box, and it will show which parameter you have selected to keyframe. For example, if you selected the "Local Transformation X" parameter of the object, it will display "kine.local.pos.posx". It

NOTE Interpolation can be tweaked in many ways using the animation editor, to create the most satisfying in-between; see Chapter 11 for more information.

looks confusing at first, but it will be very useful, as you become more familiar with it. If there is more than one parameter selected, it will display "MULTI".

f. The button with the triangle icon, to the right of the marked parameter display, is called the marked parameter button. To mark a parameter, first you need to select an element you want to animate. Second, left-click on the mark parameter icon, and a property explorer window will open up, from which you can choose which parameter you want to keyframe, such as the Pos (position) folder icon for translation or the Ori (orientation) folder icon for rotation. Just like in the Explorer view, left-click on the + and - signs to look for the property you want to keyframe. Left-click on the name of a parameter to mark it. You can click one more time to cancel the mark on a property. If you hold Shift or CTRL, you can select multiple parameters to keyframe at once, which can be very convenient. An empty green box next to a parameter means that that parameter doesn't have any keyframes set. As soon as you keyframe the parameter, the previously empty box will have a curve in it. It's a very quick way to distinguish which parameters have keyframes, and which don't.

g. The button with the keyhole icon is for locking the marked parameter, so the particular parameter you want to keyframe stays marked. This tool is very useful to keep certain parameters marked even you use the transformation menus (which would otherwise automatically become the marked parameter). To unlock the marked parameters, simply left-click on the keyhole icon again.

h. The CLR button will clear any marked parameter, so no parameter is selected. If parameters are locked, the clear marked parameter icon simply doesn't work. Unlock parameters before using CLR. This icon only unmarks parameters; it won't delete existing keyframes.

KEYFRAMING BY USING THE PROPERTY EDITOR

Alternately, you can use the property editor to add and delete keys. The property editor can be opened by right-clicking any element in the Explorer or Schematic, and choosing the specific property you want to keyframe, such as an Animation property or a Modeling property. The property editor can also be opened by clicking on the Selection button in the middle of the MCP, then selecting which property page you want to view. You will notice that the Property Editor has exactly the same keyframe icon, auto-keyframe icon, and next/previous key icon at the top, just like an animation panel, and green boxes next to parameters like the property page.

You can keyframe using two different methods in the property editor. The first method is highlighting the name of the parameter by left-clicking on it (not the green box, but the name itself). The keyframe icon lights up. Move the timeline to where you want to keyframe and change the value of the parameter to your liking. You can just click on the keyframe icon to set a key at your current frame. The second method is clicking on the green box; the parameter next to it will be keyframed at the current frame on the timeline. The green box will turn red and will have a curve inside it. By clicking one more time, the keyframe will be removed.

NOTE The easiest way to mark parameters is to highlight the corresponding transformation cells in the MCP, which automatically marks that parameter to be keyframed. The only drawback to this method of marking parameters is that only scale, rotate, and translate have these large transformation cells. If you want to keyframe a more complicated parameter, such as material color or shape, you need to use the more complex methods of marking parameters, detailed above.

CLEARING KEYFRAMES

There are a few additional ways to remove keyframes and animation. First, I will explain how to remove a keyframe using the animation panel. To remove a single keyframe, select the element, mark the property by clicking the mark parameter icon, and the property editor will pop up. Move the timeline or use next/previous keyframe buttons until you come to the frame with the keyframe you want to delete. The keyframe icon should be highlighted red. Left-click the animation button in the animation panel and select "Remove Key" from the menu. Voila, that particular keyframe of the current frame is removed! If you choose "Remove Animation" instead of Remove Key it will remove all the keyframes of the selected property.

The property editor also lets you remove individual keyframes and animation. Open the property editor by right-clicking on the element in the Explorer or Schematic window, and choose the corresponding property. Select a property by left-clicking on the name of the property. Use the timeline or next/previous keyframe to move to the keyframe that you want to remove. The box next to the selected property should become tinted red. Right-click on the keyframe icon at the top of the property editor. Choose "Remove Keyframe" to remove a single keyframe at the current frame or "Remove Animation" to remove all keyframes. You can select multiple properties by holding the CTRL key, and remove keys from multiple properties at once.

TIMELINE

The timeline is a tool that lets you move through frames. It looks like a slider bar with numbers, at the bottom of the interface. The red line on the timeline is called the playback cursor, and indicates the current frame. You can move the playback cursor by either clicking on the desired frame on the timeline, or click-and-dragging it there. You can also use the arrow keys to change frames. Right arrow will move to the next frame and left arrow will move to the previous frame. The numbers in the boxes at the left and right of the timeline indicate the first and last frame of the timeline. You may type a number directly in these boxes to specify the first and last frame of your animation.

PLAYBACK CONTROLS

The playback control panel is for previewing your animation, using controls similar to a VCR. Let's look at each icon from left to right.

a. The button labeled "Playback" contains a dropdown menu with various playback option settings, most of which are found elsewhere in the playback control panel, such as First Frame or Display All Frames.

b. The pair of smaller arrows to the immediate right of the playback menu moves the current frame backward or forward.

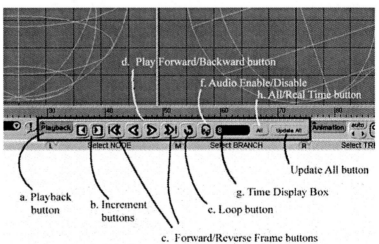

Playback control lets you preview your animation

c. To the right of the next/previous frame arrows is a set of four larger arrows. Clicking on the first or last arrow (the ones with the vertical line next to them) will take you to the first or last frame, respectively. The inner two arrows are like the Play button on a VCR, except that one is play forward and the other is play in reverse.

d. The icon with a thin, curved arrow is for loop play mode. If loop play is highlighted, when the animation reaches the end of the timeline, it simply goes back to the start and plays all over again, until you manually stop it.

e. The button with the headphone icon will toggle sound on and off while the animation is played.

f. The dark gray box is very useful. Instead of clicking on the timeline to select the frame you desire, you can just type the number in the box and hit the Enter key.

g. The button labeled "All" toggles between playing all frames or real-time playing. If you click on it the icon will change to "RT", for real-time, meaning that XSI will play the animation back at the speed you set (default is 30 frames per second), even if it has to skip frames to play that fast. The default is All, which means XSI will display all the frames, no matter how long it takes to update each frame. All is useful for checking the motion of your animation, while RT is useful for checking the timing.

h. Using the "Update All" button, you can choose what kind of element will update during playback. Clicking this button toggles between "update all" and "update selected".

PRACTICE TIME

Let's practice using these tools by keyframing some simple movements.

1. File→New Scene to clear up your previous work.

2. Get→Primitive→Surface→Sphere to create a NURBS sphere. Close the property window by clicking on the X button at the top-right of the window.

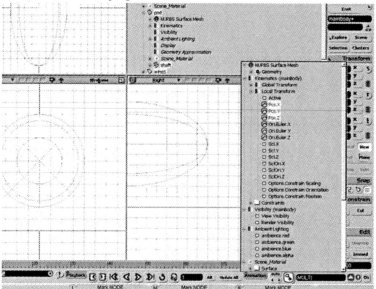

3. Let's mark parameters to keyframe. Click on the Mark Parameter button (the button with the triangle icon, in the bottom-right of the interface) to get the property explorer. Expand Local Transform in the list by left-clicking on the + sign next to it. Mark the parameter Pos (position/translation) by left-clicking on the name; it should become highlighted yellow. You should also see "kine.local.pos" in the marked parameter display box. You just marked the local translation parameter.

In this example, "Pos" (Position) is marked. "kine.local.pos" appears in the marked-parameter display

4. Set the current frame to 1 by typing 1 in the box below the timeline (to the right of the headphone icon), or simply click-and-drag the red line on the timeline to the far left.

5. Click on the keyframe icon to key the position of the sphere at frame 1. You noticed the keyframe icon is now colored red. That means there is a keyframe for the marked parameter (local translation, in this case) at the current frame.

6. Move the current frame to 30. The key icon turns green; this means that a keyframe exists for this parameter, but not at the current frame.

7. Move the sphere by typing 5 in the X-axis box of the translation menu. The key icon now turns to yellow, to indicate the parameter has been changed since last keyframe.

8. Let's key again, but this time we are going to use the property editor. Open a property editor for local transformation, either by clicking on the Selection button in the MCP and choosing "Local Transform", or by

right-clicking the sphere in Explorer or Schematic view and selecting Animation Parameter. You will see Position parameter X, Y, and Z all have a green box with a curve. Click on the box for the X-axis. The X-axis position parameter is now keyframed. Left-click on the name (as opposed to the box) of the Y- and Z-axes; their names now highlight in yellow. Left-click once on the keyframe icon at the top of property editor. Now the Y- and Z-axes are keyframed. X, Y and Z in the Position column should all have a red box.

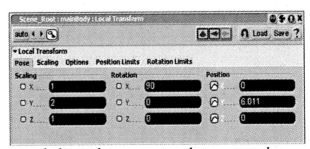

The box with a curve means that parameter has keyframes set. This object has keyframes set for its position in the X-, Y-, and Z-axes

Congratulations! To view this animation, you need to use the playback control. Try playing your first animation. Do you see the sphere moving? Change last frame to 30 by typing 30 in the box on the far right of the timeline. Click on the loop button, then hit play.

LEAD ZEPPELIN: AT A GLANCE

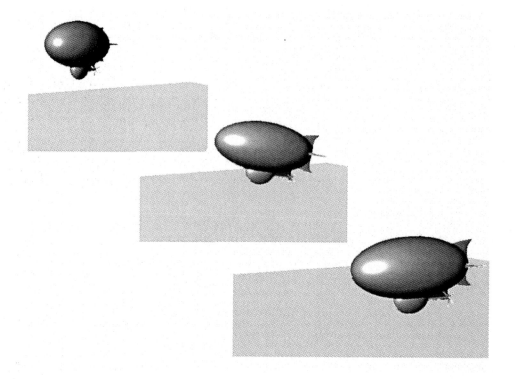

TOPICS COVERED

Now, it's time to create a simple model with moving parts and animate it. We will create a model of a blimp with propellers and fly it across the screen. This tutorial will let you familiarize with various animation tools in XSI.

You'll learn how to:

- Create a blimp out of NURBS primitives
- Animate a blimp using the animation panel
- Use the marking widget to keyframe specified parameters
- Preview your animation using the playback control

LEAD ZEPPELIN

As the title of this tutorial suggests, we are going to model and animate a classic rock group. Okay, maybe later. Instead, we are going to construct a blimp with a cockpit and moving propellers. The hierarchy technique we learned in the last chapter will help our animation tremendously.

CREATE THE BLIMP:

STEP 1. CLEAR THE SLATE
File➔New Scene to clear up your previous work.

Make sure you have four viewports open: Top, Front, Right, and Perspective.

NOTE Make sure you are using View transformation mode by clicking on the View button in the Main Command Panel.

STEP 2. CREATE THE MAIN CHAMBER
Create a NURBS sphere by selecting Get➔Primitive➔Surface➔Sphere.

We will turn this blimp 90 degrees on the X-axis, because we want to have the poles of the sphere point to the front and back of the blimp. Close the property page and rotate it by typing 90 in the X-axis box of the rotate panel in the MCP.

Scale the blimp on its Y-axis so it has an elongated, football shape. The general shape of the main chamber is done.

It is always good practice to name any objects you create. Rename the sphere "mainChamber" by right-clicking on the sphere in the Explorer window and choosing Rename from the list. Type mainChamber in the box and hit the enter key.

STEP 3. CREATE THE COCKPIT
We will simply copy the mainChamber, scale it, and move it down.

Duplicate the main body by selecting Edit➔Duplicate/Instantiate➔Duplicate Single.

Scale the duplicated sphere down so it's about the quarter the size of the main chamber. Make sure to check all four views for the proportion.

Translate the sphere downward using Front or Right view so the top half of the sphere is hidden inside the mainChamber.

Rename it "cockpit" as we did for the mainChamber.

STEP 4. CREATE THE PROPELLER SHAFT
Get a polygonal cylinder by selecting Get➔Primitive➔Polygon Mesh➔Cylinder.

The default cylinder is too big; let's scale it down by using the property page. In property view, change the radius to 0.2.

Rotate the cylinder 90 degrees on the X-axis, and translate it to just behind the cockpit, using the Right view.

Rename the cylinder "shaft".

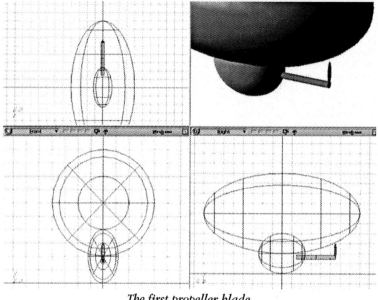

The first propeller blade

STEP 5. ADD PROPELLER BLADES

Get→Primitive→Sphere, and change its radius to 0.5.

Using all orthogonal views, shape it into a propeller blade by changing its scale, and translate it so the bottom tip of the propeller is at the end of the shaft. Make sure it isn't so long that it will hit the blimp.

Name the blade "propeller1". We name it this way so that successive copies will have consecutive numbers automatically.

We are now going to make multiple copies of this propeller blade. Before we make copies, we need to move the pivot point of the sphere to the tip closest to the shaft. That way, we can make copied items rotate around the shaft as they are duplicated. It saves some time, since we don't need to manually turn each propeller blade.

Click on the Center button located at top of the main command area. This activates center mode; now you can translate the center of the blade to the shaft. Activate the translation panel, and using Middle Mouse Button, drag the center to the bottom tip of the propeller.

Click on the Object button to return to object selection mode.

All the propeller blades

Let's make five copies of the propeller blade. Select Edit→Duplicate/Instantiate→Duplicate Multiple. You will get an option window. Change Number of Copies to 5 by typing or using the slider.

Click on the transform tab in Duplicate Options. Change Z rotation value to 60. This will turn each newly duplicated propeller blade 60 degrees. Click OK. Now you have six propeller blades 60 degrees apart. Each successive propeller blade is named automatically: propeller2, propeller3, and so forth.

STEP 6. ADD TAIL FINS

The airship should have two sets of back tail wings, to make it look cool. To make our life easier, let's use a NURBS sphere again: Get➔Primitive➔Sphere.

Change the scale, so it looks thin and elongated in the X-axis.

Change translation using the top view to place it at the back of the blimp.

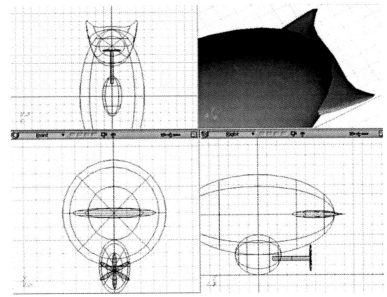

A simple tailfin, molded from a sphere

We can make it more fin-like by selecting a point at the tip of a sphere and moving it back. Click on the Point button in the main command area, and the points of the sphere will be displayed.

To select multiple points on both edges, make a small marquee box around two points at the extreme edge of the sphere, while holding Shift key.

Using the top view, move those points in the -Z direction until you get the desired fin shape. Name this Wing1.

Select Edit➔Duplicate Single. Change Rotation Z value to 90.

STEP 7. ASSEMBLE THE PIECES INTO A HIERARCHY

Remember how to create a hierarchy? We can use the Explorer window to speed up the process. Open Explorer by left-clicking on the Change View icon at the top-left of the viewport, and choose Explorer. You can hold the Middle Mouse Button to drag a child-to-be element into a parent-to-be element, to make a hierarchy. Middle-mouse-drag the cockpit into mainChamber. You should see a + mark show up to the left of mainChamber. Show the whole hierarchy by left-clicking on the + sign. You will see the cockpit in the mainChamber hierarchy.

Make the shaft a child of the cockpit by middle-mouse-dragging the shaft into the cockpit.

Using the same method, make the wings children of mainChamber.

Make the propeller blades children of the shaft.

You should now be able to select the whole hierarchy by middle-click-selecting on mainChamber. You can also select particular branches of the hierarchy; for example, middle-click-selecting the shaft will select the propeller shaft and all the propeller blades below it.

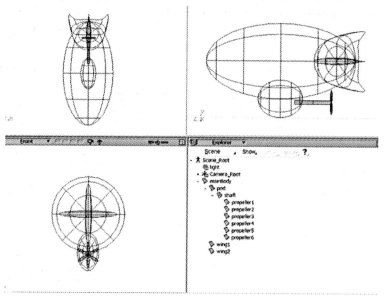

The finished blimp hierarchy

ANIMATE THE BLIMP:

STEP 1. LIFTOFF

Okay, the modeling is done! Now you are ready to animate the airship! We will make this airship slowly launch up, and then circle up into the air. First, type 100 in the box to the right of timeline. Leave the start frame at 1, the default. You want at least 99 frames to make this animation.

Select the entire hierarchy by middle-mouse-selecting the mainChamber. We will keyframe the transformations of the blimp to make it fly. Translate the ship up in Y-axis using front or side view, so the bottom of the cockpit is just a little above global center; this will be our starting point.

Make sure the translation menu panel is still highlighted and you can see kine.local.pos displayed in the marked parameter display box. By selecting the translation menu panel, you are effectively marking local position X, Y, and Z. Now click on the keyframe icon. The first frame is keyed.

Change the current frame to 30, and move the ship about 10 units in Y-axis. Click the keyframe icon. Now the blimp is lifting up! Try previewing the animation by moving the playback cursor to 0 and pressing the play button.

STEP 2. FULL SPEED AHEAD

Move the playback cursor to frame 50. After changing top view to right view, move the entire ship a little forward and up. Don't move it too much since you only have 100 frames - a little more than 3 seconds - for your animation. Click the keyframe icon.

Change the current frame to 80 and move the ship to your right using front view. Click the keyframe icon, or press the hotkey K. Go to frame 100 and move the ship to your left and up. Set another keyframe. Try to frame the shot in Camera view, so you can see the blimp take off and come towards the camera, then fly away from the frame. If your animation doesn't let you frame that, try to re-keyframe it by setting keyframes over the existing ones.

STEP 3. ADD ROTATION

Now it's time for the rotation of the blimp. Select the rotation panel. Make sure it's highlighted and you see "kine.local.ori.euler" in the marked-parameter display box. Go back to frame one and click the keyframe icon.

Move to frame 10 and click Key.

Move to frame 20 and rotate slightly in the X-axis, so the ship's head is toward the ground. Click Key.

At frame 40, rotate in the X-axis, so the blimp's head is pointed skyward. Let's start using the AutoKey function. Click on the "auto" button, so it's highlighted in red.

At frame 50, point the blimp's head back a bit and rotate it in the Y-axis, so the tip faces slightly toward you.

At frame 70, make the blimp's head point toward the direction it is translating. Turn the head 180 degrees so the blimp can head in its direction at frame 100. End AutoKey mode by clicking on the auto button again. Preview the animation. You can spend time tweaking it to your liking.

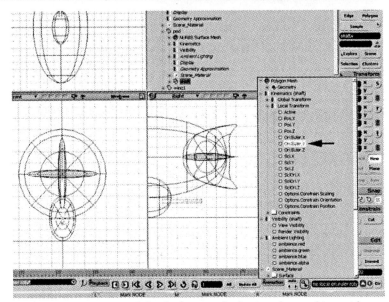

The Y-axis rotation of the shaft is marked using the marking widget

STEP 4. SPIN THE PROPELLERS

We should keyframe the shaft's rotation, so the propeller moves. The rotation menu panel should be still highlighted.

Middle-click on the shaft to select it. This will select the shaft using branch mode; all of the propellers are selected as children also. You can keyframe only the rotation of the shaft, and the whole branch will rotate because of inherited transformations.

Let's mark the shaft's rotation Y value by using the marking widget. Click on the Mark Parameter icon in the animation panel. Expand Local Transform node by clicking the + sign next to it. Expand Ori node also by above method. Click on Y to mark rotation Y value.

Make sure you are at frame 1, and click the keyframe icon.

Move to frame 20 and set a keyframe. Since you keyframed at the same value between frame 1 and 20, there is not much movement in these frames.

Move frame to 100 and type 36000 in Y rotation box. Set a keyframe. That will turn the propellers 100 times in 80 frames. Preview the animation and make changes as you wish.

Save your scene and name it "blimp"; we'll use it in future exercises.

You have learned basic keyframe animation principles using XSI's animation function. You've marked which parameter to keyframe by either highlighting a transformation panel, such as translation and rotation, or by using the marking widget. Then the keyframe icon is used to keyframe the animation. The initial state is keyframed at frame 1, and changes in the parameters are keyframed later; that way the computer can create interpolation between two different values of the parameter, thus creating animation.

All is well. You may want to tweak the animation more to make the blimp lively. We'll take a look at some animation techniques to help you tweak the animation in the next section.

ANIMATION TECHNIQUES AND TERMINOLOGY

In terms of character animation technique development, we owe a lot to Disney animators. There at the Disney studio, extremely talented animators applied real world physics to their animation, while the acting skill of characters was sharpened to tell stories effectively. These techniques are still very applicable to 3D computer animation. Let's discuss some of them to use them later in your animation. A list of books to further study technique follows this section. You may not be able to apply these theories right away, but when you become more familiar with the animation tools of XSI (especially the Animation Editor that you will study in Chapter 11), these principles will help immensely.

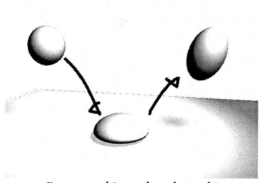

Exaggerated "squash and stretch"

THE LAW OF INERTIA

Even if you are creating cartoon-style animation, it is vital to follow the basic physical law of inertia to suspend the belief of your audience. The law of inertia states that objects in motion tend to stay in motion, and objects at rest tend to stay at rest. Imagine you are on a subway train. When the train leaves the station, your body will try to remain still, so you have feeling of being pushed backward. When the train stops, your body remains moving, your body will tip forward. The same law applies to a human body. If you animate Bruce Lee punching Mr. T in the face, you won't animate his whole body being punched back at once, because his body will try to remain at the same position. First his head will be punched back, then his upper body follows, finally the lower body is pulled back by the upper body.

SQUASH AND STRETCH

Squash and Stretch means exaggerating the change in shape of a moving object, while keeping the volume of the object constant. A ball bouncing is a good example. When a ball hits the ground, it will squash to show the mass of the ball pushing itself down. When it bounces back up, it will stretch to show the elasticity of the ball pulling it up.

Anticipation helps create more believable motion

ANTICIPATION

Anticipation happens when the action requires the subject to shift its center of gravity. Imagine a warrior with a huge warhammer, and he is trying to swing it down over a goblin's head. To deliver a powerful blow, he can't just swing the hammer from above his head. He must recoil back and swing the hammer forward using his whole body. The backward motion is called anticipation. It helps to emphasize the action by charging kinetic energy.

OVERLAPPING ACTION

When a character moves, no parts should arrive at the new spot at once. For example, if a character raises his hand, his arm will reach above his head first, and then his hand will straighten up. It's because the movement of his arm is motivating the motion of his hand. The law of inertia is at work here. This multiple movement is called overlapping action, and delay in the action is called secondary action, discussed next.

GOOD   BAD

Silhouetting is a good way to check if a particular pose is easily read

SECONDARY ACTION

Secondary action refers to the delay in the overlapping action of a secondary object that is following the animation of a primary object, such as a picture frame tilting when a door slams, or a little girl's pig-tails bobbing as she skips down the street. Secondary actions are the details that make animation realistic and convincing.

FOLLOW-THROUGH

Follow-through is a close relative of anticipation. It is the motion after the action, where anticipation is the motion before it. When our burly warrior's warhammer makes contact with the poor goblin's cranium, the hammer doesn't just stop. Again, the law of inertia is at work, and the hammer tends to stay in motion, until the friction of the surrounding world (the warrior's pull, the goblin's head, the ground, etc.) is enough to stop it.

MAKE A STRONG POSE-TO-POSE ANIMATION BY SILHOUETTING

When you set up a keyframe pose, make sure that pose could be easily read if the pose was converted to a silhouette. You want the audience to immediately recognize your character's current action, so it is very important to create visually strong poses.

TIMING

Without good timing, you will not be able to create convincing animation. Good timing can only be achieved by the daily study of movies, sports, theatre, and everyday life all around you. When you have a good chunk of time to kill, carry your sketchpad and stopwatch and time how long certain actions take. You can time how many seconds it takes a person to walk onto the train, take a bite out of a hamburger, wave at a taxi, or anything else you can think of.

Studying pantomimes like Charlie Chaplin extensively will also enlighten you as to how the great actor communicates with his audience through timing, and exaggerated and expressive poses.

BIBLIOGRAPHY AND SUGGESTED READING

Thomas, Frank and Johnston Ollie. Disney Animation: <u>The Illusion of Life</u>. New York: Abbeville Press, 1981 - This is the most important book to get. It is currently out of print, so call around used bookstores, or contact the publisher and demand it be reprinted.

Blair, Preston. <u>Cartoon Animation</u>. Walter Foster Publishing, Inc. Laguna Hills, California. 1994 - Greatest exercise book about cartoon animation. Lots of theories and techniques are discussed in this visual treasure.

Culhane, Shamus. <u>Animation from Script to Screen</u>. St. Martin's Press, New York. 1988 - Insightful book about the animation process. Lots of text, but extremely well-written.

CONCLUSION

In this chapter you learned some basic principles and terminology of animation, and several methods of setting keyframes in XSI. You learned a whole new sets of tools, such as the Animation Panel, Timeline and Playback Control, to keyframe and preview your first animation. Comprehension of the tools and principles covered in this chapter will be very important later, when you work on more complex animation sequences.

QUIZ

True or False

1. A FRAME IS THE SHORTEST UNIT OF TIME IN ANIMATION.
    a. True
    b. False

2. NORTH AMERICAN NTSC VIDEO FORMAT DISPLAYS 24 FRAMES PER SECOND.
    a. True
    b. False

3. KEY POSES ANIMATORS CREATE ARE CALLED IN-BETWEENS.
    a. True
    b. False

4. THE COMPUTER'S METHOD OF CREATING IN-BETWEENS IS CALLED INTERPOLATION.
    a. True
    b. False

5. CEL ANIMATION AND 3D COMPUTER ANIMATION BOTH HAVE UNLIMITED FREEDOM TO CHANGE COMPOSITION.
    a. True
    b. False

6. THE AUTOKEY BUTTON WILL CREATE ANIMATION FOR YOU, JUST SIT BACK AND RELAX.
    a. True
    b. False

7. THE MARK PARAMETER BUTTON IS VERY USEFUL TO CHOOSE WHICH PARAMETER WILL BE KEYED.
    a. True
    b. False

8. YOU CAN ONLY SET KEYFRAMES USING ANIMATION EDITOR.
    a. True
    b. False

9. A RED KEYFRAME ICON MEANS THAT A KEY EXIST FOR THE SELECTED PARAMETER AT THE CURRENT FRAME.
    a. True
    b. False

10. WHEN YOU WANT TO PLAYBACK ALL FRAMES, CHOOSE "RT" MODE.
    a. True
    b. False

6 MATERIALS, LIGHTING, AND RENDERING

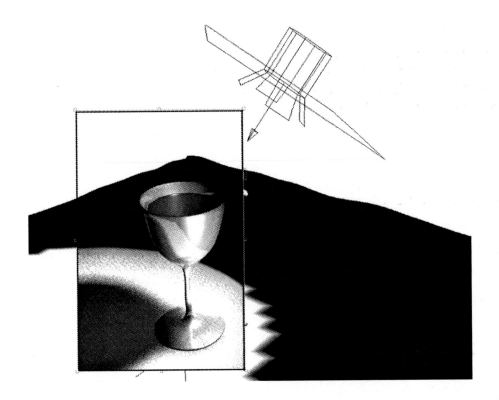

IN THIS CHAPTER YOU WILL LEARN ABOUT:

- How to apply materials (surface shader) to objects.
- What are shading models?
- How to use Render Region to preview only one section of your scene.
- How to light a scene effectively.
- How to set up the camera for rendering.
- How to render a file, and render settings.
- How to use Flipbook and Image Clip Editor.

INTRODUCTION

To make your scene realistic, or just to give it the look you want, you have to add light, color, and texture to your characters and sets. In this chapter we will discuss various tools to create surface color, edit characteristics such as transparency and shininess, and basic lighting technique, to really make your scene come alive. We will also explore rendering techniques to region-render, create a single picture, and then successive rendered images. In the end, we will discuss how to preview those images as a movie.

Let's begin with coloring an object.

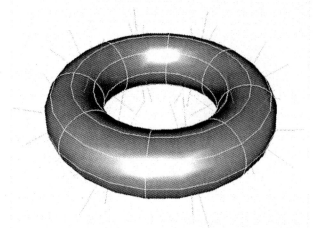

Surface normals indicate which side is facing out

SURFACE SHADER

When you want to color a 3D object, you will apply a surface shader to that object. A shader is a tool programmed to work with the renderer to affect the final rendered image of an object. You can assign different values to surface shaders to represent different colors, and other characteristics such as shininess, transparency, and reflectivity. We will discuss how to edit shader attributes later.

Surface shaders give surfaces characteristics depending on where lights are relative to an object, and which way the object's normals are facing. You can see the surface normals, which are represented by thin blue lines, by selecting an object and choosing Show→Normals (that's the Eye menu) in the top menu bar. The blue lines' direction indicate which direction the surface is facing.

DEFAULT SURFACE SHADER

Newly-created 3D objects start with a default surface shader. As soon as you create any primitive object, it has a shiny gray color when rendered or viewed in Shaded mode. This one default shader is shared by ALL objects that don't have their own material, so changing the color of one object with the default shader changes the color of all of them.

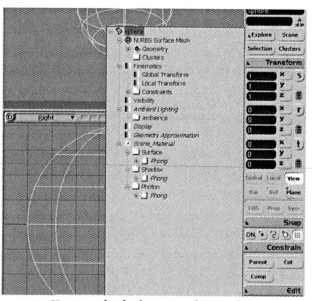

You can edit shaders using this window

You can take a look at this surface shader by selecting an object and clicking on the Selection button on the MCP. There will be a property called Scene_Material, and cascaded under that, folders for Surface, Shadow, and Photon. Under those properties, there is default surface shader called Phong. Clicking on the Phong node in the property editor will prompt you to create a copy of Scene_Material surface shader instead of editing the default Phong node.

By copying the default shader, you can change the color or other characteristics without having to worry about affecting other objects. Generally speaking, it is not a good idea to edit the default Phong node, since that is the color inherited by all newly-created elements.

Therefore, let's try the next method to view and edit a shader property page.

CREATING A NEW SURFACE SHADER

You can create a whole new surface shader by selecting the object and choosing Get➔Material➔ in the toolbar at the left. The Get➔Material menu has different material shaders which are all appropriate for different uses, which are enumerated later in this chapter.

If you choose Get➔Material➔Phong, a shader property editor will open, which will allow you to change the many characteristics of the surface shader. There are many tools available in this window. It has a keyframe tool like any other property editor, at the top-left. There is an Undo button, as well as Load and Save Presets buttons, at the top-right. There are three property tabs for all the types of material shaders - Illumination, Transparency/Reflection, and Indirect Illumination - which will be discussed following an explanation of how to set color values.

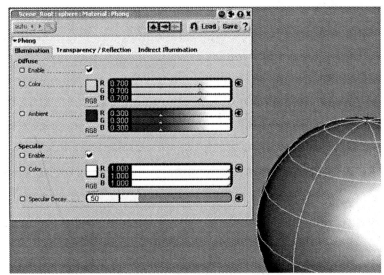

Basic Phong shading model

THE ILLUMINATION TAB

Diffuse color controls the color of the surface that is illuminated by the lights in your scene. If you want your object to be red, you would set its diffuse color to red. One thing to keep in mind is that if the color of the light something other than white, the final render will mix the color of the light and the diffuse color of the object.

Ambient color is the shadowed area of an object. XSI sets a default ambient value of 0.3 (30% gray). Frequently, you will want to set the ambient color lower than that, to create a crisper shadow area.

Specular color is the hot highlight area found on shiny objects. One parameter unique to specularity is the Specular Decay slider. The higher the specular decay value, the smaller the shiny spot. Non-metallic shiny materials, such as plastic and porcelain, tend to have smaller specular spots compared to rough metal, which has a broader specular area.

EDITING COLOR BOXES

You can change colors by dragging the sliders on the color bars. The default method of selecting a color is by editing individual RGB (Red/Green/Blue) values. This method is not particularly intuitive, and there is no easy way to make the color lighter or darker after you choose the hue. Instead, you can use the HSV (Hue/Saturation/Value) editing method, by clicking twice on the RGB button left of the slider. The HSV method can achieve a desired color faster and more accurately than the RGB method.

You can also edit a color by clicking on the color box to the left of the slider, which opens a small window with a color chart and various tool buttons. You can click on any color in the editor to choose a color. You can also pick any color from your scene by using the color picker (eyedropper button) located on the bottom-left of the window. The "..." button expands the window, giving you more selection options, tools, and feedback.

Another great use of the color boxes is that you can copy a color from one color box to another simply by click-and-dragging the color chip (colored box) you want to copy on top of the box you want it copied to.

THE TRANSPARENCY/REFLECTION TAB

Transparency controls whether or not you can see through the object, and exactly how "see-through" it is. When you are in HSV edit mode, you can make the object more transparent simply by dragging the V (value) slider to the right. Diffuse color and other surface characteristics are lost if you make it too transparent. Transparency Value 0 is a totally opaque object, and Value 1 is an absolutely transparent object. You need to render or preview to see the transparency accurately.

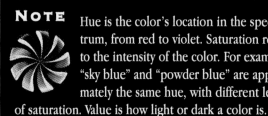

NOTE Hue is the color's location in the spectrum, from red to violet. Saturation refers to the intensity of the color. For example, "sky blue" and "powder blue" are approximately the same hue, with different levels of saturation. Value is how light or dark a color is.

If you are using the RGB color system, you can change all three sliders by holding CTRL while dragging one slider.

Index of Refraction controls the refractive property of the object. Refraction is the bending of light through a transparent object. When you put a straw in a glass of water, it appears to bend at the point where it enters the water. Water is denser than air, causing the light to travel through it at a different angle. The default refraction index is 1, which is the density of air. The refraction slider is very sensitive, so you probably won't need to slide it very much to get the desired effect. 1.3 approximates the density of water. Diamond has an index of refraction of 2.2. XSI calculates refraction by casting additional rays (secondary rays) from the point on the surface where the initial ray first hits it. This can create very accurate results, but accuracy requires that you increase the ray depth from the default of 2 to the number of surfaces you want the ray to bend through (usually 4 will do.) You can set this in the Render Module, in Render Options under the Optimization tab. Increase the Raytracing depth refraction, and then make sure that the Maximum ray depth is equal to or greater than the refraction depth you set.

Reflection controls how reflective an object is. When an object is not at all reflective, the color of the surface is taken entirely from the Diffuse, Ambient and Specular color. As the objects becomes more reflective, the color of the surface becomes blended with the color of the objects surrounding it. When the slider is 1, the object is completely reflective, like a pristine mirror. XSI calculates reflection by casting an additional ray (at least one, perhaps more than one) from the surface out to the rest of your scene.

Be aware that use of transparency, refraction, and reflection can increase rendering time considerably, since XSI will have to cast many more rays.

THE INDIRECT ILLUMINATION TAB

Translucency adds a thin, silk-like surface appearance. By moving the Translucency slider to the right, you add diffuse color to the far edge of the ambient color, creating a semi-transparent look. Translucency changes with the direction and distance to the lights. If you put a light directly inside a translucent object it will glow beautifully.

Incandescence gives the appearance of a light source within the object, even if no lights are in the scene. You can specify a color, and the Intensity slider controls how much internal glow the object has. Incandescence simulates an object that is self-illuminating, like a fluorescent tube or a firefly.

SHADING MODELS

There are eight basic material shaders available in the Get→Material menu. Let's look at the characteristics of each shader, and what they are frequently used for.

Constant has only diffuse and transparency parameters. Objects with a constant material color tend to not have any 3-dimensional appearance, since ambient (shadow) coloring is not present. Constant material works well for a backdrop object, such as sky texture, since your light-

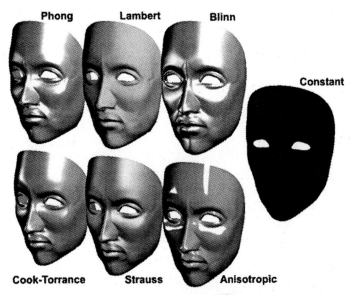

Various shading models for different surfaces

ing does not create any highlight or shadows on it. Any texture applied to an object with a constant material will be displayed as-is, with no shading.

Lambert has diffuse and ambient colors, but no specular highlight. That is, it simulates a matte surface, such as cotton clothing or tree bark. Lambert is used for most objects that are not shiny or glossy, and works well for skin.

Phong is used as the default surface shader. It has three basic characteristics: diffuse, ambient, and specular. It's very versatile and easy to edit. Phong can be used for any smooth, shiny object, but tends to make objects look like plastic.

Blinn is similar to the Phong shading model. It has diffuse, ambient, and specular colors. However, sometimes it offers better quality when simulating metallic surfaces, thanks to more accurate and complicated algorithms. It works especially well for a metallic object with sharp edges.

Cook-Torrance creates a smooth surface with a somewhat subdued specular highlight. It does not have a specular decay slider to control the size of the specular area. When its Roughness value is above 0, it loses specularity.

Strauss is the perfect solution for a frosty metal surface. Instead of ambient color or specular decay sliders, it has specular smoothness and metalness sliders. Smoothness controls the size of a specular highlight, 0 being a large specular area. However, you will lose diffuse and specular color when the slider is set to 1. The metalness slider controls the balance between diffuse and ambient color. Setting metalness to 0 will differentiate between diffuse and ambient color, so the surface will look like very frosty, shiny metal. Setting metalness to 1 will make the object more glass-like, since the diffuse and ambient colors will be the same.

Anisotropic simulates objects with tiny grooves such as a CD or brushed metal. The glossy slider controls the smoothness of transition between diffuse and specular, and can create a long streak of specularity, using either U or V coordinate mapping.

PREVIEWING THE SCENE USING RENDER REGION

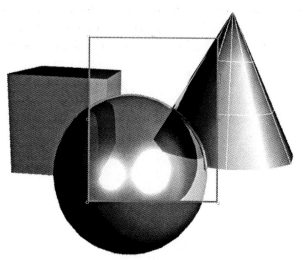

You may have noticed that the regular viewports do not always display shaders accurately. Transparency, refraction, and reflection do not show up at all in these windows. That's because these displays are created with an OpenGL accelerated video card. While this display mode offers extremely fast interaction, it does not support transparency, refraction, reflection, or even smooth shading of specularity. To accurately view how your scene looks, you need to display it using a software render. XSI's mental ray renderer offers highly realistic and speedy software rendering.

The render region tool lets you interactively preview the scene

To quickly and interactively view your scene, we are going to use a tool called render region.

To activate render region, first make sure the tool bar is in Render mode (hotkey F3), and click on Render➔Region➔Region Tool; or, you can use the Q hotkey. Render region mode is activated, and the mouse pointer becomes a transparent arrow attached to a white square with a black sphere inside. Left-click-and-drag to draw a marquee box around the region you want to render, in the viewport of your choice. A yellow box with blue control points will appear where you drew the marquee box. Immediately after you release the mouse button, mental ray starts and renders an image of the selected region. This render is truly interactive, meaning if you change any value, such as diffuse color, or placement of the object or light, render region automatically updates to the change.

The blue squares on each edge and corner of the yellow box are control points. You can left-click-and-drag on them to resize the render region. If you left-click-and-drag on any of the yellow borders, you can translate the render region around its viewport. The rectangular blue box at the top-right modifies the sampling level of the render region. If you hover the mouse pointer over the box, it becomes a slider bar. Lowering the slider gives you a less-detailed, faster render. If you move the slider up, the render is smoother and more detailed, but slower to update.

The Region menu offers a few more tools. If you turn on Render➔Region➔Track Selection, the render region will automatically move and resize to frame any object you select. If you toggle on Render➔Region➔Render Selection Only then only that object will be rendered in the region. This option speeds up the region considerably.

Render➔Region➔Auto Refresh automatically refreshes the render whenever something is changed in the scene that affects the selected area. The default is on, but if the constant updating is slowing you down too much, uncheck Auto Refresh. You can refresh the render by moving the camera or redrawing the render region.

You can also view only the color or alpha channels of the render by checking the corresponding menu option on Render➔Region. The default is Show RGB + Alpha, which draws the rendered pixels on top of a transparent background so that the Wireframe shows around the rendered parts. If you prefer to see your render Region on a black background, check on Region➔Show RGB. This helps when you are looking at transparent items, smoke, fire, glows, etc.

Render➔Region➔Options lets you edit various settings for the render region tool. This is where you need to turn on Caustics and Global illumination if you want to see these effects in your Render Region, and where you can turn other effects on and off to further speed up the region.

FORTUNE TELLER: AT A GLANCE

TOPICS COVERED

In this tutorial, you will get hands-on experience on how to apply a shader to an object and how to use the render region.

You'll learn how to:

- Apply shaders to objects
- Edit shaders to create the desired effect, using the shader property editor
- Use render region tool to render interactively

TUTORIAL: FORTUNE TELLER

So far in this chapter, we learned the basics of what a shader does and how to edit them. We also learned how to use render region to accurately see what a shader will look like in the final render. Let's apply this knowledge to create a fortune teller's crystal ball. We will use shader property editors to tweak a sphere's diffuse color, ambient color, specularity, transparency, refraction, and reflection. While we edit shaders, we will turn on the render region tool, so we can predict the results of our editing.

ASSEMBLE TABLE-TOP OBJECTS

STEP 1. CREATE A CRYSTAL BALL.

First we will create a NURBS sphere. Get→Primitive→Surface→Sphere. Leave the default settings for now.

It will be easier to add other props later if the top of the table is at 0 on the Y-axis. Translate the sphere in positive Y so the bottom of the sphere touches the thick X- and Z-axis line (the Y translation should be about 4).

Rename the sphere "crystalBall".

STEP 2. CREATE A STAND.

Let's make a stand for the crystal ball. A torus will make a great stand. Choose Get→Primitive→Surface→Torus.

Translate the torus up in the Y-axis, so the sphere will sit nicely and the bottom of the stand is at the thick X- and Z-axis lines.

Rename the torus "stand".

STEP 3. CREATE A TABLE.

Next, a table is needed, so crystalBall isn't floating in space. Choose Get→Primitive→Polygon Mesh→Cube. Scale it, so its not too small compared to the crystal ball. Around 3 times as big in the X and Z directions each is a good size.

Translate it down on the Y-axis, so the top of the cube meets the bottom of the stand.

Name the cube "table".

STEP 4. ADD MORE PROPS ON THE TABLE

Using other primitives, such as cones and cylinders, make some more interesting props for your tabletop.

Check all orthogonal views, to make sure that all the objects are sitting on top of the table. Don't forget to add a couple of props behind the crystal ball.

COLOR THE OBJECTS BY APPLYING SHADERS

STEP 1. ADD A SHADER TO THE CRYSTAL BALL

Press F3 to enter the Render module. (If this doesn't work, you need to change the keyboard mapping. Use the command File→Keyboard Mapping and change the Key Map drop menu in the top right to "SI3D Key Map".)

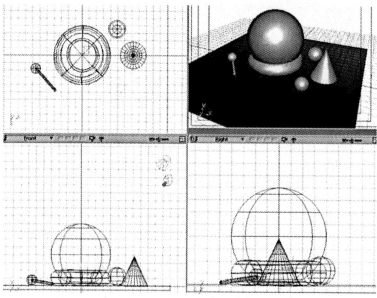

An assortment of models

Add a Phong shader to the crystal ball: select crystalBall, then choose Get→Material→Phong. Open the property page for the Phong with the Selection button on the MCP.

Let's change the color of the ball to purple. Click twice on the RGB button to the left of the slider for the Color property so it says HSV. Crank up the S (saturation) slider. The Hue bar will display the color spectrum; move the slider to purple. If you haven't already, change the perspective viewport to Shaded mode.

The shadow looks a bit grayish, and not clear enough. Lower the Ambient value to about 0.1, so the shadow looks darker and crisper. (Note: There is some ambient light added in by the renderer. To change the amount and color of this 'garbage light' use the Modify→Ambience menu cell in the Render module.)

STEP 2. ADJUST THE TRANSPARENCY OF THE CRYSTALBALL

Let's make the crystalBall more glass-like by increasing its transparency.

Click on the Transparency/Reflection tab on the material property editor.

Change from RGB mode to HSV mode for the Transparency Color property.

The Value slider controls the amount of transparency. The higher (whiter) the value, the more transparent the object; slide it to about half (0.5).

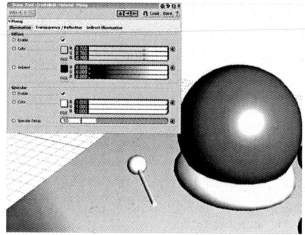

Ambient controls the color of the shadow area

Whoops! You can't see the transparency of the crystal ball, since the 3D hardware rendering used for the Shaded mode viewport display doesn't support it. You need to use the render region tool to check the amount of transparency.

USE RENDER REGION:

STEP 1. DRAW A RENDER REGION

Activating the render region tool is a snap: press the Q hotkey! The arrow cursor will change to an outline of an arrow, with a box at the bottom of it.

Left-click and drag to draw a marquee box around the crystalBall. The area inside the marquee box is rendered smoothly, and transparency is shown.

Choosing Render→Region→Show RGB will make the background black.

Try dragging each blue box at the corners of the render region to resize it.

Drag on the yellow border to move the render region.

STEP 2. EDIT THE RENDER REGION TOOL

Let's tweak the sampling level to see smoother rendering. Hover the cursor over the rectangular box at the top-right of the render region, and a vertical slider will show up. Drag the slider to the top, and the render is much more detailed, but very much slower. Drag the slider to the bottom, and rendering is really quick, but the picture looks very blocky. When you are working on the scene with render region on, you need to find the best balance between speed and quality to clearly see what you are editing, while not being bogged down by the interactive rendering. For now, keep the slider around the middle. (What this slider really does is adjust the number of rays that are cast per pixel. When the image looks chunky, the renderer is casting one ray for a group of pixels, when it looks smoother it casts one ray per pixel, when it looks really smooth it is casting more than one ray per pixel. This is called antialiasing.)

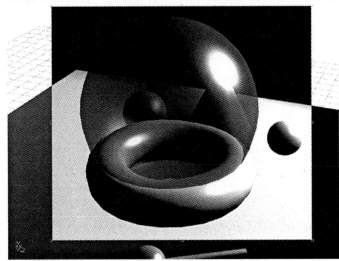

Render region properly displays transparency, unlike the Shaded view mode

ADD REFRACTION AND REFLECTION TO THE CRYSTALBALL

STEP 1. ADD REFRACTION

A transparent objects rarely looks believable without refraction, because it doesn't look like it has any volume. The reason for this is simple: the default value of the index of refraction is 1, which is the density of air.

Slide the Index of Refraction slider in the Transparency/Reflection tab. The crystal glass index of refraction is around 1.2 (If you don't know the index of refraction of the substance you are working with, you can just keep adjusting the slider until it looks good).

STEP 2. ADD REFLECTION

Another way to add realism to the scene is by making the ball reflective, so it will show a bit of the surrounding props.

In the Phong property page, find the Transparency color sliders, and make sure you are in HSV color editing mode. Like transparency, the V (value) slider controls the amount of reflection. Set the crystalBall's reflectivity to about 0.5. Now you can see the props reflected on the surface of the crystalBall.

ADD SHADERS TO ALL OBJECTS IN YOUR SCENE

STEP 1. ADD SHADERS TO OTHER OBJECTS

Refraction makes your crystal ball more realistically transparent

Add more shaders to other objects, by selecting an object and choosing Get➔Material, and use whichever shading model is suited to the object.

Save the scene and name it "fortune".

You have learned how to add a material shader, and edit each parameter of shaders in the property editor. You also learned how to interactively preview the result of editing by using the render region tool. A very important thing to remember is that those shaders don't just control the color of objects, but all the surface characteristics of an element, such as reflectivity and transparency. In the future we will learn how to put a picture on the surface, which is called texture mapping.

LIGHTS AND GOOD LIGHTING TECHNIQUE

When you see diffuse, ambient, and specular color on that crystal ball, what you are seeing is interaction between the shader of the ball and the lights in the scene. Without a light, you wouldn't even be able to see the ball. The color of the surface is blended with the color of the lights that shine on it, depending on how far away they are, how bright they are, and the angle of the object surface to the light. This is called "Shading".

Lighting is the most important aspect of rendering. No matter how hard you work on tweaking a shader, or how beautifully you paint and apply a texture map, bad lighting will make it look, well... bad.

WHAT'S IN THE LIGHT MENU CELL?

You can create a light by choosing Get➔Light. There are five types of lights available in the light menu cell. All of them are useful, depending on the situation. Let's take a look at each light and what each is used for.

INFINITE

An infinite light is like an abstracted Sun: it exists infinitely far away from the scene, and illuminates the entire scene evenly and from the same angle. Because it is "infinitely distant", moving it won't actually have any effect; but you can change direction the light is coming from, which determines the angle of the light rays in the scene. A hidden default infinite light is created when you create any new scene. You can unhide it with Shift-H on your keyboard.

SPOT

A spot is, as its name implies, like a spotlight. It shoots out light in a cone shape, pointing at a null called its interest, which is created automatically along with the light. You can control the position of a spot light, the position of its interest, the angle of its cone, and the distance away from the spot that the light will travel (called falloff or attenuation).

POINT

Point lights act like a bare light bulb: it casts light in all directions, out from a single point. You can control its position by translating it, and like spot lights, point lights have a falloff parameter.

LIGHT BOX

This type of light simulates a film studio's light box. It creates a nice, soft, and diffused light, for a more real, less computer-generated look. This is really just a point light with Area lighting turned on.

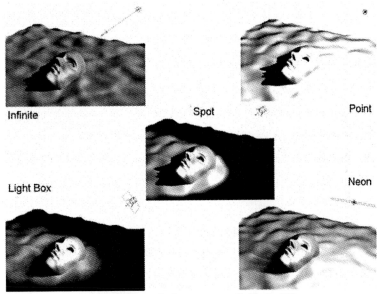

Infinite   Spot   Point

Light Box   Neon

The different light types available in XSI

NEON

If you want to simulate fluorescent or neon light, a neon light is the way to go. It works just like a point light, except that it has a longer and wider light source, creating a softer shadow and less harsh, focused light.

This also is an area light, with a very long and narrow shape (check out the Area tab of the Light property editor.)

EDITING LIGHTS' PROPERTIES

Let's examine the property pages of a light. Do Get→Light→Spot, and open the property editor.

Lights can be changed to spot, point, or infinite on the fly, by selecting Light Type.

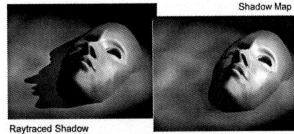

Shadow Map

Raytraced Shadow

Raytraced and shadow map shadows

Cone Angle controls the width of the beam on a spot light. Spread Angle controls how diffuse the outer edge of the beam is. A lower spread angle creates a more focused beam of light, and a high spread angle creates a more faded, diffuse light. It is extremely useful to turn on View→Cones in the top menu bar if you have spot lights in your scene.

You can set color of the light with the Color slider, the same way you edit material shader colors. An important thing to remember if you use HSV mode is that the Value slider controls how intense the light is. You can type directly into the Value box to "overdrive" the light's intensity to greater than 1.

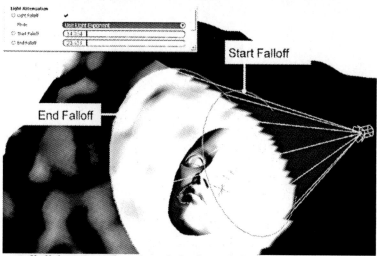

Intensity also determines the strength of the light: the higher the Intensity, the brighter the light. This control is redundant to Value if you are using HSV color editing, but necessary if you are using the RGB method.

Lights don't cause objects they illuminate to cast shadows unless you check the Shadows Enabled box in the soft_light tab of the light property editor. Umbra controls the darkness of the shadows cast: the smaller the

Falloff determines how far a light shines before it loses its intensity completely

number, the darker the shadows. The default shadow type is raytraced shadows, which create highly accurate, but harsher-edged shadows. Alternately, you can use shadow-mapping, which is often called depth map shadow mapping. This type has a control to make shadows softer, and renders faster, but it is not as accurate as raytraced shadows. You can enable shadow-map by clicking on the Shadow Map tab at the top next to General and checking the Use Shadow Map box. Resolution controls the quality of the shadow map: higher Resolution gives higher quality, but slower render time. To view the shadow map in render region, you need to change the setting in the option box: choose Render➜Region➜Options and click on the Shadows tab. Check the Enable box under Shadow Map.

Light Attenuation, also called falloff, is used to determine at what distance a light diminishes in brightness. To use falloff, you need to check the Light Falloff box, set the Light Attenuation Mode to Linear, and set Start and End Falloff values. Start Falloff is the distance at which light starts to lose its brightness, in Softimage units, and End Falloff is the distance at which the light has faded completely. The Start Falloff is generally set to near zero, while the End Falloff should be close to the width of the scene.

Let's practice what we've learned by creating some lights and editing their properties, in the following tutorial.

NOTE Changing the Falloff Mode to Use Exponent will let you set the rate at which the light falls off relative to the distance traveled. The default light exponent is 2, meaning that the light will fall off as the square of the distance (distance raised to the 2nd power.) This makes for really rapid falloff, and you will need very intense lights to see any results. A light exponent of 1.2 makes it easier to control while still falling off in a more accurate fashion. Advanced lighting enthusiasts may experiment with Exponent and Intensity to create fantastic and intense lighting effects.

GOOD LIGHTING: AT A GLANCE

TOPICS COVERED

We learned what kinds of lights are available to us and how to control them using the property editor. In this tutorial, we will create a three-light setup as a starting point of good lighting technique.

You'll learn how to:

- Create lights, and place them in a basic three light set-up
- Edit several parameters of lights
- Add shadows and explore different kinds of shadows
- Create a negative light to create a mood

MATERIALS REQUIRED

Fortune Teller tutorial scene

TUTORIAL: 3 POINT LIGHTING

Without good planning, lighting a scene can become very time-consuming. In this tutorial, we will learn the three-point lighting technique used widely by lighting designers to create a basic light setup that enhances the 3-dimensionality of the stage or character on the stage set. The three lights are named the key light, the fill light, and the back light. This setup does not work on every occasion, but it is a good, organized way to start lighting you scene. We will also create a negative light, a light that casts darkness, to obscure part of the scene.

CREATING A KEY LIGHT

STEP 1. LOAD THE SCENE
Load the scene you created in the previous tutorial, "fortune".

Have three orthogonal (Top, Front, Right) and one camera view on your viewports.

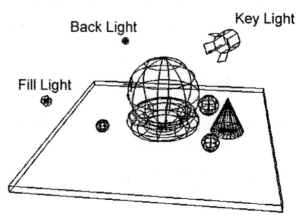

STEP 2. CREATE A KEY LIGHT
First, we will create a spotlight, which will be the key light. The key light is the brightest of the three lights, and casts shadows. Choose Get→Light→Spot.

The three-point lighting technique is a good foundation to build on

We need to move the spotlight to illuminate the scene correctly. Activate the translation tool and move the light up in the Front view, and to the bottom-right of the Top view. Make sure the light is shining on the crystal ball, by translating its interest to the center of the crystal ball.

Alternately, you can change one of the viewport to SpotLights→Spot to see through the spotlight as if it were a camera. Aiming the light can be much easier using this technique; just track, dolly, and orbit around the scene to change light's direction. Don't forget to switch back once the light is where you want it, though.

You can view the changes interactively by creating a render region around the crystalBall (hotkey Q).

STEP 3. EDIT THE KEY LIGHT
Let's give the spot key light characteristics. Open its property page and change its Cone Angle to about 40. This will narrow the beam and focus more on the crystal ball.

We will make the light a little brighter using the Intensity slider. Slide the slider all the way to the right (1). You can directly type in a higher value like 3 if you wish.

Enable shadows by checking the Enable box, and lower the Umbra to somewhere around 0.3, so the shadows will be darker.

Light Attenuation is next. Check the Light Falloff box to enable falloff. Oops, where did the light and shadow go? Because default Start Falloff is 1, light starts to lose its brightness only 1 unit beyond the spotlight. Adjust the Start Falloff and End Falloff so that the scene is sufficiently illuminated, yet the light is gradually diminishing in intensity. If you have View→Cones turned on, there will be rings indicating the Start and End Falloff drawn on the spot's cone, which is extremely helpful when editing attenuation.

Change the color of the Key Light to be slightly yellowish or yellow-orangish.

FILL LIGHT

STEP 1. CREATE A FILL LIGHT

Choose Get→Light→Point to get point light to use as a fill light. The purpose of a fill light is to smooth out the harsh shadow area created by the key light. Often when you observe a photo shoot, an assistant is holding a large reflector panel to cast light opposite of the main light source. This way, the shadow made by the main light source does not obscure the subject's shape.

Move the fill light. It should be placed about 45 degrees apart from the key light. Also, it does not need to be as high as the key light.

STEP 2. EDIT THE FILL LIGHT

Lower its intensity to about 0.5; you don't want the fill light to overwhelm the key light.

The fill light doesn't need to cast shadows. Rather than having to go to great lengths to minimize shadows, we can simply not check the Enable box.

The fill light also doesn't need to cast a specular highlight, which would give away its position. In the Light tab of the Property Editor, check off the Light Contribution Specular check box.

Adjust the fill light's attenuation as desired.

Make the color of the fill light slightly bluish.

BACK LIGHT

STEP 1. CREATE A BACK LIGHT

A back light is used to create an outline on the subject. It produces a more 3-dimensional illusion by separating the subject from the background. The light is even weaker than a fill light, and it doesn't cast shadows.

Choose Get→Light→Point to create a point light.

Translate the back light, so it is placed at the back of the scene, and little higher than the key light. Name it "backlight".

STEP 2. EDIT THE BACK LIGHT

Lower its intensity to be even weaker than the fill light, around 0.3.

You may want to edit the placement, intensity, and color of the lights to experiment with different effects. Another great technique for lighting is called negative light. Frequently, you won't want to illuminate everything in your scene. In Softimage|XSI, you can cast darkness by using negative light, which is a technique unique to computer animation.

NEGATIVE LIGHT

STEP 1. CREATE A NEGATIVE LIGHT

Create a spotlight. We use a spotlight because they are easy to aim and control.

Translate the spotlight and its interest so it's aimed at the back corner of the tabletop.

To create negative light, type in a negative value in the Value slider. Change RGB mode to HSV mode, and type "-1" directly into the box next to the V slider. Intensity should be 1.

You can help create a more dark, mysterious mood by using several negative lights to conceal the edges of the table.

You just learned how to light a scene in an organized manner using the three-light setup. It is a good idea to plan in advance what kind of lighting you will use in a particular scene. Lighting can create a mood and suspense if used wisely. It is highly recommended to pick up a book that deals specifically with lighting techniques for cinema or photography to study this subject further. The next section will deal with framing a camera and rendering out a sequence of images, so we can see fully rendered moving pictures.

SETTING UP A CAMERA

Another very important aspect of rendering is camera setup. The images you render are defined by where the camera is looking in the scene. You can manipulate and edit your camera to its maximum effect. Let's discuss the different controls built into cameras.

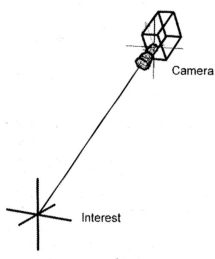

A camera and its interest

CREATING AND EDITING A CAMERA

Choosing Get→Camera→Perspective creates a camera which resembles the default camera. You can create an unlimited numbers of cameras, as you desire. Other camera types include Telephoto, Wide Angle, and Orthographic.

Doing Get→Camera creates a camera, and a null object called the camera's interest. You can move a camera around like any other object in the scene, but it always points in the direction of its interest, like a spot light.

To look through the new Camera, choose a view and in the View name drop menu at the top left, click on the Cameras submenu option to see your new camera listed. Select it to set the view to look through your camera.

EDITING A CAMERA

Most of the parameters used to define a camera can be found in the camera's property page. Select the Camera in the 3D views or in the Explorer, and use the Selection button in the MCP or if you have a view looking through the camera, then click the Camera shaped icon in the top of that view menubar, and choose the Properties command to open the Camera property editor.

You can rename a camera by typing in its Name field.

Format controls what picture resolution and aspect ratio the camera records. If you are planning to output to video in North America, and you want to preview exactly what the final render will look like, you want to set the Format to Video NTSC. By clicking the down arrow at the right, you can select other standardized formats for the camera, or manually set a custom aspect ratio in the Picture Ratio field.

Field of View determines what focal length your camera is using. The default is 41.5 degrees, which is about the same as a 35-mm lens. Moving this slider has the same effect as zooming in our out with the Z hotkey in a perspective view.

Clipping Planes tell the camera to stop displaying objects that are beyond (or closer than, in the case of Near Plane) a given distance, in Softimage units. If you want to find out the distance between a camera and an object accurately, find out the name of

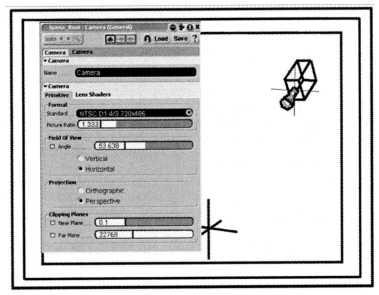

Camera property editor, and the Field Guide

the camera from which you want to measure the distance, such as Camera1, and choose Render→Options, and click on the Format tab. Choose the correct camera name in the Output Camera field and click on View→Distance to Output Camera in the top menu bar. Now you will see the distance between the output camera - the camera that does the final render - and selected objects in any viewport.

Another important tool is the Field Guide. Objects close to the edge of a camera's field of view run the risk of getting distorted or cut off when viewed on a television monitor, and the field guide will help you avoid cutting or distorting anything important. You can activate the field guide by clicking the Show menu of the camera viewport you are using and selecting Visibility Options - or by pressing the Shift + S hotkey - then select the Grid tab and check the Field Guide box. The camera view will display three black rectangles. The outermost box is exactly the resolution you have selected (usually NTSC, which is 720x486); anything outside this rectangle will definitely be cut off. The second, middle rectangle is the Safe Action box. Anything outside this box still has a chance to be cut off or distorted, so be sure any important action is inside this rectangle. The innermost rectangle is called the Safe Title box. If there is anything in your scene that absolutely cannot be distorted or cut off, such as text, it needs to be inside this rectangle.

RENDERING THE FILE

There's one more subject to cover before we are ready to actually render pictures and view them with the Flipbook tool: setting the render properties. Choose Render→Options from the left-side menu stack of the Render module, and we'll look at a few of the important tabs.

OUTPUT TAB

You'll need to tell XSI where to save images, and what to name them, by entering a path in the Image File Name field in the Output tab.

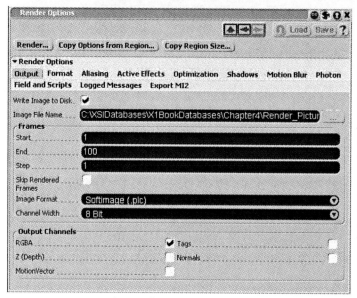

The Render Options window

Frames determines the start and end frame that mental ray will render. If you want to render a 30-frame animation starting from frame 1, you set Start to 1 and End to 30. If you only want to render frame 30 as a single image, you would enter 30 for both Start and End frames.

You can select what type of picture file you want to produce by choosing one from the Image Format menu. The default is Softimage PIC file, but if you want to use a program like AfterEffects to composite the movie, you need to set it to a more standard format, such as TIFF or JPEG.

FORMAT TAB

You need to tell XSI which camera you are using to make the final render by choosing one from the Output Camera menu.

Picture Standard is similar to the Picture Format camera property. If you are producing content for the North American video standard, it needs to be set to Video NTSC.

Image Resolution controls the actual size of the image file. You can type in the value directly to create smaller rendered images for testing animation, or larger images for high-resolution stills. This setting overrides Picture Standard.

ALIASING TAB

Anti-aliasing smoothes the edges of rendered images. The higher the Sampling level, the smoother the edges will be, though rendering time will be increased as well. The Sampling level determined how many rays will be cast to each pixel. Because the rays arrive at different places on a single pixel, casting more rays will produce a more accurate color for the pixel. Setting the Max Level to 0 shoots one ray per pixel, 1 gives you 4 rays per pixel, 2 gives 9 samples, 3 gives 16 samples and so on. The greatest difference you can set between Minimum and Maximum Sampling is 3.

Jitter makes anti-aliasing less artificial, by randomizing sampling.

Filtering further improves picture quality by smoothing out color transitions.

SHADOWS TAB

The default setting will create shadows by raytracing. However, if you are using the shadow map method, you need to turn it on by checking the Enable box.

Once all the parameters have been set, you can start rendering your sequence by choosing Render→Current Pass.

BLIMP 2: AT A GLANCE

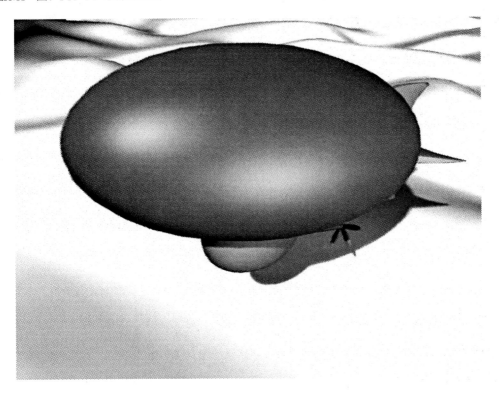

TOPICS COVERED

Using what we learned in this chapter, let's render out a sequence of images to create a small movie of the blimp we made in Chapter 5. We will edit shaders, lights, cameras and render properties.

You'll learn how to:

- Edit render properties
- Render a sequence of images
- View animation using the Flipbook tool

MATERIALS REQUIRED

Lead Zeppelin tutorial scene

TUTORIAL: BLIMP 2

In this tutorial, we will create a final render of the flying blimp animation. A material shader needs to be applied to the blimp, and lights need to be set up. Then, after the rendering properties are set, images are created frame by frame and we will view them as a movie using the Flipbook tool.

ADD SHADERS, LIGHTS, AND CAMERA

STEP 1. LOAD THE SCENE
Load the blimp scene you created in the Chapter 5.

Have three orthogonal and one camera view on your viewports.

STEP 2. ADD A SHADER TO BLIMP'S SURFACE
Add shaders to each part of the blimp. You can color each part one by one, or all at once by selecting the blimp hierarchy as a branch (middle-click-select the root) and adding a new material to it. Children below the mainChamber will inherit its color.

Create a NURBS grid and scale it to be much larger; this will be the ground surface.

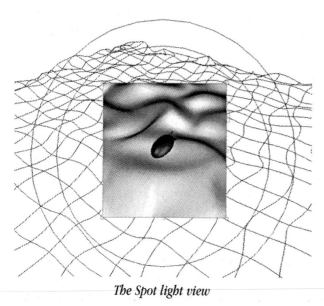

The Spot light view

STEP 3. CREATE A SPOT LIGHT
Add a spot light to the scene. Change one of the viewports to spot light view and make sure the blimp is illuminated throughout its animation sequence. The blimp should not move out of the cone angle circle in the spot light view.

Make sure to turn on shadows by checking the Enable box under Shadow. Set Umbra to around 0.3.

Preview the scene using the render region tool

STEP 4. ADD A NEW CAMERA
Choose Get→Camera→Perspective to get a new camera.

Make one of the viewports a Camera1 view by choosing Cameras→Camera1 in the viewport mode selection menu.

Frame the view, so you have an interesting perspective on the entire animation sequence.

RENDER THE SEQUENCE

STEP 1. EDIT RENDER PROPERTY
In the Render Module, choose Render→Render→Options to open the render options.

Make sure you are rendering to the Render_Picture folder of your database in Image File Name. Change the name of the output image from "default" to "blimp".

Set Start to 1 and End to 100, which should be the default. Keep everything else as-is.

Change Image Resolution of X and Y to 320 and 240 respectively. This is a test, so we want to render small images.

STEP 2. RENDER THE SEQUENCE
Render the images by choosing Render→Render→Current Pass.

TO VIEW RENDERED SEQUENCES:
To view the rendered images as animation, you need to use a tool called the Image Clip Viewer. Let's try viewing the blimp animation.

STEP 1. OPEN A CLIP VIEWER
To open an Image Clip Viewer, click on the View Name drop menu on any viewport and select Image Clip Viewer.

Select File→Load from the window and choose the path to the rendered images. Inside the Render_Picture folder, there should be a file named blimp.[1..100]. Highlight the file and click OK. If you double click the file, you will be able to see individual frames, but opening individual frames won't let you view animation.

Click on the Play button at the top of the Viewer window, and the animation is displayed. Clicking on the Loop button will play the animation again and again until you stop it. The framerate maintained by the Clip Viewer is printed to the right of the VCR style playback buttons in the titlebar.

Extra Credit: You can also drag and drop images into the Clip Viewer. Change another view to be a Browser, and find some other images to look at. Click on an image in the browser with your Left Mouse Button and drag it to the middle of the Image Clip Viewer and then let go. It loads into the viewer! You can drag and drop all kinds of image files, including AVI and QuickTime movies, into the Image Clip Editor.

CONCLUSION

Congratulations! In this long and complex chapter, you learned how to add surface shaders to objects, preview using the render region tool, how to add light to the scene, how to create and edit the camera, and how to render a single picture and sequence of pictures by editing render options. In the end, you learned how to play the sequence of images by Image Clip Editor tool. These techniques are still pretty basic compared to what you can add to each step. Some people spend their entire careers making a study of just cinematography or lighting, and the same principles can be applied to computer graphics. However, knowing and studying the workflow covered in this chapter will certainly enhance the speed and quality of your work.

QUIZ

1. BLINN IS A GOOD SHADING MODEL FOR RUBBER.
   a. True
   b. False

2. ONE SHADING MODEL WITHOUT A SPECULAR COLOR IS:
   a. Phong
   b. Lambert
   c. Anisotropic

3. NORMALS INDICATE WHICH SIDE OF A SURFACE IS FACING OUT.
   a. True
   b. False

4. THE BENDING OF LIGHT THROUGH TRANSPARENT OBJECTS IS CALLED:
   a. Reflection
   b. Referencing
   c. Refraction

5. AMBIENT IS THE PRIMARY COLOR OF THE MATERIAL.
   a. True
   b. False

6. SPOTLIGHTS AND LIGHT BOXES COME WITH AN EXTRA CONTROL OBJECT CALLED:
   a. Locator
   b. Interest
   c. Director

7. THE DARKNESS OF SHADOWS IS CONTROLLED BY PENUMBRA.
   a. True
   b. False

8. THREE-POINT LIGHT SETUP USES:
   a. Key Light
   b. Negative Light
   c. Neon Light

9. THE LIMIT OF A CAMERA'S VISIBILITY CAN BE CONTROLLED BY THE CLIPPING PLANE PROPERTY.
   a. True
   b. False

7 PATH ANIMATION

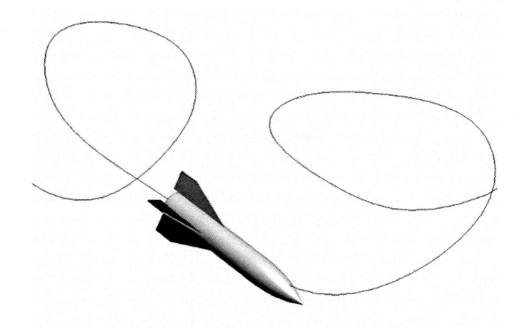

IN THIS CHAPTER YOU WILL LEARN ABOUT:

- How to animate objects on a path.
- How to save keys on path.
- How to use orientation and tangency to control an object's movement.

INTRODUCTION

Path animation is another useful animation tool. By drawing a NURBS curve, you can animate any object, camera, or light along a path. In addition, you can adjust how the object travels through space by moving the control points of the curve, animate the orientation of the object along the path, and change the timing of path animation.

SETTING PATH ANIMATION

Path animation is a type of constraint. You can imagine the path as having a magnetic attraction to the animated object: the object can be moved along the path, but not away from it, and if you move the path curve, the object moves with it.

There are two ways to set path animation. The first method is by drawing a curve, and then attaching an object to that curve. The second way is setting translation keys on an object, and telling XSI to create a path based on that movement. Let's try the first method:

ANIMATING ON A PATH BY PICKING

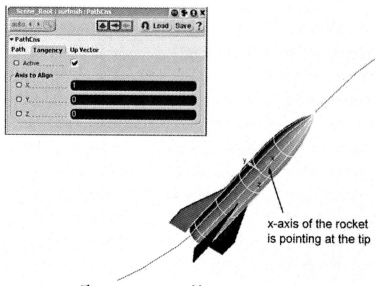

First, either draw a curve using Create➔Curve➔Draw CV NURBS, or choose one of the pre-defined curves under Get➔Primitive➔Curve. Make sure you are using an orthographic viewport, rather than a perspective-corrected one, when drawing a curve, and avoid any particularly small, tight kinks or twists. Then, select the object you want to animate. You can also branch-select the root of a hierarchy, for a more complex object to animate on the path. Next, switch to the Animation module (F2) and select

x-axis of the rocket is pointing at the tip

There are many variables in setting a path

Create➔Path➔Set Path. You will be prompted to enter the start and end frame of the path animation. There are two check boxes under the start and end frame slider. By checking the Linear box, the object will travel on the path at a constant velocity, meaning no ease-in or ease-out, which can be very useful. For example, if you path-animated a camera around a model to show a 360-degree view of the model, and you want to loop the animation for several revolutions, you wouldn't want it to slow down and stop every time it finished turning around. The Tangent box keeps the X-axis of the object aligned to the curve, so it stays pointed "forward" on the path. Click OK to accept these values and move forward to the last step.

Finally, pick the curve you created. The object (or hierarchy of objects) that was selected will jump to a position on the path you picked. Now, when you scrub the time slider, you should see your object animating along the path.

To modify the path animation, Open the PathCns property editor with the Selection button in the MCP. You will have to click on the small plus sign next to the Constraints folder to open up the Constraints properties and see the PathCns property. Click on the square icon to the left of the PathCns property to pop its properties into a Property Editor. The Path Percentage slider tells you where on the path the object is, 0 is the start of the path and 100 is the end. The Path Percentage property is automatically keyed at 0 and 100 for the start and end frame, respectively, that you chose earlier, but you can set Path Percentage keyframes at any time to change the animation's timing.

Under the Tangency tab of the Property Editor you can toggle Tangency on and off to align one axis of the object to the direction of the path. (Which axis that is, is determined by the Axis to Align text boxes.)

Examine your object to find out which axis you want to align to the path by selecting the object and clicking on the Translate menu cells so that the Manipulator icons show up. Observe the orientation of the manipulator and figure out which axis you want aligned with the path. Then put a 1 in the Axis to Align section of the PathCns property page that matches the axis you want aligned, and a 0 in the other boxes. This tells XSI which axis to line up.

The Up Vector tab has a similar arrangement designed to control which axis is facing up (or pointing at another axis). You can also animate the roll of an object here.

SETTING KEYS TO CREATE A PATH

Alternately, you can save keyframes and create a path according to the motion created by that animation. First, move the time slider to the frame where you want animation to start, and translate the object to that place. In the Animation module, select Create→Path→Save Key on Path. The selected object's translation is now keyframed at its current position and frame. If you go to a different frame, move the object, and Save Key on Path again, you will see a curve between the two places you set keys, which can be adjusted to alter the object's interpolation between the two points. This method is very useful when you need an object to be at a specific location at a specific frame.

EDITING PATH
ANIMATION

Since the objects are glued to the path, you can edit the curve's shape any way you like, and the object will just follow the new path. You can edit a path by adding or deleting points, moving points, or modifying its properties.

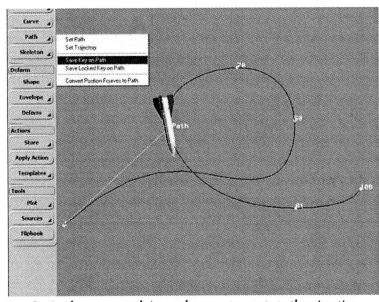

Setting keys on a path is another way to create path animation

VIEWING A PATH

You can display the controls for a path animation by selecting Show→Relations in the viewport in which you want to view the controls. The numbered white squares are saved keys on the path. Clicking on the dotted white line and pressing Enter will open the PathCns property editor for the selected curve.

REMOVING PATH ANIMATION

If you want to delete path animation altogether, select the object with path animation and choose Constraint→Remove Constraint from the bottom-right of the Main Command Panel.

NOTE You can also use Save Locked Key on Path. The difference is that when you use Save Key on Path, any modification to the curve will change the timing of the animation. For example, if you move the last point on the path curve, the objects will end up at in a different location than where you set the keyframe. Save Locked Key on Path will make the object always pass through the point where you keyed, at the frame you keyed, even if you edit the curve. Both methods are useful, depending on what you are doing.

SMART BOB: AT A GLANCE

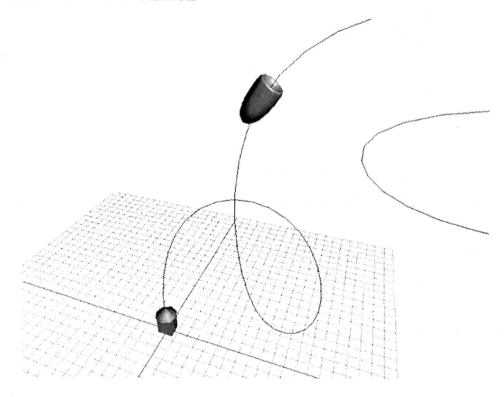

TOPICS COVERED

We will model a rocket and a target, and draw a curve between them. The animation of the rocket hitting the target is achieved by path animation on the curve.

You'll learn how to:

- Create path animation
- How to use tangency
- Viewing and editing path animation

TUTORIAL: SMART BOB

Let's create a rocket named Bob and hit an outhouse precisely, using the path animation tool. We will also use the tangency tool to keep Bob's head pointing toward the curve.

MAKING THE MODELS

STEP 1. MODEL THE ROCKET
Choose File➜New Scene to clear the slate.

Since we'll be doing modeling first, enter the Model Module.

We are going to create a profile curve of Bob and revolve it around the Y-axis.

In the Front view, draw a profile of the rocket, using Create➜Curve➜Draw CV NURBS. Make sure to draw the curve from bottom to top, or the resulting revolution will be inverted.

In Model mode, select Create➜Surface➜Revolution Around Axis. Pick the curve.

Open the Revolution property page, and choose Revolve Around Y in the Revolution Axis menu.

If the surface of the rocket is dark (in shaded mode), it's probably inside-out; show normals to check. If it is inside-out, choose Modify➜Surface➜Invert Normals.

Name the rocket Bob.

STEP 2. MODEL THE OUTHOUSE
Get➜Primitive➜Polygon Mesh➜Cube to get polygon cube.

Scale and translate the cube, so it's bit smaller than Bob.

Rename the cube outHouse

Add a roof using Get➜Primitive➜Polygon Mesh➜Cone.

Again, scale and translate the cone, so it fits on top of the cube.

Name it roof and make it a child of outHouse.

STEP 3. CREATE A GROUND PLANE
Create a grid using Get➜Primitive➜Surface➜Grid.

Scale the grid in X and Z to cover the ground surface.

Name the grid ground.

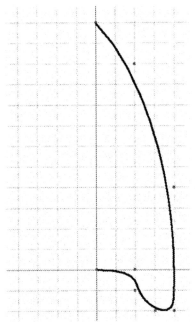

Draw profile curves bottom to top, or you'll end up with an inverted surface (you could Modify➜Surface➜Invert Normals, but why not save yourself the trouble?)

PATH ANIMATION

STEP 1. CREATING THE PATH

Zoom out in Front view, so you have enough space to draw a curve for Bob to travel along.

Select Create➔Curve➔Draw CV NURBS, and draw a curve starting about 50 units to the right of the outhouse. That's where Bob will be launched.

Add more points. Be sure to make it fun! Bob can do a few loop-de-loops or other aerobatics on the way to his target. As long as there are no extremely tight corners or kinks in the curve, he will follow it smoothly. End the curve at the center of outHouse.

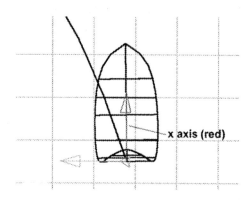

STEP 2. PUT BOB ON THE PATH

Select Bob, and change to Animate mode (hotkey 2, or F2 in SI3D mode). Select Create➔Path➔Set Path. Keep the defaults on the window that appears, then click OK and pick the curve as prompted.

Preview the animation. Oops, Bob is not heading toward the curve! We need to constrain Bob's tangency to the curve.

Open the PathCns (path constraint) property page, and click on the Tangency tab.

Check the Active box, and Bob's direction (tangency) is constrained to the curve. Preview the animation.

A little better, but that still isn't right. Bob's tangency is constrained to the curve, but the wrong axis is facing forward. Back in the PathCns property page, under the Tangency tab, change the value for X to 0, and Y to 1., and then preview the animation.

VIEWING AND EDITING

STEP 1. VIEWING PATH CONTROL

You can view a path constraint by choosing Show➔Relation, and selecting Bob. The white rectangles with numbers next to them represent the location and frame of where you set a key, and a dotted white line connects them.

Select the dotted white line, then hit Enter key. This is an alternate way of opening the PathCns property editor.

Under the Path tab, the Path Percentage slider will let you move Bob back and forth on the curve. Let's create additional keyframes using this property page.

Move the time slider to frame 20 and slide Path Percentage to 0. Click on the keyframe button next to the slider. You just added an extra keyframe. Bob remains at 0 percent of the curve translation, so he won't start his launch until frame 20.

Let's make him fly slower in the beginning before picking up speed: move the time slider to frame 50, and change the path percentage to around 14 percent. Click on the keyframe button next to the slider.

Play the animation and you will notice there is a "frame 50" white rectangle added to the path, and Bob is flying slowly when he starts out.

One of the most useful aspects of path animation is that you can make changes to the path after you constrain an object to it, and the object will follow the new curve. You can experiment by editing Bob's path curve. Hold down the M hotkey and drag points of the curve around to see this in action.

Great! Now he is flying really smartly, and dead on target!

CONCLUSION

In this chapter you learned how to create path animation. You can edit animation by editing points on a curve or adding another key on the path. Path animation is the most intuitive way to set motion to an object.

QUIZ

1. PATH ANIMATION IS A KIND OF CONSTRAINT.
   - a. True
   - b. False

2. YOU CAN'T EDIT PATH ANIMATION BY ADJUSTING THE CURVE AFTER YOU SET THE PATH ANIMATION.
   - a. True
   - b. False

3. TO SET PATH ANIMATION ON A HIERARCHY, SELECT:
   - a. root by node
   - b. root by branch
   - c. child by branch

4. CHECKING THE LINEAR CHECK BOX IN THE SET PATH DIALOG WILL LET YOU CREATE:
   - a. smoother animation
   - b. constant-speed animation
   - c. un-editable animation

5. THE TANGENCY CHECK BOX WILL CONSTRAIN THE Y-AXIS OF THE OBJECT TO THE CURVE'S SLOPE.
   - a. True
   - b. False

6. SAVE LOCKED KEY ON PATH WILL MAINTAIN:
   - a. Timing
   - b. Shape
   - c. Tangency

7. ADDING POINTS TO THE PATH CURVE WILL:
   - a. erase the path animation
   - b. give more control over the path shape
   - c. make the animation less smooth

8. CHOOSING SHOW→RELATION FROM A VIEWPORT MENU WILL LET YOU SEE:
   - a. picture of your parents
   - b. F-curves
   - c. Path animation information

9. CONSTRAINT→REMOVE CONSTRAINT WILL ERASE:
   - a. a path
   - b. an object
   - c. path animation

10. SETTING KEYFRAMES ON PATH PERCENTAGE WILL MODIFY THE:
    - a. length of the path
    - b. timing of the animation
    - c. size of the object

11. WHITE NUMBERED BOXES ON A CURVE REPRESENT SAVED KEYS ON THE PATH:
    - a. True
    - b. False

8

BUILDING SETS AND MODELS

IN THIS CHAPTER YOU WILL LEARN ABOUT:

- The terminology of modeling in XSI
- How to look around you to find inspiration for modeling shapes
- How to organize your work so that you are most effective and productive
- How to build and modify NURBS curves
- How to make Revolutions, Extrusions, Lofts, and Four-Sided patches

INTRODUCTION

Because Softimage XSI is an integrated package, which includes all aspects of the computer animation process, you will find a high degree of synergy between the modeling tools, the animation tools, and indeed all the other modules. In XSI you may mix and match animation and modeling as you create your scene, by animating the properties of the modeling tools to create animation effects, and by using animation tools like Animated Duplicate and Spline Deformation to create new models. While the ability to go back and forth so easily is empowering, it can also become overwhelming, and lead to a lot of down time as you explore new interactions in the program. It is good workflow policy to organize your project into discrete stages, and stick with the plan. Usually, that means that modeling is the first step. Enter the Model module to get ready.

MODELING

Everything you use in your 3D scenes first has to be made somehow, by someone, usually yourself. That's one of the first cold hard truths in 3D animation. Traditional artists have asked me 'Can't you just, like, get some pre-made stuff?', to which I usually respond, 'Sure, but would you paint using color by numbers? Or design using only clip art?' Some high-quality 3D models are available for purchase or download, but most of the time you'll need to build your own models from scratch to fit the needs of your specific scene. That means that everything in your storyboards that the camera will see must first be made. The process of making objects, set pieces, props, and characters for your production is called 'modeling'.

Modeling is defined as the action of creating all the objects that will form the set for your production. Each object that will be seen in your finished animation has to be manufactured in the computer before you can use it. That means that the walls and windows must be designed and constructed, the glasses, plates, and silverware must all be made, the light switches, light fixtures and light bulbs have to be modeled. In short, everything you want to see, you must first make.

Since there are many different kinds of objects with many different shapes out there in the world, you will have to develop a variety of different techniques, and use a variety of different tools within XSI to build them all. The tools and techniques discussed in this chapter are in no way a complete and exhaustive set. Every year, more modeling tools are developed, and other methods of using them are discovered.

Regardless of the modeling tools and techniques you develop and practice, there are certainly some standard and very helpful ways of organizing your work. If you don't bother to organize your modeling tasks, and instead just jump right on a workstation and start rubbing the mouse you are likely to find that after many bleary eyes hours contemplating the screen you really don't have much done.

PLANNING OUT YOUR SCENE

Scenes can generally be broken down into three parts: the environment, the props, and the characters. Examine your storyboards, and make a list in each of the three categories, to determine what you will need.

ENVIRONMENT

The environment is the area surrounding the action. It gives place and context to the action. Generally, it is a very good idea to keep this as simple as possible, since the actual world is a huge place and the effort that would go into modeling a realistic world would be immense. Ask yourself 'what needs to be seen to validate the action?' If you are doing broadcast logo development, the answer is probably that you don't need an environment at all, since the on-air graphics will be composited on the backgrounds later. Next time you go to the theater, the Opera, or a play, pay attention to the sets used. The sets are the environment for the action, and due to the constraints of the stage, set designers are generally quite talented and innovative in their reduction of complexity. In many productions, the environment can be a blank stage, with a black curtain and darkened wings. This setup concentrates the attention of your audience on the area of the action.

Often while modeling your environment, you will be tempted to keep extending the complexity further and further away from the area of the action. One good way to limit this crawl is to light only the areas you want people to look at. You will have no need to build any environment past the limits of the pools of light you use to illuminate the action.

A great way to add ambience and a sense of place to your environment is to find a suitable image and texture map it onto a plane or cylindrical wall as a backdrop. If you blur the image first (using the XSI image editing tools, or another program) your viewers will understand that this blurred backdrop is intended to set the time and place, but can be ignored beyond that.

If your scene takes place indoors and you must create an architectural setting, draw out the floor plan on graph paper and get the dimensions of the space right before beginning work. Whenever possible, research a similar building plan, and crib from the dimensions there by roughly estimating, using ceiling tiles (usually one foot square) or by walking it off in strides (usually about three feet). Getting the proportions of a space right is tough, and if you get it wrong, your characters will look out of place in the environment.

The environment could include pillars and supports, fences, trees, bookcases, desks, flower vases and other set dressings that will make the space look lived-in (or not) and believable.

THE PROPS

Your characters will probably interact with objects: sitting in a chair, opening a blind, throwing a ball, flipping cards, etc. Each of these objects must be modeled separately, and stored for later use in the scene. It's lousy workflow to wait until you actually need a model to go back and make it. Start by creating a list of all the props you will need, eliminating non-essential ones and brainstorming about how to make the ones you keep more interesting.

THE CHARACTERS

If you are doing character animation, then you'll need to model or otherwise acquire your characters. Characters can be as simple as a primitive cube, or as complex as a fully developed human character with clothes and hair. Keep your characters as simple as you can. Simple characters are actually more effective at creating the suspension of disbelief necessary to pull off successful stories, because they have a wider range of expressive possibilities than real human characters, and because creating realistic human figures is so darn difficult. Representing the human form in painting or sculpture is a lifetime achievement for a classical artist, requiring a solid understanding of human form, proportion, anatomy, and movement. Think about how much work must have gone into Michaelangelo's statue of David next time you get a hankering to create a realistic human figure. And he was naked...

The most effective animated characters in the world (Beavis and Butthead, Ren and Stimpy, Wallace and Gromit) have all been very simply designed, yet capable of incredible acting range and emotion. Remember also that any object can be made into a character using XSI.

DECONSTRUCTING YOUR SURROUNDINGS

The first step in mastering the art of modeling is to observe. Look at the objects that surround you and inspect their construction. In general, greater attention to detail will make your work more interesting visually. For instance, a room detailed in 1960's Spartan cubist furniture will often look less appealing and more "computery" when rendered than a drawing room outfitted in Victorian fashion with an ornate fireplace and grandfather clock. One drawback to detail is that good modeling requires skill and time to complete. Another is that as you model in more detail to your scene you generally increase the amount of polygonal and patch geometry and your computer becomes less responsive and takes longer to render images of that scene.

As an artist you will have to choose where to add the detail, and determine where detail isn't needed, or can be added with texture maps.

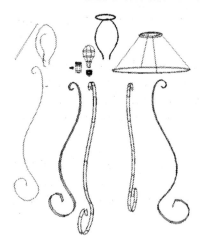

The individual parts of a floor lamp

When you are working on an important project it is often a good idea to do some real-world research about the items you'll be modeling. The easiest (and most fun) way to do this is to get a cheap digital camera or Polaroid, and go on a scavenger hunt field trip, looking for the items on your modeling list. When you find objects that fit both the descriptions of the item and the style to fit your scene, snap a picture. Then, back at the production studio you can tape up all the images as reference to guide you in deconstructing them into constituent parts. Another great source of ideas for props is the Ikea furniture catalog, which has thousands of items that are generally attractively designed, yet simple in construction.

For each object on your modeling list, examine it to see how it can be broken down into smaller components. This works best if you can see a real version of that object to examine how it was constructed. For instance, a light bulb can be broken down into the glass bulb, the metal base, and the wire filament. A floor lamp can be broken down into the base, the pedestal, the bulb, the wire guard for the bulb, the switch, and the lampshade.

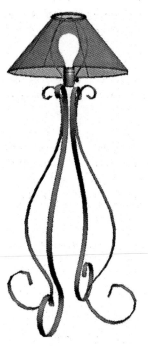

The finished lamp, with different modeling methods used for different parts

Each of those parts was manufactured or created in a certain, usually simple, way. Examine each to get an idea of how it was done, giving yourself clues about possible modeling techniques in the process. Was the shape stamped out of a flat piece of metal? Was it lathed out of a piece of wood? Molded out of plastic? Extruded from a metal tube?

After going through this exercise a few times you will find yourself automatically deconstructing the ordinary objects you come in contact with throughout your day.

In general, objects that are round or circular about one axis can best be made with a modeling revolution. Objects made of pipe or with a consistent cross section can be extruded. Plastic parts with complex organic surfaces can be lofted, and parts stamped out of a flat sheet of metal or cut from fabric can be made with the four-sided tool.

For each object in your modeling list, conjure a mental picture of its component pieces and how you will make each of them. The final bits and pieces can easily be stuck together in a hierarchy, and then modified all together for final scale. One of the great things about XSI is that once a model is built, it takes no effort at all to duplicate that base model into as many different shapes, sizes and colors as you wish.

SAVING MODELS EXTERNALLY FOR A MODEL LIBRARY: MODEL→CREATE→MODEL, AND FILE→EXPORT MODEL

After you have exhaustively planned out all the different items you will need to make, and planned the construction process for each part of each item, you will be ready to get started making them. Since you will want to re-use your models many times throughout the scenes you make, it's a great idea to start creating your own model library. The best way to do this is to create a library scene in XSI that will have certain default elements that are useful for making models.

In your reference library scene, start by creating several elements that will provide a sense of scale while you work. Create a default floor rug area about 10 units by 8 units (8*10 feet), a yardstick 3 feet high standing in the middle of your scene, and a pyramid representing a human that is 5 feet 8 inches tall - a standard average human height. These elements will give you a visual reference for the size of individual objects as you model, so you can make all your models to the same scale.

There are also a few things you can do to make your modeling work easier. They all involve turning on feedback options so that you get better information about what you are doing, and can make better decisions.

• The default gray lighting doesn't show contour or direction of the surface very well. Create three point lights, one bluish, one yellowish, and one reddish. Imagine a circle laying on the floor grid of your scene. Place each light at thirds around the circle so they form a triangle about 50 units from the center. Since you made them and placed them in the top view, they all lie at zero in Y. Take the yellowish light and elevate it 50 units up in Y. This simulates the sun. Leave the blue light where it is, and lower the red light 20 units to light the bottom of objects.

• Turn on some feedback options in different view windows. In the Camera view, in View→Visibility options (the bottom menu command of the Eye menu), look for the Attributes tab. Under the Selected Objects area turn on Normals, so you can see the direction the surfaces are facing.

• Turn on Boundary Flags. Curves have a beginning and end, and a direction from start to finish along their length. Normally you cannot see this information, but it sometimes becomes useful. You can also turn on the Show Boundaries option for any whole view. The start of the curve is a colored red/green section of the curve when viewed in Wireframe. It's a good idea to leave this on all the time so you know which direction your curves are going.

• In the Unselected Object side, turn on Name, which will show the names of unselected objects in the Camera view. We'll assume that if the object is selected you know what it is.

• Change one of the views to the Schematic view. The Schematic should be your constant companion, useful for organizing your work, naming, and selecting objects.

• Show Points; if you can't see the vertices or control points that make up an object, it will be pretty hard to manipulate them. If you select an object but still don't see points at the intersections of the surface edges and parameters, look to the top of the window you are working in, and toggle on Show Points.

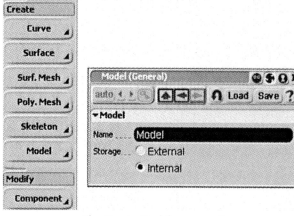

The Create Model menu cell

Then, as each object is completed and parented together into a hierarchy, you can create a 'model' out of it with the Create→Model command. A model is like a tree in the hierarchy, except that the elements in a model have a unique namespace, and these models can be saved individually to disk so that you can pull them back in later. A model can contain objects, animation, expressions, and constraints. In the Model property page (which appears automatically when you create a model, unless you have disabled the auto-PPG feature in the user preferences), you can choose whether the model is stored internally or externally. Internally means that the model is bound into the scene file like everything else, while external means that the model is saved separately to disk, and can be easily reloaded into another scene.

There are two kinds of Models: regular (static) Models and Referenced (dynamic) Models. Both are stored the same way, with File→Export→Model, but differ in how they are Imported. When you use the regular File→Import→Model, the modeled object you import becomes part of your scene and will not ever change.

If you use File→Import→Referenced Model, the model retains a link back to the original model that you exported to disk. Should you need to, you may go back to the original and modify it in any way you wish. When you are done modifying it, re-export it to save the changes, and then in the scenes where you imported the referenced model, use the Model→Update Referenced Model command to bring the new changes into each scene.

That way you can share one base model between many scenes, and later make changes at will that ripple through many scenes in your animation.

DRAWING NURBS CURVES

XSI uses NURBS curves as the basic elements in patch modeling. You can draw NURBS curves in any window, using several different tools, all located in the Model module, under the Create Curve menu cell.

If you choose the Create→Curve→Draw CV NURBS, you can point to an area of the screen and click the Left Mouse Button to drop the first control point. Point somewhere else and click again to drop the next control point. Four control points are required to define a CV NURBS curve, so if you drop less than four points, XSI will add some in for you. The control points, also known as control vertices or CVs, influence the curve, but the curve does not have to pass right through them. The NURBS curve is sort of a best fit through the points you lay down. This method makes controlling the placement of the curve and the tangency of the curve very easy, and always maintains a smooth, gentle arc.

While you are laying down points you can keep the mouse button down and drag to see the curve update dynamically, before you commit to a point location by letting up on the button. If you click with the Middle Mouse Button you can add a point to the middle of the curve wherever you click, and if you click with the Right Mouse Button you can add a point to the beginning of the curve.

If you choose the Interpolating NURBS option from the Create Curve menu cell, a different method is used to lay down points. When you click the second point, a full set of four NURBS CVs are created. As you create more points, the location in space of the curve is modified. Both methods are equivalent, so you can use either tool to create curves; they are provided to give you a personal choice in what you prefer.

The Create Curve➔Linear option draws straight-line NURBS.

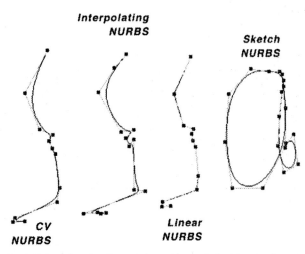

The different kinds of NURBS curves and the shapes they make

You can constrain the placement of a point to snap to the grid by holding the CTRL button while dropping points, which can make it much easier to achieve precision results.

You can also use the CTRL snapping hotkey to snap to other objects, lines, midpoints, surfaces and much more by modifying the options of the Snap menu in the MCP.

ADDING AND DELETING POINTS

After a curve has been drawn, you can go back to it and add more points to either end, or in the middle. The Modify➔Curve➔Add Point command performs this magic, and with the command active, the status bar informs you that the Left Mouse Button adds points to the end of the curve, while the Middle Mouse Button adds points to the inside of the curve, and the Right Mouse Button adds points before the first point. This command can also be used to add detail to a patch surface that has already been created. The Modify➔Curve➔Delete point tool command will remove points from a curve.

INVERTING CURVES

Since curves have a start and an end, it must be possible to swap them. This is called inverting the curve. If you have a car that must travel down a path you have drawn, but the car drives in reverse, you can simply invert the path curve that you drew. To do this, use the Modify➔Curve➔Inverse command.

MOVING POINTS

Individual points on a curve (or surface) can be moved interactively by choosing the Modify Component➔Move Point Tool command. With this command active, when you click on a specific point in one of the view windows, you can drag the point to a new location. Because this command is so useful, it has a hotkey assigned to it: M. You can also hold down the CTRL key while dragging to make the point snap to grid intersections, assisting in accuracy.

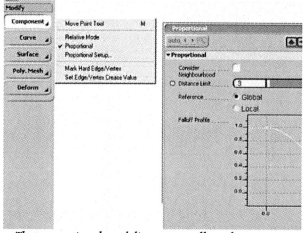

The proportional modeling menu cell, and a property page showing the falloff graph

In production work, you will want to keep your menu command picking to a bare minimum, since it takes your eye off the object you are working on. Practice holding the M key with your left hand and picking and transforming vertices until it is simply second nature. Currently, XSI logs each move you make as a separate Move Component operator, under the geometry mesh operator of the object. Freezing the operator stack will cook all these move operators down into a base mesh, when you want to simplify your scene.

If you want to avoid creating a lengthy operator stack altogether, you can toggle on the Immed. button in the MCP, which turns on the Immediate mode. While in Immediate mode, all changes you make will be added without creating an operator in the stack at all.

TAGGING POINTS

Sometimes you will want to operate on more than one point at a time. Tagging points is a method of selecting multiple points at once, that can all be moved, rotated and scaled together relative to the center of the selected object. You must be in Point selection mode to operate on these points. If you use the T hotkey, XSI will automatically place you in the Point selection mode, but you can do it yourself by clicking on the Point button in the top section of the MCP, just under the large selection arrow. Now the transformation controls such as scale and translate will apply only to the points that you have selected.

PROPORTIONAL MODELING

Proportional modeling solves a tremendous problem in organic modeling. Often, an object will have hundreds of points, making some types of editing difficult and tedious. For example, simple changes in the facial expression of a complex model could require manual manipulation of each of dozens of points. As a modeler, it would be great if you could grab just one point and have the other points in the area stretch to follow the selected point, like grabbing the edge of a rubber mask to distort the features. Proportional modeling accomplishes this feat. When you move one point, all the points in vicinity (set by you) are also affected. Nearer points are effected more than distant points, and the rate of falloff can be changed with a spline curve profile. This feature works for polygonal meshes as well as for NURBS models. If you are working on a polygon model, the area of influence is measured in 3D space, along all X, Y and Z axes. If you are working on a NURBS surface, the effect of the proportional modeling can be set to the 'neighborhood', which measures distance in U and V rather than the XYZ system, to calculate how much a point's neighbors move when you move the point.

Toggle on Proportional modeling in the Modify→Component menu. Now each move operator will also have an italicized link to a proportional operator. You can set the default distance used by the Proportional operator with the Modify→component→Proportional Setup menu command. Each proportional operator can be modified independently at any time to change how much the surface responds to your movement of vertices, by finding the Proportional operator in the Operator stack (look in the Selection button of the MCP) under the Move Component folder and under each Move Component operator.

COPYING CURVES

You can also create a curve from another curve, or even from a NURBS surface that already exists in the scene. If you choose the Create→Curve→Extract Segment command, and then pick on a curve, a new curve will be created that looks exactly like the previous one. Additionally, if you open the Extract Curve Segment property page for the new curve, you can now modify the starting and ending points of the curve so that you end up with any portion of the original curve.

You can pull a curve off of the surface of an existing object with the Extract from Surface command.

Select a curve and execute the command, then pick one CV on the curve for the new starting position, and one CV for the new curve ending position. After you pick the second CV, a new curve will be created that extends between the points you picked.

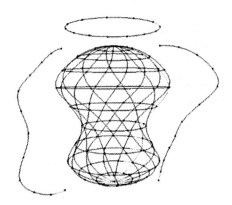

The Extract tools make a new curve either from a surface, or another curve. The copied curve matches the contours of the original perfectly

The property page for the new curve allows you to choose an even more precise position for the start and end of the new curve segment, so that you don't have to start and end exactly on Control Vertices.

An extracted curve can also be created from any Isoline anywhere on the surface, using the Create→Curve→Extract from Surface command. This feature is very useful for matching one shape to another while modeling. For example, if you have modeled the hood of a car, you could extract the base of the hood to get the starting curve of the windshield. Each of these modeling tools retains a relational operator connection to the original curve. If the starting surface changes, your extracted curve will also change. You can freeze the operator stack of the new curve to disconnect this relationship.

CONNECTING CURVES TOGETHER

You can change one curve so that the beginning or end snaps to the beginning or end of another curve in your scene with the Create Curve→Merge command.

The property page for this operator offers controls for picking which end snaps to which end.

CREATING CURVES FROM ANIMATION

You can also create curves from the paths taken through space by animated objects or even tagged vertices in your scene. As an example, imagine a fighter jet twisting and corkscrewing through the sky, leaving trails of vapor from the tips of its wings. This feature is located in the Animate Module and is called Tools→Plot→Curve. If you have an animated object selected, the curve will be generated using the center of that object as the reference. If you are in Point mode, and have one or more vertices selected, a curve will be generated for each vertex. The dialog that pops up after you choose the command offers you the chance to name the curves, the ability to set at which frame the curve starts and stops being generated, and the how often a control point is placed (Step). You should also note that if your object isn't moving at a constant speed, perhaps due to the natural ease-in and out of spline interpolation, the control points won't look evenly distributed in space, and will bunch up at the beginning and the end. You can fix this in the animation editor by making the function curve linear before you plot the motion.

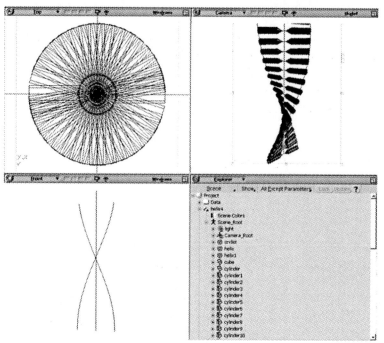

This helix was made by animating the center crossbar and then plotting the ends with Plot→Curve

RESAMPLING AND CLEANING CURVES

You can dynamically clean up curves that have either too many or too few control points by either cleaning the original curve or by fitting a new curve to it with a new number of points.

To create a new, matching curve with a different number of points use the Create→Curve→Fit on Curve command in the Model module. In the property page for this command you can interactively determine how many points the new curve has. If the new curve has too few points, it may not perfectly match the original curve.

You can add a Modify→Curve→Clean operator to an existing curve to clean it up, reducing its complexity and simplifying its shape. This feature is tremendously useful for patches as well, and allows you to better control how much detail you are modeling into a surface.

OPENING AND CLOSING CURVES

An open curve is one where the beginning and the end do not meet. Many surface shapes will require using a closed curve as a construction element. Imagine creating a garden hose from a circular profile curve. If the circle isn't closed, the hose will leak. The Modify→Curve→Open/Close command simply opens or closes the selected curve by moving the point of the end to the same position as the point of the beginning, and insuring that the correct continuity is preserved so that the seam is invisible. You can toggle this operator on and off through its property page.

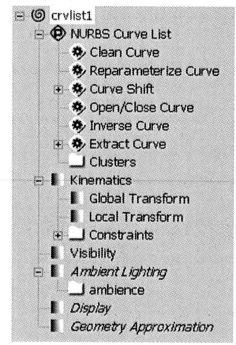

This is the transient selection explorer (the Selection button in the MCP) showing a curve with a bunch of operators on it

MAKING SURFACES OUT OF CURVES

Working with curves is a broad description of the majority of the modeling commands in Softimage 3D. The concept is simple enough: by drawing curves and connecting them together, surfaces can be created. Because of the rich variety of curve shapes, an infinite number of unique surfaces can be made with this method. There are four major categories of surfaces created from curves in XSI, described by the method of creating them: revolutions, extrusions, lofts, and four-sided patches.

Each glass was made by modifying the same curve. Then each glass had its operator stack frozen, severing the connection to the generator curve

Each is made in a different way, and works better for certain kinds of models, but they all rely on curves as a basic construction element.

When you make a surface from a curve, the resulting surface is permanently related to the generator curve, so that if you then change the shape of the curve, the shape of the surface made from it will change. This relationship is profoundly useful, because it means that you can refine the shape of your surfaces after they have been made, when you can see whether or not they look like what you had in mind when you drew the curve.

In 3D modeling, the more iteration you make between the design and the completed shape, the better the model is going to look. It also means that in real life when your Art Director or client comes in to look over your work, and wants to make changes, you don't have to start from scratch. Relational modeling makes your life easier.

Softimage|XSI can keep a complex chain of relational links between different operations, so that the results of changes at any step are automatically sent down the chain to the finished model.

For example, if you drew a curve and revolved a surface from it, then extracted a curve, then inverted it, and extruded a third curve along the extracted curve, all those steps would be stored in a relational hierarchy. You could go back to the original curve and change it, and the results would ripple through the revolution, the extraction, the inverse, and the extrusion to change the final product.

Relational modeling is also a potent animation tool. If you were to save different shape keyframes for that original curve at different points in time, the resulting modeled surface would animate over time as well.

The best part of relational modeling is that it is the automatic behavior of XSI for almost all modeling operations. In fact, you only have to know that it is on when you want to disable the relationship between a surface and the curves that generated it. To do this, just select the surface and click the Freeze button in the bottom of the MCP, or use the Edit menu from the MCP and choose the Freeze Operator Stack item (both are the same). The relationship of the surface to the other curves will be deleted, and the surface will become a stand-alone shape.

NOTE If you have a hierarchy of splines used in creating a model, and the model blows apart like an exploded view diagram when you move the hierarchy, you will need to freeze the operators used in the modeling. This is because the surface is getting double transformations when you move it. It moves once, and the curves used to generate it move. Therefore, the surface moves away from the curves and the model comes apart.

VIVA LA REVOLUTION!

The first surface creation tool to master is the revolution. A revolution is a surface that is symmetrical around a central axis. Think of a revolution as the kind of surface that would come out of a lathe.

REVOLVING A NURBS CURVE

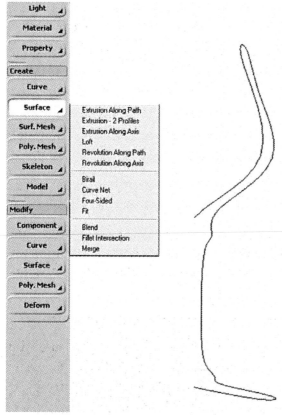

A NURBS curve can be drawn in any view, and then revolved around either a global axis or around another axis that you draw with a NURBS curve.

To revolve a curve around a global axis, use the Create→Surface→ Revolution Around Axis command, while if you wish to draw your own axis of revolution, you can use the Create→Surface→Revolution Around Path command. Most often you'll draw your revolution profile close to a global axis (usually the Y axis) and use the Create→Surface→ Revolution Around Axis command. You can change the axis used for revolution in the property page for the Revolution operator after the fact if you need to use a different axis.

To perform a revolution around the global axes, just select the revolution profile curve and execute the Surface→Revolution Around Axis command. You can also do it in the opposite order - execute the command with nothing selected, then pick on the revolution profile.

A revolution curve and the menu cell

If you want to specify the axis of revolution with another curve, you can draw that with a two point linear spline, then select the original profile, run the Create→Surface→Revolution Around Path command, and pick the custom axis with the Left Mouse Button. Now the revolution will be made relative to your custom axis.

I tend to build my revolutions in the front view, next to the global Y-axis, and revolve them around Y. Revolving a shape in the front view around the X-axis can make other interesting shapes, like car tires.

Open the Revolution operator from the Selection button in the MCP to adjust which axis is used, how far around the revolution extends, the number of U and V subdivisions and whether the resulting shape is open or closed in U and V. The Revolution Angles determines how far around the object is lathed. If you choose 360 degrees, it will be completely circular, and the edges in the U direction will become closed together. If you revolve less than 360 degrees, the U parameter will be open.

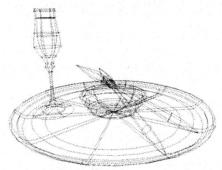

Revolved objects are extremely easy to create, and quite commonly found in the real world. Keep an eye out for

A variety of revolved surfaces

objects made of revolutions as you go through your day, and when you find one, consider the axis it was revolved around and what the cross section would look like if it was sliced open.

ALL ABOUT EXTRUSION

The first surface creation tool in the Surface menu, and possibly the most useful, is the Create→Surface→Extrusion command. Extrusion takes a generator profile and extends it into the third dimension along an axis or another curve, to create a surface. Extrusions can also be made along two different paths, so that the resulting shape stretches between both rails. Extrusions can be performed on open and closed curves.

The extrusion process is easy to think of as a pasta machine (or a Play-Doh machine if your inner child is still stronger than your inner yuppie). The shape of the extrusion profile determines the shape of the object that gets pressed through it. Keep in mind that like pasta, extrusions in Softimage|XSI do not have to be rigid - they can follow curved extrusion paths.

Look around you right now and analyze the objects you see. Those that are symmetrical around one axis make good candidates for extrusion. Try looking at objects end-on from different sides to see if you can visualize the extrusion profile. The most overused extrusion example is flying text, but rain gutters, tube metal, wires, pipes and electric cords are all good examples of extrusions.

NOTE You can set shape keyframes for the revolution profile, and cause the resulting shape to animate over time.

The Mesmer logo, before and after a simple extrusion

EXTRUSION ALONG AXIS

Start by drawing a NURBS extrusion profile in the front view (try something simple, like a swirling curve). Then with the first profile selected, choose the Create➜Surface➜Extrusion Along Axis command from the Model module, open the Extrusion property page created by the operation, and look at the new shape that was created in your scene.

The Extrusion Axis determines the direction that the profile is pushed to create the shape. If you choose X, Y or Z, the extrusion will be a rigid object symmetrical around that axis.

The Length slider can make the extrusion taller in one axis, but you can change this later by simply scaling on one axis, so you don't have to worry about getting it right at the moment.

The Subdivisions sliders allow you to add in just the right amount of detail to your extrusion, and the extrusion shape can be either open or closed.

EXTRUSION ALONG PATH

You can also create Extrusions that meander along a path, keeping their profile shape.

You'll need to draw two curves, one for the profile and one for the path it will follow. To make the Extrusion, first select the profile, then run the Extrusion Along Path command, and finally pick on the extrusion path. A new object will be created. Select it and inspect the Extrusion property page, which is similar to the Extrusion Along axis PPG, but also has two new toggles for Snap to Profile and Rotate Profile. If Snap to Profile is checked on, the new object will begin in space exactly where the extrusion profile still is, instead of building it at the global origin. If Rotate Profile is toggled on, the extrusion will be tangent to the path at all times.

The Length slider can be animated to grow the extrusion along a path.

MAKING TRACKS: AT A GLANCE

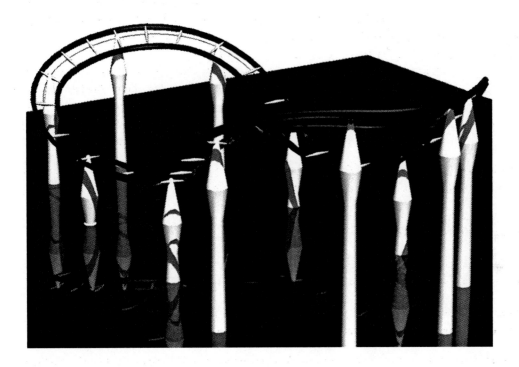

TOPICS COVERED

The prototypical use for guided extrusions are roller coaster tracks. In this tutorial, however, we'll throw in a curve ball - the tracks will be animateable so that they build themselves dynamically. The tracks will extrude themselves along the guide rails, while the cross bars in between them pop into existence at the same time.

You'll learn how to:

- Extrude along one axis
- Extrude a profile along a curve
- Attach objects to a path
- Animate the visibility of an object
- Make changes with the modeling operators

TUTORIAL: MAKING TRACKS

Here's the short game plan – next will follow detailed instructions. You'll draw a center curve for the overall shape of the tracks. Next you'll create a central cross bar, and animate it down the central track. You will tag the ends of the cross bar, and use a Plot function to make new curves for the left and the right track exactly where the ends of the tie travel through space. You'll draw a cross section of the rail, and use a guided extrude command to make the tracks, setting keys so that the tracks grow into existence right behind the animating railroad tie. Then, using Duplicate Multiple, you'll make 50 of the cross members, keeping them live on the path. For extra credit, you could animate the scale and visibility of these cross members, so that they seem to appear and grow into position as the animation progresses.

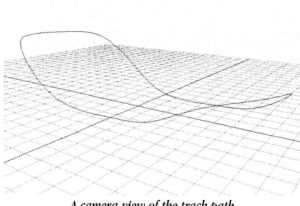

A camera view of the track path

STEP 1. DRAW THE OUTLINE OF YOUR TRACKS.

Using the NURBS curve drawing tools, plot out the shape of your tracks in the overhead (Top) view window. The tracks can follow whatever shape you want.

Unless you want your riders to plummet off the track at the end, use the Modify→Curve→Open/Close tool to make the track a closed circuit.

In the front and side windows, raise some of the points of the curve to make hills and drops in the track (use Show Points in a view title bar to make points visible).

STEP 2. MAKE A CROSS MEMBER FOR THE TRACK

Next you'll design a cross bar that will link the two tracks together. Get a primitive polygon mesh cylinder, and in the Geometry property page, adjust the number of V parameters to 4, so we have some detail on the cylinder to model with.

Tag the points at the top and at the bottom of the cylinder, and scale them smaller in X and Z by holding just the Left and Right Mouse Buttons down as you scale, so the tips of the cross bar are narrow.

Untag the points, select the cylinder again as an object, and scale the whole cylinder until it looks like it will be the right size and shape for the curve you drew in Step 1 (Remember - you can make it thinner by holding just the Left and Right Mouse Buttons, and you can scale it uniformly by holding the Shift button).

STEP 3. ATTACH THE CROSS MEMBER TO THE TRACK

You want the cross member to be attached to the path that runs down the center of the tracks, animating along the length of the path from the beginning to the end.

Now with the cross section selected, enter the Animation module and choose the command Create→Path→ Set Path. In the dialog that pops up, leave the animation Start at 1 and the End at 100, and check on the Linear and Tangent boxes.

Click OK to dismiss the dialog, and finish the command by picking on your path. The Linear option will remove the ease-in and ease-out so that the cross bar moves at a constant rate along the path. The Tangent option will make the cross bar rotate as it follows the curve around.

Open the PathCns property page if it didn't pop up automatically (click on the Selection button in the MCP and look under Kinematics/Constraints/PathCns).

Click on the Tangency tab. When Tangency is active, the cross section changes orientation at different points along the path to remain correctly oriented between the rails. The Tangency command can align any axis of the cross section to the track, so in the Tangency tab of the property page type a number 1 in the axis you want aligned, and a zero in the two others to let XSI know which axis to align. If you want to know which is correct before trying it out, turn on Show Centers, and zoom in on the cross section. Look at the colored arrow that you want to be aligned to follow the curve: Red, Green, or Blue. If you want the Red axis aligned to the curve, put a one in the X text box of the Tangency section. If you want Green, put the 1 in Y, while for Blue you would use Z (RGB = XYZ). The correct axis here is the X-axis.

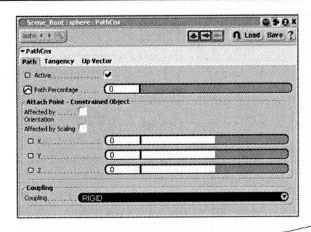

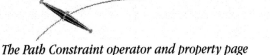

The Path Constraint operator and property page

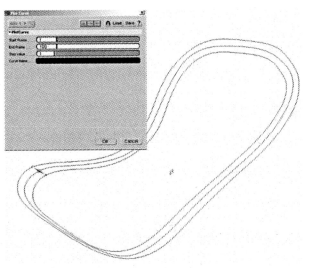

The new rail guides, after plotting

NOTE When you use the Create→Path→Set Path command in Animate mode, the cross bar will be stuck on the path you made, and the point of attachment will be the local center of the cross section. That's what we want in this case, but it's nice to know that you can change where an object is stuck onto a path. Just move the center in Center mode with the translate keys, or you could just tag all the vertices of the cross section and use the Move Center to Vertices command, located in the Transform menu of the MCP.

Now that your cross section is aligned to the path, check that it is facing up in the right direction. If it isn't, you can go to the Up Vector tab of the PathCns property page, and check the Active box to enable the Up Vector. The axis with a 1 in the entry area will be the axis aligned up in global Y. You can modify this by changing the numbers (Z up is what we need - put a one in Z and a 0 in X and Y), and by adjusting the roll.

Back in the Path tab of the PathCns property page, see that the Path Percentage is animated. This is what actually moves the cross section along the path. Scrub in the timeline to see the cross section move and the values change.

STEP 4. MAKE SOME PATHS FOR THE RAILS

We need two more paths for the rails to follow, one inside of the center path and one outside. We can't just duplicate the original, because then the rails would overlap. We can't duplicate and scale the original, because then the rails might not maintain a constant distance between themselves. What we can do is use the animated cross bar to define two more curves that follow the ends of the cross section as it moves through space. This is called Plotting. XSI can plot the position of objects from their centers or from tagged points, creating a path by dropping a new point in space at intervals in time.

Zoom in really close on the cross bar, and Tag just one point on each end of the cross section (if you tag more than one point you'll make more curves than you need, since the curves will be drawn from the tagged points).

Now with the two Tags still active (showing in red), in the Animate module, near the bottom under the Tools section, choose the Plot→Curve command. Leave the Start and End frame properties at the defaults, and change the Step Value to 5, so that a point is created on the curve every 5 frames. Click OK to execute the command.

Do a Modify→Curve→Open/Close on each of the new curves, so they form an unbroken loop.

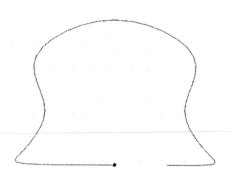

The cross section of the rails. Note the point where it will attach to the curve

STEP 5. DRAW THE PROFILE OF THE TRACKS.

In the right view, draw the cross sectional profile of the rails that your roller coaster will run along. Imagine that you just cut a slice out of the tracks, and imagine the shape of that slice. Keep the shape of the profile fairly simple, with less than 8 points, as the complexity of the shape will have a huge impact on the complexity of the final tracks, and complexity will mean a slowdown for your computer.

Make sure that you create the curve in the Right view. Also, it is good to know that the Extrude command will place the extrusion on the path using the first point of your profile for placement, so if you want the rail to run exactly down the middle of the path you should add a first point in the middle of the rail profile.

STEP 6. MAKE THE PATH EXTRUSIONS FOR BOTH TRACKS

With the track profile selected, execute the Extrusion Along Path command from the Create→Surface menu.

Pick one of the two new track curves created in Step 4. Open the Extrusion Property page if it did not open automatically (If the tracks are dark, maybe they need to be inverted; check the normals and if they seem to pointing inside the surface, invert them).

We want the track to grow out, starting small and reaching all the way around back to the beginning at the last frame. The Length slider in the extrusion property page accomplishes this. Set the slider to 1 at frame 1 and click on the small green animation divot to the left of the word Length to set a key.

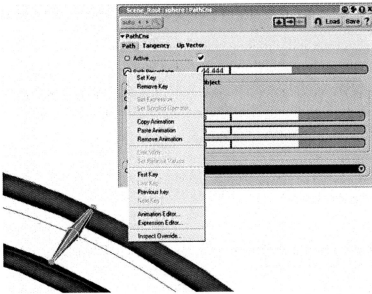

Removing the animation from the Length parameter in the Path Cns property page

Move the time slider to frame 100, set the Length to 100, and set another key. You may also adjust the U and V Subdivision to make a smooth track if you need to. Keep the Subdivision as low as you can to avoid slow-downs in interactivity, while having enough subdivisions to be able to maintain the shape of the curve.

Repeat Step 6 for the other curve created in Step 4. You now have two sets of tracks!

STEP 7. MAKE MORE CROSS SECTIONS

Back in the Path tab of the PathCns property page for the cross bar, the path Percentage slider controls where along the path the cross bar is. Since we want 50 of them, all at different places along the path, we won't really want this one animated along the path, but rather we'll want it stationary at the beginning of the path.

Drag the timeslider to frame 1, then click with your Right Mouse Button over the animation icon to the left of that slider, and when the pop up menu appears, choose the Remove Animation option. Now when you scrub in the timeslider, the cross bar should remain stationary at the beginning of the path.

We want 50 (total) of the cross sections, so we need to make 49 more, all at different points on the path. Fortunately, XSI will do this for us automatically, so we won't have to do the same thing over 49 times.

NOTE A simpler way to create multiple cross bars at different points along the middle path would be to use the Duplicate from Animation option. However, the point of doing it this way is to use a formula inside of a property page. This technique can be applied to almost any property, so it's more flexible than Duplicate from Animation.

Go to the Duplicate/Instantiate Options item in the edit menu at the bottom of the MCP, and make sure that the Constraints property is set to 'Copy & Share Input'. When we duplicate the cross bar this will ensure that the path constraint that we set is duplicated along with it.

Now, select the cross bar and from the Edit menu at the bottom of the MCP, choose Duplicate/Instantiate→Duplicate Multiple, and make 49 more copies, with no changes at all to the size, placement, or rotation. The result is that all 49 new cross bars should all lay in the same place on the track.

With all 49 new cross bars selected (they should still be all selected, unless you have clicked on something else after making them - if they are, the selection box will say "MULTI(49)"), open the property page for the Multiple Selection→Kinematics→Constraints→PathCns using the transient selection explorer in the MCP (hint: expand the Kinematics property page to see the Path Constraints).

Now any changes we make to the Path Constraint will be applied to all of the selected cross bars.

What we really want is for each to have a different position along the path, starting at 2 and going up to 100. Click directly into the text entry area of the Path Percentage slider and type the formula L(2,100) which means "make this value different on each cross section, changing linearly from 2 to 100". Hit the Enter button to execute the change. The cross sections should all be in different places, evenly spaced along the center curve! If they don't seem to change, force a refresh of the scene by dragging in the timeline.

Try animating the length of the extrusions and the making the cross sections become visible as the tracks build past them for extra credit! The roller coaster is an example of flexibly using both axis extrusions and path extrusions to construct a set. Since the modeling tools are dynamic, they can also be used to animate the construction of the path.

LIP SERVICE: AT A GLANCE

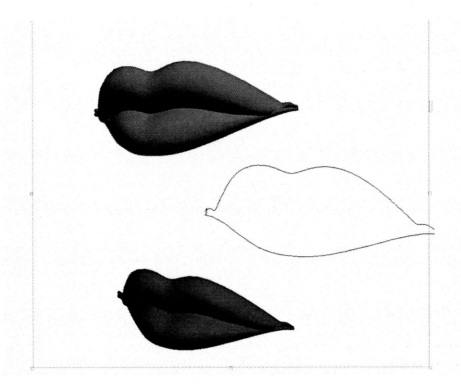

TOPICS COVERED

Let's make some lips, using a variation on the Extrusion tool.

You'll learn how to:

- Perform a Birail Extrusion
- Use the Guided Extrude

TUTORIAL: LIP SERVICE

Other forms of extrusion along a curve are the Birail and Extrusion - 2 Profiles commands. Both use an extrusion profile, and two extrusion paths, one for each side of the profile. As the profile extrudes along the two paths, the profile gets bigger or smaller as needed to connect them together. This differs from the standard extrusion, which just follows one profile. Birail extrusions are great ways to make boat hulls, bananas, saxophones, and other shapes where one profile changes size as it sweeps along two guides. Here we'll use Create→Surface→Birail to make a set of lips.

The Birail and the Extrusion-2 Profiles commands are sensitive. If the ends of the profile are not very close to the ends of the two rail curves, the tool won't work, and a simple ball will be created.

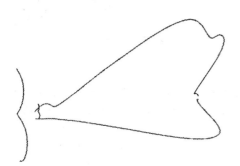

The contours of the lips are the two guide splines

STEP 1. MAKE THE SPLINE GUIDES

Run your finger along the top edge of your lip, and then draw that shape with a NURBS curve in the Front window. This shape will become the top extrusion path.

Trace your bottom lip edge, and draw that as well, starting from the same side as before. Your splines should now look like an outline of a pair of lips.

STEP 2. MAKE THE LIP SHAPE CROSS SECTION

Move to the Right view. Now, using the lines you just drew to help with scale, draw a cross section of your lips at their middle, fullest, tallest point. This will be what we extrude.

Translate the cross section in X to line up exactly with one end of the lip curves you drew in step one.

You now need to scale the lip cross section down in Y and in Z so that it starts very small. It should match the gap between the top and bottom lip profile. Turn off the grid with the G hotkey to help yourself here. You will probably have to zoom in close to make sure that it looks good.

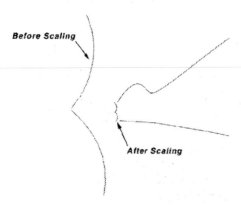

The cross sectional piece of the lip must then be scaled to fit the corner of the mouth

STEP 3. MAKE THE LIPS

With the single cross section selected, execute the Create→Surface→Birail command and then pick on the top and bottom lip profiles. The pair of lips is made!

You can open and adjust the detail in the lips with the Birail operator on the object, under NURBS Surface Mesh in the Operator stack to make smoother lips.

STEP 4. TWEAK THE RESULTS

If the surface of the lips are dark, they may be inside-out; show normals to check. If the normals are facing the wrong way, choose Modify→Surface→Inverse Normals.

You can interactively adjust the lips by modifying the curves, by changing the curves' position or shape (including the cross-section).

When you are happy with your lips you can select them, and do a Freeze Operator Stack from the Edit menu to remove their dependence on the profile curves. Birail is a simple tool that is very powerful and useful. Plant leaves also make great candidates for Birail Extrusions.

LOFTED SURFACES

Some shapes in the real world aren't symmetrical around any axis at all. Revolving or extruding a profile curve can't make these shapes. However, they can be made by drawing a series of cross sections slicing through the object.

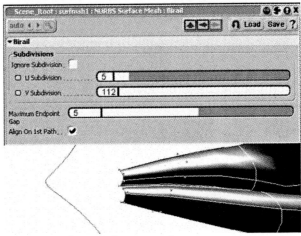

The Birail menu and property page

To visualize this, imagine a stick of celery. Lay the mental vegetable down on an imaginary cutting board, and starting at the top, cut it into slices about a half-inch thick. Each individual slice is a cross section. When the celery is all cut up, imagine carefully stacking the slices back together and wrapping a sheet of plastic tightly around them. That's what a lofted surface is, a spline patch stretched over a series of cross sections.

Another good visualization of a loft (or "skin") is the roof of your house. First, the cross-sectional ribs of the roof are constructed out of two by fours, and then a waterproof skin of tar paper and shingles is lofted over them to form the roof.

Human shapes can also be made from skinning cross sections. Visualize the cross sectional shape of your leg, starting at the thigh and moving down the leg about 6 inches at a time. A skin made from circles made to the shape of the cross sections of your leg would look just like the real skin stretched on your frame.

Lofts can be created from at least two NURBS curves with any number of control vertices. Although the cross sections don't have to share the same number of points, it's often good workflow to start with one cross section (called a rib), then duplicate and modify it to for the next, the next, and so on.

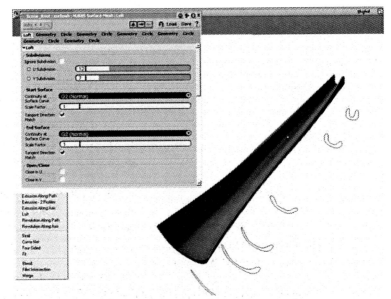

The celery cross sections change shape as they go

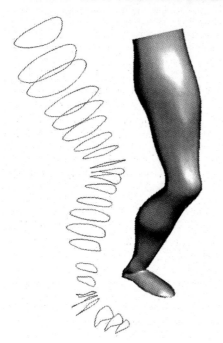

When you have a few cross sections, and have placed them apart from one another in space, choose the Create→Surface→Loft menu cell to activate the command. You must now pick each of the cross sections in order, from first to last, with the Left Mouse Button. If you accidentally pick one out of order, hit the ESC key to cancel the command, select the first one, and do it over. If you forget which mouse button does what, look at the status bar to see how to choose the cross sections. When all the cross sections are picked, use the Right Mouse Button to finish the command and bring up the Skin dialog box. You can also use the new Freeform tool (hold down hotkey F9) to select the profiles in order, by drawing one line with the tool through them all, from start to finish. The order is important. If you loft some members out of order there will be a strange pouch in the lofted skin. If you make a mistake when selecting ribs for a loft, use the Escape key to cancel the Loft tool without creating a loft, and do it over again.

A human leg, and the curves that made it. A drawing of a leg was used to match proportions

After the Loft is complete, open the Loft property page in the Property Explorer from the MCP to adjust the Subdivision, Continuity and other properties.

If the surface is dark, it's probably inside out. Check by showing the Normals. They should point outward from the surface. If they do not, use the Modify→Surface→Inverse Normals command to flip them.

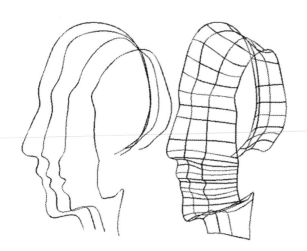

A human face can be drawn using contours as loft curves

GETTING A HEAD IN XSI

Skinning is also a great way to make human faces. Look in a mirror, and imagine drawing lines from the center of the top of your head down your face and under your chin, about a half an inch apart. Then turn these curves projected onto your face sideways in your mind so you can look at them in a side view. The shape of each line is the contour of your face at that longitude, with the top of your head and under your chin being the poles. Another method is to locate one of the poles inside your mouth, and the other at the rear of your head, and imagine the contour lines coming from inside your mouth and over the top of your head to the back.

THE FOUR SIDED TOOL

The 4-Sided Patch tool is the most useful and least utilized of all the XSI NURBS modeling tools. It is designed to create a NURBS surface from four different splines that represent the four sides of resulting surface. Each one of the splines can be a different shape, and even have a different number of control points (although it's a good idea to make opposite sides having the same number of points). Why is this important? Imagine that you are modeling a human character, and have divided the chest area up into squares for the pectoral area and the stomach area. The bottom edge of the pectorals needs to exactly match the top of the abdominal section, and the edges need to line up over the kidneys. You could draw simple surface curves over a polygonal shape to define these areas, then use the four sided tool to turn them into NURBS surfaces prior to binding them all together in a surface mesh.

Using the tool is easy. Draw the four sides out of separate splines, and try to get the end of one side at least close to the start of the next curve, so that XSI can correctly guess which end of the curve to connect to the next curve. The direction you draw the curves is not important.

Finally, choose the Create→Surface→Four Sided command from the Model module, and pick each of the four sides in a consistent order, clockwise or counter-clockwise. If you pick the sides in the wrong order - i.e. one side, then the opposite side, then the next pair of opposite sides - the patch will be mangled.

When you pick the last (fourth) spline boundary, the surface is completed! Open the property page to modify the U and V subdivision, making the 4-sided surface follow the contours of the splines more closely.

Modeling is an art form, and these tools are just the basic elements you will use to practice your craft. Each can be combined with other, more specific tools in Softimage XSI to perform unique functions. Some techniques work miracles in some circumstances, and don't work at all in others.

As the artist, you should experiment with all of them to find the tools that work best for you.

PSYCHO: AT A GLANCE

In this tutorial, we will create a part of a bathroom scene, using many different modeling tools to create and assemble the pieces of a bathtub and shower curtain.

You will learn:

- How to use the Four-Sided tool
- Further application and practice on the use of Extrusions and Revolutions

TUTORIAL: PSYCHO

STEP 1: CREATE THE FLOOR AND WALLS

We need to create some simple floor and wall area for our scene. For the floor, use Get→Primitive→Surface→Grid to create a floor plane. Type '2' in all three scale axes' entry boxes to make the grid twice as big.

For the walls we want only two walls that will be the back of the tub and shower arrangement. In the Top view, choose Create→Curve→Draw Linear, and holding down the CTRL button to enable the grid snap, place 5 points along the edge of the grid in an L-shaped configuration.

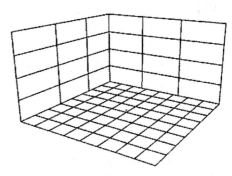

The grid floor, and the extruded walls

Now extrude this linear L shaped segment up in Y to make the walls, using the Create→Surface→Extrusion Along Axis command.

By default it will extrude in the wrong direction, so in the Extrusion property page, check only the Extrude Along Y box (check off the others) and make it snap to the placement of the L spline by checking the Snap to Profile option. You can make the walls shorter with the Extrusion Length slider, or taller with the Scale in Y menu cell. Change the U and V subdivisions if you want to. Make the floor the parent of the walls, and change their names in the schematic view to keep the scene organized.

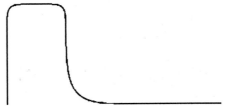

The revolution profile for the bathtub. The CTRL key made the points snap to the floor, keeping the line straight

STEP 2. MODEL THE BATHTUB

The tub will be a revolution for the basic shape, with some simple tagging and moving points to make it squared off. In the Front view, draw a cross section of a tub using Create→Curve→Draw CV NURBS, including the inner and outer walls, as if you sawed through one with a hacksaw.

Make the outside of the spline end straight down at the floor height. Make the inside end stretch towards the center Y-axis, with four or more control points so the floor of the tub will have some detail. Leave the last point just shy of the Y-axis, so there will be a hole in the middle of the tub (at the Y axis) for water to drain through. Again, you can use the CTRL key to drop points right on the grid so that the tub has straight sides and a level floor.

Make the Tub with the Create→Surface→Revolution Around Axis command. If you drew the profile in the front view, it should be revolved around the Y axis, so open the Revolution PPG and make sure that Y is the axis of revolution. If the surface is dark, it may need to be inverted, using the Modify→Surface→Inverse Normals command.

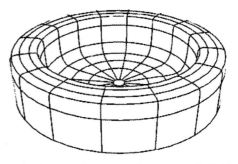

The tub after revolution, with more U subdivisions

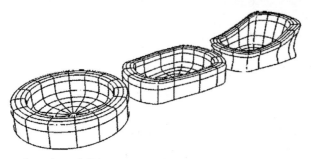

The tub in different stages of tagged and moved points,
sculpting its shape

Open the property page for the new NURBS surface. Make the U Subdivisions 16 so we have a smooth tub, with enough points to sculpt. Check the Close U box to make the tub sealed all the way around.

Now we'll sculpt the tub into a more rectangular shape by tagging points and moving them in space. In the Top view, show points and tag one half of the tub (using the T hotkey), minus the two rows of points around the middle hole.

With the points tagged, drag them in global Z only (which will keep the tub straight) to elongate the tub into a nice shape.

With the same points selected, scale the tub in X only to make the foot of the tub slightly thinner. If you wish, you can make the head of the tub a bit taller than the foot. Tag the points in the front half of the tub, then deselect all those at floor level, and tag the remaining points up in Y only (Are you a perfectionist? Tag the points around the hole and translate those down in Y slightly, so the tub will drain correctly).

Untag those points, and tag only those points near the floor of the tub, and carefully holding both the Left and Right Mouse Buttons, scale the bottom of the tub inwards slightly to make a graceful shape.

When you are done sculpting the tub, use Edit→Freeze Operator Stack to get rid of the Move components and simplify the tub geometry.

The tub probably isn't in the right place, or the right size for the floor and walls. Scale it down and place it in the corner (remember - Shift constrains scale to work uniformly so you don't dent the tub accidentally).

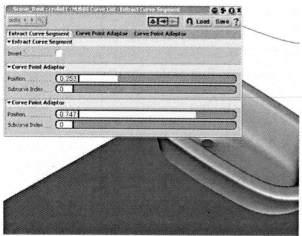

The extracted curve after moving it up in the air, and
the property page that created it

STEP 3. MODEL THE SHOWER ROD
The shower rod is a circular tube of metal that should follow the curves of one half of the tub, and hang above it to hold the curtain. We'll grab a curve from the tub as a guide, and use an Extrude Along Path to make the tube.

First, with nothing selected, run the Create→Curve→Extract From Surface command and pick on the tub shape. A new curve is created on the tub. If it's running in the wrong direction, open the Extract Curve property page for the curve that was created (use the transient selection explorer in the MCP) and switch the direction from U to V (or vice versa).

Look in the Camera view to see the new curve. In the Extract Curve operator property page, adjust the Position slider to pick a position along the top inside of the tub, so the curtain will hang inside the tub and prevent water damage.

When you're happy with the curve, translate it in Y to the top of the walls. There's are two problems, however. We only need half of the curve, and it needs to be straight across all at the same height.

With the curve selected, run the Create→Curve→Extract Segment command to get a new curve that is just a portion of the original. The command will wait for you to click on the base curve to define where you want the beginning and the end of the new segment to be. Pick points on the curve along just the outside of the tub, away from the walls.

To make the curve level, Change the scale in Y to be zero.

Name this curve 'rodTop'.

The final rod, made from an extrusion along an extracted, modified path

Finally, Get→Primitive→Curve→Circle, scale it to an appropriate cross section size for the shower rod, and use the Extrusion command, picking the half-tub curve as the extrusion path.

Adjust the size of the circle as needed, and invert the surface if it's dark.

STEP 4. MODEL THE SHOWER CURTAIN
If we make the shower curtain out of a Four-Sided patch, using the same curve as the rod for the top and bottom, we'll be able to animate various effects and keep the curtain flowing.

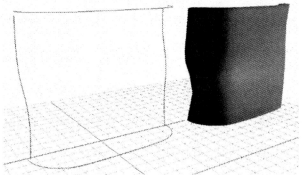

The four sides of the curtain, and the resulting Four-Sided surface. Try moving the points on the curves after making the surface!

Copy the 'rodTop' curve and name it 'rodBottom'. Move it down into the tub.

Draw another curve with five or so points, in the Front view, stretching vertically from the top rod curve to the bottom rod curve.

In the Top view, translate it to one end of the two rod curves, and name it 'leftEdge'

Duplicate the left edge and name it 'rightEdge', then translate it to the opposite end of the rod curves.

Choose Surface→Four-Sided, and pick each of the four curves, in order (it doesn't matter which curve you start with, but continue clockwise or counter-clockwise. For example: "left, top, right, bottom" works, but "left, right, bottom, top" does not).

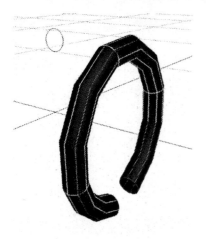

A four-sided surface is created. Adjust its position so it hangs from the bottom-center of the rod. You can also move points on the curves you used to create the curtain, to make it wavy.

STEP 5. MODEL THE SHOWER CURTAIN CLIPS

Shower clips look a bit like rings that don't connect all the way around. A simple way to make them is to get a primitive circle, move it off center from the global Y axis, and revolve it not quite all the way around so there is a gap for the curtain.

Select the circle you used as the Extrusion profile for the curtain, duplicate it, and name it 'clipcircle'.

The clip is an incomplete revolution of a curve offset from an axis. Adjust it by modifying the size and height of the revolution circle

Translate it in Y one half-unit, and revolve it with the Revolve around Axis tool. In the Revolution property page, set the Revolution Axis to X (only - uncheck Y), the start angle to 200 degrees and the Revolution angle to 330 degrees.

Move the resulting shower clip to a position on the shower rod so you can see what it looks like. Select the circle it was revolved from, and adjust it, scaling it smaller and moving it along the Y axis to change the dimensions of the clip until you are happy.

Make 8 or so more clips and position them along the top rod to hold the shower curtain, and rotate each of them in Y so they face the right direction (perpendicular to the rod).

STEP 6. SHOWER HEAD AND HANDLES

The shower head is a great object to revolve. Draw a revolution spline like in the picture, revolve around Y and then either bend the head manually by tagging points, or with a Bend deformation, adjusting the Bend Angle, Radius, and Offset in Y to make the showerhead bend so that it can come out of the wall but still spray down into the tub.

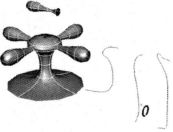

When finished, rotate, scale, and translate it into place on the wall.

The shower head is a revolution that has been deformed with a Bend operator

The knobs could be simple revolutions, or perhaps a revolved center stalk with four revolved knobs parented to it. Examine the parts diagram, make the parts, parent them together, and then duplicate the finished knob hierarchy for the other side.

NOTE Want to have more control over the appearance of the curtain? Well, the curtain is too straight because it doesn't have many points along the top and bottom. You could go back, and use the Create→Curve→Fit On Curve tool to make new top and bottom curves with more points. Then you could run the Four-Sided command again, and move these points back and forth in the top view to make more ripples in the curtain.

GIVE YOURSELF A HAND: AT A GLANCE

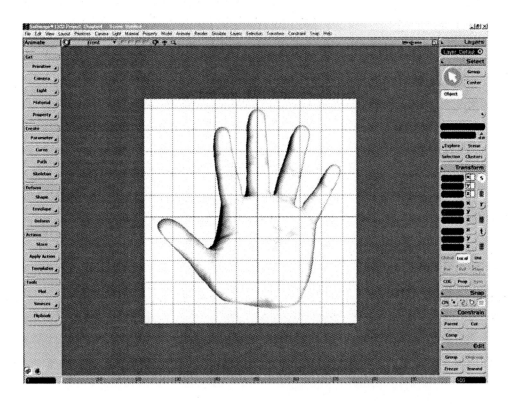

In this tutorial, we will learn how to create a realistic humanoid hand model using a couple of powerful NURBS tools built into Softimage|XSI.

We will learn how to:

- Use the Rotoscope view to create an image plane to use as a modeling reference
- Use the Revolution command to create fingers
- Use the Fillet Intersection to fillet between the fingers and the palm, creating a smooth blend

TUTORIAL: GIVE YOURSELF A HAND

STEP 1. CREATE AN IMAGE PLANE (ROTOSCOPE)

Unless you have a photographic memory, it can be hard to model something as complex as a human hand from scratch. Especially when modeling human body parts, the proportions of the model are difficult to get just right. One way to make your job a lot easier is to import an image into XSI, and use that image as a backdrop to model over. This technique is called Rotoscoping. There are many picture formats you can import to XSI. In this example we have used the JPEG format.

Scan your hand on a flatbed scanner, or use the picture from the Project for this book posted on the Mesmer web site.

In the Top viewport, click on the view style button in the top right corner (it says "Wireframe" if you are in Wireframe mode), and select Rotoscope to put the view into the Rotoscope mode. The Rotoscope Options page will appear. Using this option page you can tell Softimage|XSI what image file you want to use as a background in the view window.

 NOTE You can scale, offset and otherwise edit the actual image you imported by clicking on the "Edit" button. This is also the same as right-clicking in the clip window to show the context sensitive options and choosing "Clip Properties". If you closed the Rotoscope Window and want to open it again, you can get it from Wireframe➔Rotoscopy Options.

Click on the New button and select New From File to load an image. Browse to the picture of the hand you are using, and select it. Close the Rotoscope Options page.

When you zoom or track in Rotoscope view, you will notice that the picture does not change size or placement with the grid (and objects in the scene). Let's track the camera, so the middle finger stays right on top of the center Z-Axis line.

Hold the Z key and using the Left Mouse Button, align the center Z-Axis line to the middle finger. This step is important because we want to revolve a NURBS curve along that axis.

STEP 2. CREATE THE FINGERS

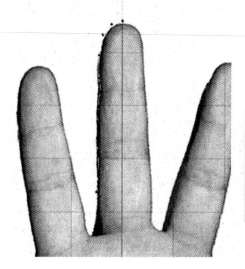

Maximize the Top view so you can really see what you are making (left-click on the resize viewport button at the top-right of the view).

Make sure your tool bar on the left is in Model mode. Select Create➔Curve➔Draw CV NURBS.

 NOTE Since the backdrop picture does not zoom or track, it is important to align the View window using the Rotoscope to your satisfaction, and then discontinue using zoom or pan in that window.

Plot about 15 points starting from the tip of the finger toward the root. Make sure to add more points around the joint areas of the finger so that it will bend well when animated.

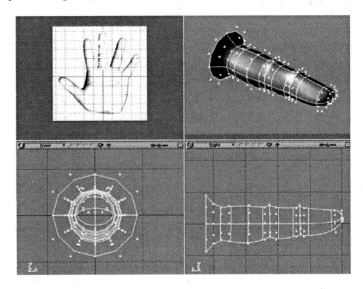

Select Create→Surface→Revolution Around Axis, and then right-click to end picking (we're going to revolve around an axis, not a curve).

Oops, it looks strange! Don't be alarmed. Open the Revolution property page, and select "Revolve around Z" (and uncheck any other axes that are marked) at the bottom of the Revolution Axis menu. Close the window.

Using your finger as a reference, edit the finger to your liking in the Right view. You can use the M hotkey to move points one at a time, or use the T hotkey to tag multiple points, and scale, rotate, and translate them in Point mode. You can check the overall appearance of the finger in the Camera view. Use the Top view to make sure the finger fits with the image plane. When you like the way the finger looks, you are done.

Switch back to Object selection mode, and choose Edit→Duplicate Single from the top menu bar. A duplicate of the finger is created in the same place as the first.

Translate the new finger in the Top view so it's lined up with the index finger on the Rotoscope image. Scale, rotate, and edit tagged points so it's the correct size and shape. Repeat this step for the ring finger, pinky, and thumb. Be sure to check the Front, Right, and Camera views during this process, not just the Top view, to make sure the fingers look accurate from all angles.

STEP 3. CREATE THE PALM
Get→Primitive→Surface→Sphere to get a NURBS sphere.

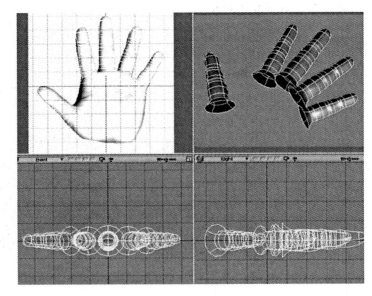

Open the property page for the sphere, change the Radius to 3, and add more detail by changing the U and V subdivisions to 12 each. Close the Sphere property page.

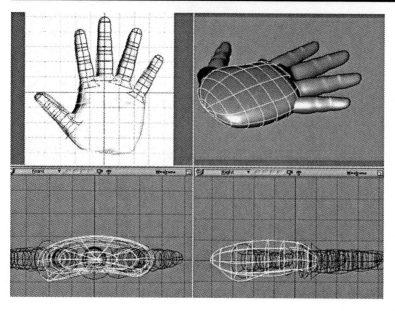

We want to have one pole of the sphere at the wrist, so we can connect it to the arm later if we want to. We have to rotate the sphere to make this happen. Rotate the sphere 90 degrees around the X-Axis. You can type 90 directly in the entry box for the X-Axis in the rotation menu cell if you wish.

Move the sphere and scale it to approximately the size of the palm, using the image plane in the Rotoscope view as a guide. Also check the thickness of the palm in the other views, and scale on one axis at a time, as necessary.

Tag and move points to conform the sphere to the shape of the palm in the image.

Make sure that the edge of each finger extends into the palm sphere surface at least a little, so we can create a good fillet.

We are going to create a Fillet Intersection, so that the finger surfaces and the palm surface will connect seamlessly. A fillet is a curved section of surface that connects two parts together smoothly, like caulk running between a floor and a wall. The fillet in the hand will make the surface of the fingers appear to seamlessly transition into the palm.

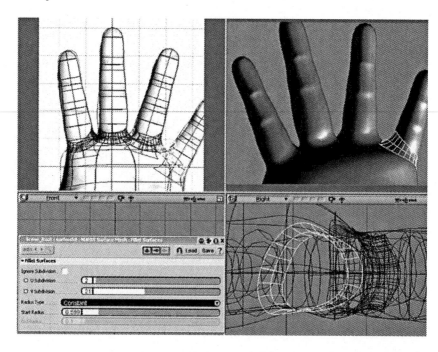

STEP 4. CREATE A FILLET INTERSECTION

Deselect everything by holding the Space bar and clicking an empty area.

Make sure you are in the Model mode, then choose Create→Surface→Fillet Intersection.

The status bar at the bottom prompts you to pick the objects you want to create an intersection between. Pick the index finger, which will highlight white. Then, pick the palm, and right-click to complete the Fillet Intersection command.

A fillet will be formed between the index finger and the palm.

Open the property page for the Fillet Intersection, change the Radius Type to Cubic, and the Start Radius and End Radius to 0.5. Keep Tolerance at 0.01. You can adjust these to see the effects on your hand.

Repeat the fillet procedure for other three fingers. For the thumb, set Start Radius and End Radius to 0.3, for a broader transition.

CONCLUSION

In this chapter we have covered the basic modeling tools in XSI, along with some strategies for using them fruitfully in real-world applications. There is a great deal more to learn about modeling in XSI, including more sophisticated patch modeling, surface meshes, and the continuity manager, but these tools will get you started in the right direction. Don't forget to plan out your modeling work carefully and use good workflow habits!

QUIZ

1. HOW DO YOU SHARE MODELS WITH OTHER SCENES?
   a. Just mark External in the model setup
   b. Use File→Export Model
   c. both a and b

2. YOU DON'T NEED TO PLAN OUT YOUR SCENE AND MAKE A MODEL LIST.
   a. True
   b. False
   c. Who cares?

3. WHICH IS NOT A TYPE OF NURBS CURVE?
   a. CV NURBS
   b. Linear
   c. Cardinal curve

4. WHICH COMPONENT LIES ON THE SURFACE OF A NURBS SURFACE?
   a. Knot
   b. CV

5. WHAT DOES PROPORTIONAL MODELING DO?
   a. Keeps the parts all together
   b. Keeps scale uniform
   c. Stretches your model like rubber when you move a point

6. WHICH CAN'T YOU DO WITH A SURFACE?
   a. Inverse
   b. Clean
   c. Extrude

7. CAN YOU SWITCH BACK AND FORTH BETWEEN EXTRUDE ON AXIS AND EXTRUDE ON PATH IN THE EXTRUDE OPERATOR PROPERTY PAGE?
   a. Yes
   b. No

8. DO THE CURVES IN A 4-SIDED PATCH HAVE TO HAVE THE SAME NUMBER OF CV'S?
   a. Yes
   b. No

9

WORKING WITH LAYERS

IN THIS CHAPTER YOU WILL LEARN ABOUT:

- How to create new layers to organize your scene
- How to move objects in your scene to one layer or another
- How to turn layers on and off
- How to select using layers
- How to render only certain layers

INTRODUCTION

After just a little bit of time working with XSI, you will doubtless be creating fairly large scenes, with hundreds or even thousands of objects. Although we've already looked at scene-wide organization tools like the explorer and the schematic view, there is still room for more productivity-enhancing organization tools. The Layer Control panel is intended to help you with just that.

USING LAYERS

Using the Layer Control panel, you can group your work into separate layers according to any scheme you devise to fit your scene. If you were building a car, you could put the wheels, tires, axles, and chassis into one layer, the engine block into another, and the body into a third. Then you could easily turn off the layers you were not working on at the time, to better focus on the layer you are working with.

If you are working on a special effects composite shot, you could place the backgrounds into one layer, the geometry into another layer, the glowing elements into a third, the particle effects into a forth, and so on, separating your work so you could easily turn on or off any combination of the effects for preview or rendering.

If you are working on a character you might have a complex IK skeleton, a system of controls for the rig, a low-res skin for working with and a high-res skin for rendering. Each could be on a different layer.

THE LAYER MENU AND THE CURRENT LAYER

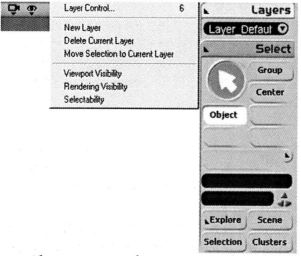

At the top of the Main Command Panel on the right side of your screen you will find the Layer tools. The Layers menu is where the commands are located for adding, removing, and managing the layers that exist in the scene. Here also is the Layer Control command (Hotkey 6) used to display the Layer Control panel, which is the most often-used part of the Layer system.

THE LAYER CONTROL PANEL

When you choose Layer➔Layer Control from the MCP, the Layer Control panel is displayed. You are free to move the Layer Control panel around the screen to any comfortable location. You can also resize it by

The Layer menu in the Main Command Panel

clicking and dragging on a bottom corner of the box, to make it larger or smaller as needed for your layers.

The Layer Control panel is a small floating dialog box divided into rows and columns. Each row is a layer. Each column is a box for a check mark. The columns are View, Render, and Selectable (Sel.). You can check

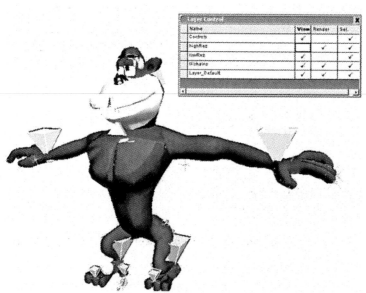

The Layer control panel

or uncheck each column box for a given layer; checking View toggles the layer visibility in the scene, marking Render makes it renderable or unrenderable, and clicking Sel makes the layer selectable or unselectable. You can have any combination of the three aspects for each layer.

If you click directly onto the name of the layer, the entire contents of that layer are selected on-screen in your other views, and will be displayed in a gray wireframe (even if the layer is currently unselectable).

ADDING OBJECTS IN A SCENE TO A NEW LAYER

To create a new layer, just select the objects you want added to the new layer, and choose the Layers→New Layer command. A new layer will be created with the selected objects as members. To change the name of

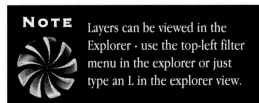

NOTE Layers can be viewed in the Explorer - use the top-left filter menu in the explorer or just type an L in the explorer view.

the layer, click on the name in the Layer Control panel, then open an Explorer view in your interface, and type an E to frame the selected element (the layer.) The layer object will appear in the Explorer, where you can right-click over it to change the name.

It is important to note that the only way to activate a layer is not located in the Layer Control panel, it's located in the MCP, at the very top, under the Layers menu cell. You can click into this drop box to see the list of layers in the scene, and quickly choose one to activate that layer. When a layer is active, that is the layer that objects will be moved to if you choose the Move Selection to Current Layer command. That layer will be highlighted in a minty green color in the Layers control panel.

MOVING NEW OBJECTS INTO AN EXISTING LAYER

When you already have a defined layer, and you just want to add some items to it, first make the target layer the active layer with the Layer drop menu in the MCP, or by clicking on the name of the layer in the Layer Control panel, then select those items you want added, and use the Layers→Move Selection to Current Layer command.

The only way to move objects from one layer to another layer is to use the Explorer view, showing layers (hotkey L), and then expanding the layer to see the list of objects within it. The objects can then be dragged and dropped to the new layer.

Another automatic use of layers is that when you merge two scenes (using the File→Merge command), each scene is placed on a separate layer.

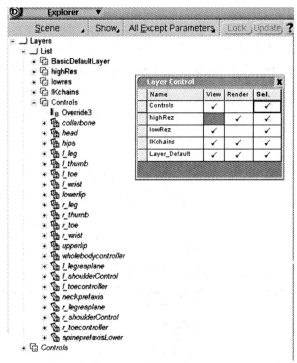

You can show the layers and their contents in the Explorer

ORGANIZING A CHARACTER: AT A GLANCE

TOPICS COVERED

In this quick and easy tutorial you will use the Layers commands to organize a character into layers for easy animation.

You'll learn how to:

- Add high-res and low-res skins to an object, then show only what you want
- Move all Inverse Kinematic skeletal chains to a layer so they can be easily hidden
- Make the control hierarchy selectable and everything else unselectable
- Make the control hierarchy invisible to the renderer, but visible to you

MATERIALS REQUIRED

The Julian_layers.scn scene (available from www.mesmer.com/books/)

TUTORIAL: ORGANIZING A CHARACTER

The Julian monkey character has both a high resolution and a low-resolution mesh. We're going to want to work with the low-res version, but keep the higher res version around so for later, higher-quality renders. We also need to make the controls selectable so you can use them, but invisible during the render. We need the other stuff to be the opposite: unselectable – and perhaps invisible – during working, but renderable for the final effect.

STEP 1. PUT THE HIGH-RES AND LOW-RES MESHES ON SEPARATE LAYERS

Show the Layers control panel. Also make one view an Explorer view, and press the L hotkey to show the layers list.

Select the higher resolution version of Julian and carefully place it on top of the lower resolution version, checking all three views.

Place the high-res version on a new layer, by making sure it is the only object selected, and choose the Layers→New Layer command. That new layer (called 'layer') will be visible in the Explorer.

Change the name of the new layer to "highres" by right-clicking on the name in the Explorer and choosing the Rename command, or by double clicking on the name in the Layer Control and typing over it.

Make the high-res version unselectable, unrenderable, and invisible by unchecking all three columns in the Layer Control panel.

Select the low-res mesh, and using the same commands, put it on its own layer.

Rename the new layer "lowres".

Make the lowres layer visible and renderable, but unselectable.

STEP 2. PUT THE INVERSE KINEMATIC SKELETON IN A SEPARATE LAYER

You will want all the IK on a separate layer so you can easily make it unselectable, since you'll be manipulating it with the control objects.

Using the selection filter, which is the small diagonal triangle in the top portion of the MCP, choose Chain_Element. This will limit the selection tools to only select IK chain parts.

NOTE Later on, you could bind the high-res to the IK. When you do that, the mesh must be selectable. Weighting the envelope also requires that the mesh be selectable.

Now, holding down the Space bar and Shift to get a multiple selection, drag a rectangle around everything in the whole scene. All of Julian's IK should be selected, and nothing else.

Place this skeleton on a new layer, change the name of the layer to "IK", and make it unselectable and invisible.

Click on the Object button in the MCP to turn off the filter, and select the other parts of Julian that you want grouped with the IK, like the skull, the diaphragm, the hips, and the collarbone.

Add them to the IK layer with the Move Selection to Current Layer command.

STEP 3. MAKE A LAYER FOR THE CONTROLS

Select all the control elements (the cones and spheres outside the Julian model), and make them into a new layer.

Name the new layer "controls".

These control elements need to be selectable so you can set keys on them easily, but you won't want them to be rendered. Change the check marks in the Layer Control to make the controls visible, selectable, but not renderable.

Now you have the elements of your scene organized into layers so that you can easily select the controls without accidentally selecting the mesh or the IK bones. You also have the power to make sure that the controls don't render, but the skin will!

CONCLUSION

The layer menu and control panel are not too hard to figure out, but they can make a fantastic impact on productivity. You can find many more innovative uses for the layers system. Try placing special effects on their own layer in a scene to make managing renders easy.

Quiz

1. Each object can be on how many layers?
   a. one
   b. two
   c. as many as you need

2. How many layers are there in XSI?
   a. one
   b. two
   c. as many as you need

3. How many objects can be in each layer?
   a. 10
   b. 50
   c. As many as you need

4. You can move elements between layers with the Layer Control panel
   a. True
   b. False

10   DEFORMATIONS, AND THE GAP

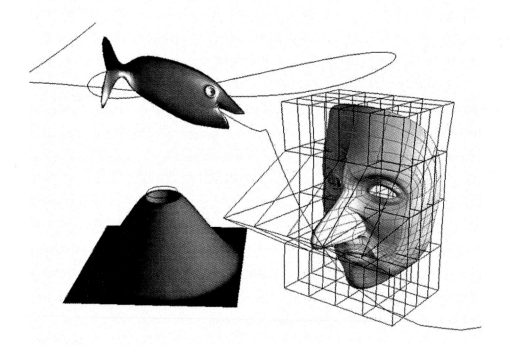

IN THIS CHAPTER YOU WILL LEARN ABOUT:

- How to use various deformers
- How to edit Bend, Bulge, Shear, Taper, and Twist properties
- How to deform by Curve, Surface, Spine, and Lattice
- How to view and edit operator stack
- How to use the Push Deformation and Weight Maps
- How to paint weight with the Generic Attribute Painter

INTRODUCTION

Deformation tools can provide a great amount of freedom to modelers and animators alike. The primary function of deformers is to give you a very easy-to-use control to deform an object. You can deform all kinds of objects, hierarchies, and even clusters. You can also animate properties of deformers to create animated deformation effects such as a wiggling snake or rippling water.

THE DEFORM MENU CELL

You can find the deformation tools in the Modify➔Deform menu cell, in the left toolbar of the Model module.

These basic deformation tools are extremely easy to create and edit. Each of them only requires you to select the object you wish to deform, and choose Modify➔Deform➔(any deformation tool). You can also get a property editor for the operation, in the usual way through the Selection button in the MCP, to edit every aspect of the deformation. Many of these deformers are perfect for creating cartoon-like physical effects or modeling complex shapes.

FUNDAMENTAL DEFORMATION TOOLS

Any time you want to edit your deformation parameters, you can go through the operator stack of the deformed object. Deformation tools are "operators", and they will be added to the properties of the objects they affect. To see the operator stack, select the object in question and press the Selection button on the

MCP. The gear icons indicate operators, which can be modified the same way as any other property, using the property editor.

Deformers can be edited interactively; any changes you make will be displayed immediately, even if there are several deformations applied to the object.

If you have deformed an object to your liking, and you don't plan on animating the deformation, it's a good idea to freeze the operator stack. Freezing

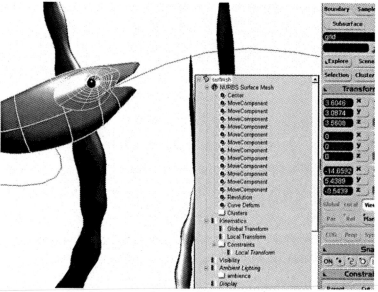

The Operator Stack lets you edit your deformations after they are applied

the operator stack will save the object's current shape and remove all the operators, freeing up some RAM and CPU load. To freeze the operator stack, select the object, and click on the Freeze button at the bottom of the MCP. You can also choose Edit➔Freeze Operator Stack from the main menu.

BEND

Just as the name suggests, Bend bends object. The Bend property page is a little bit complicated. In the Direction area, you can set both the Bend Direction and the axis of the effect. In the Amplitude area, Angle controls how much the object is bent. Radius is for how far bending occurs on the object. Offset displaces the "center" of the bend along any axis.

Bend deformation

BULGE

Bulge pulls point outward to make the object look inflated. You can change which way it bulges by checking on Deform Along... check box. Amplitude controls extent of deformation tool. Amplitude Modulation Profile is a spline graph that gives you finer control on how this deformation influences the object.

Bulge deformation

SHEAR

Shear pulls points at the top of the object, while pulling bottom points in the opposite direction. It resembles a cartoon character's anticipation before running like hell. The Shear property editor is extremely similar to the Bulge deformer's. You can change which way it shears and which axis it uses. One difference is there are only two points in the profile curve.

Shear deformation

TAPER

Taper "pinches" one end of an object on one or more axes. Deform Along... controls which sides of the object are pinched. Axis controls which direction the deformation is pinched toward, and Amplitude determines how much the object is deformed. Like Shear and Bulge, there is an Amplitude Profile curve you can edit.

Taper deformation

Twist deformation

TWIST

Twist successively rotates rows of points to wring the object like a towel. Its Property Editor looks a bit different from the previous three deformers. Angle controls how much the object is twisted, while Vortex is an effect that gradually dissipates the twist as it leaves the vicinity of the object's center, creating a shape more like a tornado or whirlpool, than a wrung towel.

PUSH

The Push deformation displaces points of the surface outward, in the direction of its normals. This deformer is very useful when used in conjunction with the weight painting tool: you can add weight interactively with strokes of the mouse to push and pull surfaces. We will discuss this in greater detail later in the chapter.

Push deformation

RANDOMIZE

Randomize moves points randomly, in the axes you specify. This deformation is great for creating landscape geometry, or other irregular surfaces with lots of bumps.

Randomize deformation

ADVANCED DEFORMATION TOOLS

There are four more advanced deformation tools. These tools require a little bit of preparation, but create stunning modeling and animation effects fairly easily.

Let's take a look at each one:

DEFORMATION BY CURVE

Keyframing something like a huge, slithering anaconda or a powerful, great white shark swimming would be extremely difficult. However, deformation by curve can achieve this effect relatively easily.

Deformation by curve will deform an object by moving the object's Y-axis along the U direction of the curve you create. The object will try to bend to follow the curve's shape (whether or not it is successful depends on the level of detail on the object, and how sharp the turns in the curve are). You can animate the object's Y translation to make the object move from the beginning to the end of the curve, and animate the control points on the curve itself to change the object's shape.

To create a deformation by curve is fairly easy:

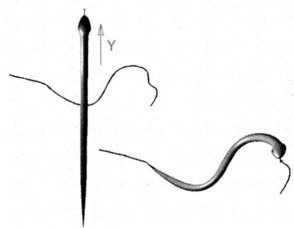

Deform by Curve can deform an object along a curve

1. Because the Y-axis will be heading toward the direction of the curve, you'll need to create the model or hierarchy facing up. If the model wasn't created facing up, you can rotate it so it is, move it to the global origin (the intersection of all three global axes), and choose Transform➔Freeze All Transforms from the MCP. This is necessary because deformation by curve requires an object's transformations to be 1 in scale and 0 in rotation and translation. Otherwise, Deformation by Curve will take the value of each cell and add them to the deformation parameters, and the object won't deform along the curve properly.

2. Create a curve. The Draw Interpolating NURBS tool is especially useful since the curve will go exactly through the places where you've assigned a point.

3. Select an object to deform. You can also select a hierarchy, model, or even a group. Choose Deform➔By Curve from the Deform menu at the bottom of the Model module.

4. The mouse cursor will turn into a pick cursor. Pick the curve you drew. Your model should have snapped to the beginning of the curve (though if it doesn't, there is a way to fix that, mentioned later).

5. Open the Curve Deform property page under the Surface Mesh object. The three sliders in the Scaling section will let you scale the deformed object in three axes relative to the curve. Roll lets you rotate the object around the curve, along its local Y-axis. The Translation section controls the movement of the object. Along Curve will move the deformed object from the beginning of the curve to 20 units forward and backward. If you want to go further each way, you can type a number directly into the box at the left of the slider. The other two sliders move the object up and down and side to side (away from the curve).

6. The Constraint tab has a special tool just in case you haven't frozen the transformation of either the object or the curve. If you moved the object and didn't freeze it before using Deformation by Curve, you need to click on the Constrain to Deformee check box. It will snap the deforming object right onto the curve. The Constrain to Deformer check box is used when you have moved the curve and haven't frozen it. If both of them were moved prior to using Deformation by Curve, you need to check on both check boxes.

We will use this tool later in the tutorial. Let's move on to the next deformation tool:

DEFORMATION BY SURFACE

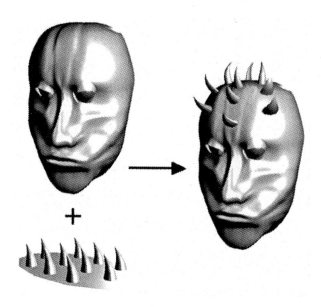

The Surface Deformation tool wraps an object around a surface

If you want to conform one surface to another surface's shape, Deformation by Surface can achieve it. For example, you could wrap some extruded text around the surface of a globe, or make a drop of water slide down a leaf.

Whereas Deformation by Curve aligns the Y-axis of the deformed object to the U parameter of a curve, Deformation by Surface aligns the X- and Z-axis of an object to the U and V parameter of a surface.

Here is how it's done:

1. Create a base surface for the object to deform on. A polygon object cannot be a base surface, since it lacks U and V parameters. You can have another deformation tool already applied to the base surface; the two will work together.

2. Select the object to be deformed. It can be a hierarchy, model, or group. Unlike the base surface, this object can be a polygon mesh. However, you may need lots of subdivisions for the object to deform correctly. Make sure the side you want facing out from the surface is facing up in global Y, and freeze the object's rotation.

3. With the object selected, and the toolbar in Model mode, select Modify→Deform→by Surface.

4. The mouse cursor will turn into the pick tool. Pick the base surface you will deform the object on.

5. You may see your deforming surface extremely (improperly) deformed, but don't be alarmed. Open the Surface Deform property page, and simply scale the object down by sliding Scaling X- and Z-axis to left. You can move, scale, and rotate using the sliders in the window. The Constraint tab works the same way as the Curve Deformation Property Editor. If you don't create (or freeze) your objects at the global center, the controls here can fix the deformation to look correct, but it's better to get it closer to right the first time.

DEFORMATION BY LATTICE

Lattices are very effective if you want to pull on part of an object, or squash and stretch an object.

A lattice is a bounding box, like a cage, that surrounds another object to take control of its entire geometry (with less control points). The only thing you need to do is edit the points on the lattice, and the geometry under it will change accordingly. It's a perfect solution for simple modeling, or animating an object with lots of detail, since a simple lattice can control complex geometry underneath. The level of detail on a lattice can be changed to suit the resolution you want to work with. You can either apply a lattice directly to an object, or create a lattice first and then apply it to something.

Here is how to apply a lattice. It's actually easier than curve or surface deformation:

The first method uses the Get➔Primitive menu cell to create a lattice, instead of the Deform menu cell.

1. Select an object, hierarchy, model, or group. There is no particular requirement on how this object is placed or oriented, unlike the other deformers.

2. Click Get➔Primitive➔Lattice. Done! A lattice object is created around the selected object.

3. Open the lattice deformation property page. Set its Subdivision to the resolution you want to work with. More subdivisions means more

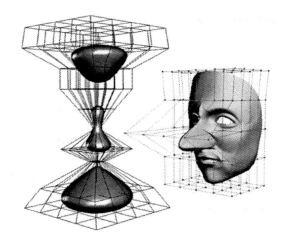

Lattices have many uses

detail, but lots of points to deal with. Too many subdivisions may mean it's not that much different from picking and moving the original object's surface points, losing the benefit of lattice deformation. Interpolation controls how points on the deforming object are weighted to the lattice. Curve will create nice smooth weighting, but if you want to have sharp and rough edges, Linear is the way to go.

4. Move, scale, and rotate the points on the lattice, and the underlying object should deform along with the lattice points. You can animate the movement of the lattice points to create animated deformation.

The second method involves creating a lattice first, and then applying it to an object.

1. With nothing selected, create a lattice using Get➔Primitive➔Lattice.

2. Select the object you want to deform and choose Modify➔Deform➔by Lattice. Pick the lattice you want to use.

3. The property editor looks very different from the first method. Deformation Scope deals with how the object's points are influenced by the lattice. All Points (SI3D) will affect all points of the deformed object. If the Points Inside Pre-Deformed Lattice option is chosen, only the points of the object that are inside the edited lattice are influenced (so, for instance, you could make the lattice into a funnel shape and animate the object passing through it). Scaling will let you decide if you want to treat the scale of the lattice as a deformation factor. The default for the option uses the lattice's center for scaling the object; Apply Scaling to Geometry (SI3D) will scale the object using its own center.

DEFORMATION BY SPINE

This last deformer can deform a surface using a curve, without putting the object on the curve. The curve will have a zone of influence as soon as the spine deformation is applied: like a magnetic power, the deforming object's points are attracted to the curve as long as points are within the curve's zone of influence. This means the curve should be fairly close to the surface. The only thing you need to do to deform the surface after that is to move the curve itself, or the points on the curve.

1. Create a curve you want to deform a surface with. The curve should preferably be in close proximity to the deforming surface, because you need to make sure its zone of influence is actually influencing the target points of the surface.

2. Select the object, hierarchy, model, or group you want to deform.

3. Select Modify➔Deform➔by Spine. The mouse cursor becomes a pick cursor. Pick the curve you created to deform the surface.

4. The deformed surface should now have clusters (points) that are displayed in blue. We will discuss clusters later.

5. Open the Spine Deform property editor. Falloff Amplitude controls how the curve influences the object's points. The left column controls the weight of the points: 1 means 100% weight, or total attraction to the curve, while 0 is "unaffected". The bottom row is the percent of the zone of influence: 0.0 is exactly on the curve, and 100 is the edge of the curve's influence. Radius sets how much the magnetic power of the curve will influence the object. Moving this slider to right adds more influence radius, thus deforming more of the surface. Longitudinal controls the influence of the curve length-wise, allowing you to control how much of the curve affects the surface.

6. Move, scale, and rotate the curve; the points close to the curve should follow its transformations.

TORO THE HAPPY TUNA: AT A GLANCE

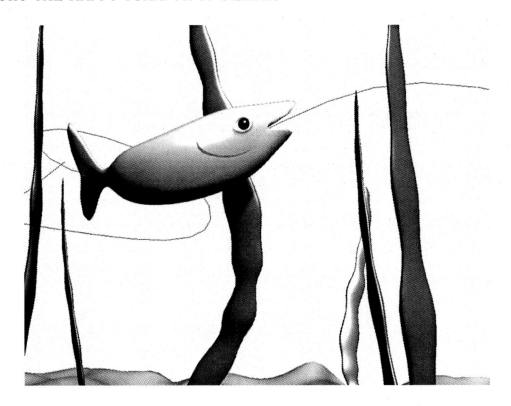

TOPICS COVERED

You learned about many deformers in the previous section. Let's practice applying them. We will model a fish and his environment using several deformers, and then make him swim around, using the curve deformation tool.

You'll learn how to:

- Model a fish using bulge and surface deformation tools
- Create an ocean bottom using the randomize tool
- Use the twist and bend deformation tools to create seaweed
- Curve-deform the fish, so he will swim like a happy tuna

TUTORIAL: TORO THE HAPPY TUNA

We will use various deformations we learned about, and apply them to modeling and animation workflow. First, we will model a fish, ocean floor, and seaweed using Bulge, Surface, and Randomize deformation tools. Then at the end we will make Toro swim around the environment using the Curve deformation tool and keyframing the translation slider along the curve.

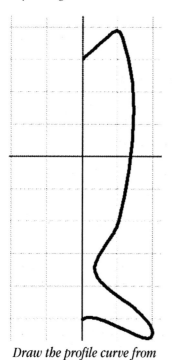

MODELING TORO

STEP 1. MAKE THE BODY

Use a Revolution to rough out Toro's body. Choose Create→Curve→Draw CV NURBS and create a profile of a fish, using the Front view. Remember, because we are going to curve deform the fish in the end, we need to model the fish with its head pointing up (in Y). Hold the CTRL key while you are plotting the first and last points, to put them exactly on the Y-axis.

After you finish the profile, have it selected, and choose Create→Surface→Revolution. Right-click to end picking, and it should default to revolving around the Y-axis.

In the surface mesh property page, increase the subdivisions in U and V as desired, to give yourself some more detail to work with.

Scale the fish on the Z-axis down, to flatten him.

Switch to Point selection mode and tag the last few rows of points at the tip of his mouth. Translate them up in Y to give him a slightly more pronounced mouth. (Note: if the point transformations don't behave as you'd expect them to, make sure your transformation mode is Global.)

Draw the profile curve from bottom to top

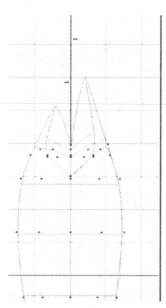

Use your own artistic senses

Scale the same tagged points a little bit in the Z-axis to make the mouth smaller.

Untag the points on the left side, and translate the right side a bit more in Y, to create a longer upper mouth.

Tag the points at the bottom-center of tail and move them up, to further define his tail fin.

Select all the points that belong to the tail and them down in Z, to flatten it.

Now Toro's body is roughed out! Name this mainBody.

STEP 2. MAKE THE EYE SOCKETS USING SURFACE DEFORMATION

We will create eye sockets for Toro using the Surface Deformation tool. Let's make an eye socket by revolution first. Create a profile of an eye socket in the Front view.

Revolve the curve and set the new surface's U subdivision to 10, V subdivision to 6, and Revolution Axis to Revolve Around Y. Scale it down to your liking, and name it "eyeSocket"

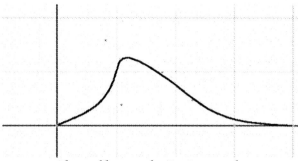

The profile curve for Toro's eye socket

Time to surface deform the eye socket. First, we need to freeze the transformation on both surfaces, eyeSocket and mainBody. Click on the Transform button in the middle of MCP and select Freeze All Transforms. Both objects' Scale should be 1, 1, 1 and Rotation and Translation should be all 0.

Make sure the eyeSocket is selected. Choose Modify➔ Deform➔by Surface, and pick the mainBody. Wow, looks crazy doesn't it? Let's edit the values in the Surface Deform Op property page.

First, make sure you are in Global transformation mode, and open the Surface Deform Op property page for the eyeSocket.

Make it smaller by sliding the X and Z Scaling sliders to the left (adjust X and Z first, and then Y - which you might end up not changing at all). You might have to scale them down quite a bit, to get the eye socket to the proper size.

Next, move the eyeSocket to where you want it on the surface by using the Translation sliders. Again, you will probably want to adjust the X and Z axes first. If the eyeSocket was not created or frozen at the global center (that is, if the Center of the eyeSocket was not inside it because it was moved before you Froze its transformations), it will be floating above the surface of the mainBody. You may need to adjust the Y translation to put the socket on Toro's surface. The closer you get the eye socket to where you want it, the more the Surface Deformation controls will make sense.

Once you have positioned the eyeSocket to your satisfaction, choose Edit➔Freeze Operator Stack, and then Edit➔Duplicate Single.

Scale the duplicate by -1 in Z to mirror it on the other side of Toro's head.

Make the eye sockets children of the mainBody. Your tuna is done!

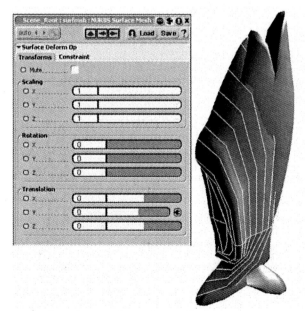

Edit the values in the Surface Deform property page to get the results you want

MODELING THE ENVIRONMENT

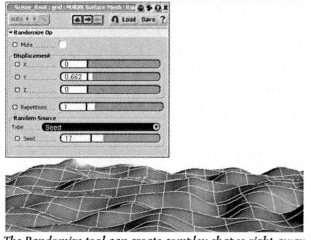

The Randomize tool can create complex shapes right away

STEP 1. MAKE THE OCEAN FLOOR

We will create a NURBS grid for the ocean floor and apply a randomize deformer to make it look more natural.

Choose Get→Primitive→Surface→Grid and set both length values to 50 and both subdivisions to 25.

Select Modify→Deform→Randomize. Experiment with the Displacement and other sliders to produce the desired effect.

STEP 2. ADD SEAWEED

In the Front view, draw a NURBS profile curve bordering the Y-axis, and then revolve it around the Y-axis.

Scale the new mesh down in the Z-axis to flatten it.

Choose Modify→Deform→Twist, and open the Twist Op property editor. Change Axis to Y-axis. Add a little more Angle, and use the Offset slider to make the seaweed sway.

Add a Bend deformation to the concoction and edit the sliders to your liking.

Duplicate this seaweed and plant them all over.

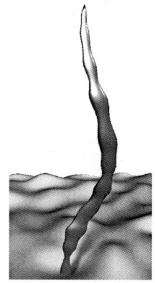

First, create a single chunky seaweed

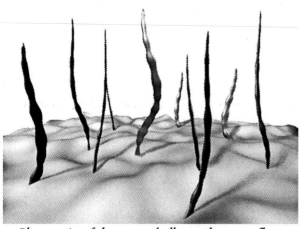

Plant copies of the seaweed all over the ocean floor

MAKING TORO SWIM:

STEP 1. CURVE DEFORMATION

Let's make a path for Toro to swim along. Using the Top view; plot a curve (using CV or Interpolating NURBS) so Toro can swim around the seaweed. Don't make any turns in the curve too tight; Toro won't deform correctly around a particularly sharp turn.

Toro won't be a bottom-feeder - translate the curve up in Y, so it weaves around the seaweed. Once you move the curve up, you can edit the points around to make the curve more three-dimensional.

Branch-select Toro. Choose Modify→Deform→by Curve, and pick the curve you just made. Oops! If Toro is in strange place, it's because we didn't freeze the transformations of the curve. Not to worry: in the Curve Deformation property editor, click the Constraint tab and check the Constrain to Deformer box. Now Toro should be at the right starting point.

If Toro is upside-down, use the Roll value in the Curve Deformation property page to correct him.

STEP 2. ANIMATE THE SWIMMING

Let's keyframe Toro swimming. We will set keys on the Translation Along Curve value in the Curve Deformation property page to make Toro animate.

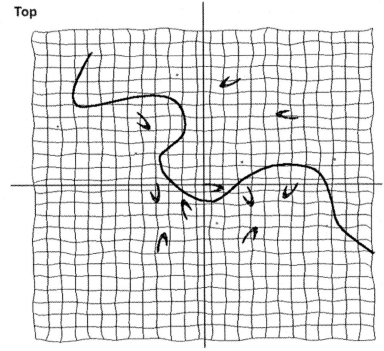

Make Toro swim around between the weeds

Make sure you are at frame 1, and click on the small green keyframe box to the left of the Along Curve value. It should turn red, and have a curve in it.

Move the time slider to frame 100, and move the Along Curve slider to all way to the right. Most likely, that's not enough value to make Toro swim until the end of his path (possibly not even close). Type a number directly into the Along Curve number entry box to make him swim to the end of the curve. When you find the value that puts Toro at the end of the curve, click on the keyframe icon to left of Along Curve again.

Now, he moves from the start of the curve to end of the curve, over 100 frames.

Frame him the way you feel is best, and preview the animation.

MUTING DEFORMERS

You can mute deformers to temporarily remove their effect from an object. On the property page of all deformations, there is a Mute check box. You can check or uncheck this box to toggle the deformation "on" or "off" without deleting it. You can also set keyframes on the Mute check box.

CLUSTERS

When you created a spine deformation, you may have noticed the points on the surface had two colors: blue and green. What are they?

The colored groups of points are called clusters. Clusters are groups of a component of an object, such as CVs, vertices, and faces. Clusters can be user-defined, and doing so can allow you to quickly and easily select and animate a specific portion of a model, without having to painstakingly select a group of points every time you want to make a change to them.

In case of the spine deformation, XSI automatically created two clusters. The blue cluster is weighted 50% or more to the spine deformation.

You can view and select clusters by selecting an object that has them, and clicking on the Cluster button at the top of the MCP, below the Selection bar.

To create a cluster, select the points you wish to group together, and click on the Cluster button at the bottom of the MCP, below the Edit bar. Name the cluster using the property editor. Note that the cluster's name is displayed at the top of the MCP, immediately below the name of the object.

PUSH DEFORMATION AND WEIGHT MAPS

A weight map is a property that is added on surfaces and clusters, and can affect how deformations behave.

The color of the weight map changes how much a deformation will affect the surface. You can paint your own weight maps to build more complex deformation effects.

To paint weight on a surface, you need to follow this procedure:

1. Select an object. If you want to sculpt the whole surface, just select the object in Object mode. If you want to affect only certain parts of a surface, select the points in that area.

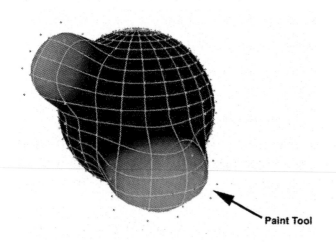

Paint Tool

Pushing and pulling a model using a weight map and the GAP

2. Choose Get→Property→Weight Map. A weight map is created for the whole object or selected points. A cluster is created automatically, prior to generation of the weight map.

3. You can't see weight maps by default. Make sure Weight Map is checked in the Show menu of the viewport you are using, and change it to Constant shading mode.

4. Open the WeightMap property page from the Selection button in the MCP. Several parameters here are very important:

Amplitude controls how far the deformer will move points. If the value is positive, it pushes points outward. If it's negative, it's pulling points inward.

Weight Map Type determines the default pattern of the weight map. You will probably want to use Constant, which is the blank base weight.

Base Weight defines what "blank" is, on the weight map. If you plan to paint on the map, set this to 0, so there's no weight (and therefore, no effect) unless you paint it there.

Weight Value Range controls how much weight can be painted (and also "unpainted" if the Min value is negative) on the map. When you move on to using the Generic Attribute Painter, left-clicking will paint positive weight, and right-clicking will paint negative weight. The scale of these values is usually 0 to 1 (or -1 to 1).

5. Now, the only thing you need to do is to switch to the painting tool. You can either get the paint tool from the Selection bar at the top of MCP, or simply use the W hotkey.

6. As mentioned before, left-clicking paints weight and right-clicking removes it. Middle-click and drag to change the size of the brush interactively.

THE GENERIC ATTRIBUTE PAINTER

The Generic Attribute Painter (GAP) allows you to paint on a 3D surface. The brush size and other attributes can be customized to suit your workflow. Choosing Get➔Property➔Paint Properties, or using the Ctrl-W hotkey, will summon the Paint Properties editor.

Diameter controls the size of the brush. You can also change size of brush on the fly by dragging with the Middle Mouse Button while in GAP mode.

Hardness, Softness lets you determine how much of a feathered edge you want.

Opacity controls how much of the value is added when you paint, similar to the pressure control on the airbrush tool of most paint applications. 100 means 100% of the Maximum weight will be painted with every stroke, so it's a good idea to set this value low, which gives you more control and lets you gradually build the surface.

USING A WEIGHT MAP WITH A DEFORMATION

You can use a weight map to modify the strength of any deformation across an object.

You must have a weight map created, and have a deformation on the same object. To hook up the weight map to the deformation, open the Property Editor for that deformation and click on the plug button to the right of the Amplitude slider (fact) and choose Connect from the drop menu that appears. A property explorer will pop up. Expand Polygon Mesh (or NURBS mesh), then Clusters, then WeightMappCls to find the Weight Map you created, and finally click right on the name of the weight map to select it. It will become highlighted in purple. Click anywhere out of the property explorer to close it.

Now the Deformation operator and the Weight Map are connected, but nothing will happen to the surface until you start painting.

ORGANIC SCULPTING WITH THE PAINT PUSH TOOL

Because all polygonal mesh objects and patch surfaces are defined by the vertices and control points that make them up, you can of course change the shape of the object by moving those points around. This fundamental concept is the basis of organic modeling. When you simply push and pull points on the surface to create the shape you desire, you have the ultimate degree of control over what you come up with. Although the experience is different, organic modeling is just like sculpting with clay, in that your talent and dedication are all that stands between you and a masterpiece.

Since polygonal meshes are usually composed of a great many vertices, sculpting in this way is pretty hard, unless you are building low poly game characters. NURBS surfaces usually have many fewer control points, and form very nice smooth shapes, making sculpting them much easier and more productive. You will want to start with a NURBS surface (or polygonal mesh) that has enough subdivisions for the detail you want to model into the object, but not more than you need since too much detail tends to be confusing and difficult to work with.

XSI has a tool designed to make sculpting easier and more intuitive. The Paint Push tool from the Property Menu cell in the Animate Module can be used in to sculpt the surface of an object into whatever form you desire. You could use this to model a human shape, paint in the valleys and mountains of a landscape, or model the creases and dents into a pair of digital blue jeans.

Select your object, and inspect the geometry property page, turning up the U and V subdivisions until you have plenty of detail to work with - usually 24 points in U and V or more.

Next, with the object to sculpt selected, choose the Get→Property→Paint Push Tool, which will automatically add a Push operator, a weight map, and activate the Paint tool. You can now start painting on you object, but let's make some changes that will make it easier.

Select your object again, then pull up the Paint options with CTRL-W or the Get→Property→Paint Properties command. Set the opacity quite low, around 10% so that you can work gradually, and adjust the brush softness to get a smooth, gradual fade of the brush shape. Click the key icon of the brush PPG to lock it open so you can make changes while you work.

The Paint Push tool should still be active, showing you a circle tangent to the surface of the object you have selected. If it is not, activate it again from the menu, or and hold down the W button, the hotkey for Paint Weights. A circle appears on your surface, following the contours as you roll your mouse. The size of the circle is the size of the brush, and can be adjusted carefully by holding down the Middle Mouse Button and dragging left to right.

Now click your Left Mouse Button to paint positive values on the weight map, which changes the value of the Push operator at that point on the surface, and displaces the surface mesh right there, under your mouse. The surface will update when you let up on the mouse button, so practice sculpting with short strokes.

The Left Mouse Button will pull out, the Right Mouse Button will push in. The total push and pull available can be changed by looking at the property page for the Push operator.

FACE MODELING: AT A GLANCE

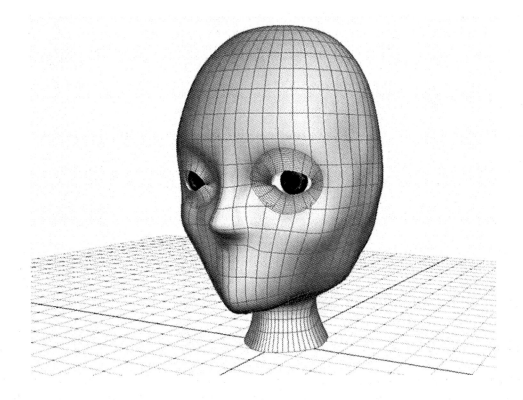

TOPICS COVERED

The Generic Attribute Painter is a fantastic tool to edit surface geometry quickly and easily. Let's use the GAP and other tools to model a face. Along the way, we will pick up several modeling techniques.

You'll learn how to:

- Shift U and V parameters of a surface
- Rough out the general shape of an object using lattice deformation
- Edit a surface using the Generic Attribute Painter

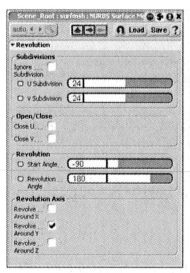

Create a profile curve for the face

TUTORIAL: FACE MODELING

In this tutorial, we will learn a basic face modeling technique using a high-density surface, the Generic Attribute Painter, and a Push deformation. Along the way we will also learn how to create basic shapes using lattice deformers, and other techniques to speed up the process.

STEP 1. DRAW A CURVE AND REVOLVE

We will revolve a profile curve to create the basic geometry. Select Create→Curve→Draw CV NURBS, and draw a profile curve just like the picture, in the Front view. Make sure you draw from bottom to top (so you don't end up having to Invert the surface) and grid-snap the first and last points with the CTRL key, so they are exactly on the global Y-axis.

Create→Surface→Revolution Around Axis and revolve the curve around the Y-axis. In the Revolution property editor, change the U and V subdivisions to 24 and 24. We really need this high-density surface (and possibly even higher) to use GAP effectively.

Next, we will cut this revolved surface in half. We want to do this because we can just model one side and mirror the other side, thereby reducing our modeling time. In the Revolution property editor, change the Start Angle to -90 and the Revolution Angle to 180. The surface is now cut in half.

Revolve the profile curve to make the basic shape of the head

You can also safely delete the lattice - it's no longer attached.

Name this surface "face".

STEP 2. USE A LATTICE TO ROUGH OUT THE SHAPE

Make sure the face is selected, and choose Get→Primitive→Lattice to create a lattice around the face.

Change to Point selection mode and move lattice points around in the Right view to get more of a general face shape.

After you have a shape you like, select the face and choose Edit→Freeze Operator Stack in the main menu bar, or click the Freeze button at the bottom of the MCP. The face loses all its operators, but retains its shape simplifying the object and saving valuable CPU cycles.

THE GENERIC ATTRIBUTE PAINTER

STEP 1. APPLYING THE GAP TO THE FACE

Select the face surface, and choose
Get→Property→Weight Map, which will create a blank
weight map on the surface. To see weight maps, you
need to enable Weight Maps in the Show menu for a
viewport (probably the Camera view), and change the
view type to Constant (as opposed to Shaded or
Wireframe).

Next, with the weight map still selected, choose
Modify→Deform→Push, to apply a Push deformation
to the face. The Push deformation values are tied to
the weight map, by default.

In the weight map property editor, change Amplitude
to 1, which means the weight map will affect the Push
deformation by a factor of one unit.

Change the Base Weight to 0, which means the default
(blank) value for the weight map is 0 – it won't affect
the Push unless positive or negative weight is painted
in a particular area.

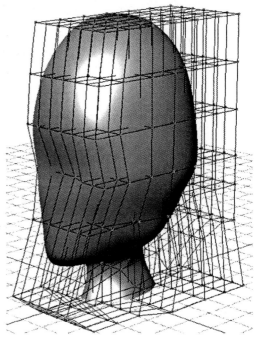

A lattice is very useful for roughing out models

Change the Minimum value of Weight Value Range to -1, which will allow you to paint a range of -1 to 1
weight on the map with the GAP, meaning you can both Push and negative-Push (or "Pull") points.

STEP 2. MODELING THE FACE BY PAINTING
Change to the Paint tool by selecting Get→Property→Paint Tool, or click the W hotkey.

The first thing we need to do is to change its opacity; right now, a single, brief brushstroke will paint weight
much too strongly to give us any fine-detail editing capability. By setting the opacity to less than 100%, you
can build up strokes gradually. Get→Property→Paint Properties, or use the CTRL + W hotkey, to open the
brush properties, and change Opacity to about 10.

Time to edit the surface. Maximizing the Camera view might help. Left-clicking (and holding if desired) on
the surface will pull points out. Right-clicking
(and holding) will push points in. Middle-but-
ton-dragging will let you change the brush
size on-the-fly.

Start from the eye sockets: push the surface
in, using right mouse clicks just below the
middle half of the face. Remember that you
need to build up details; try to avoid making
big, dragging sweeps. Keep working on an
eyebrow area and a cheek. Don't work on the
nose or chin yet, we will pull these areas out
after mirroring and merging the two face surfaces.

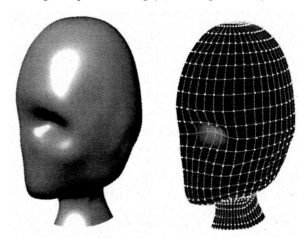

Half of the face is done

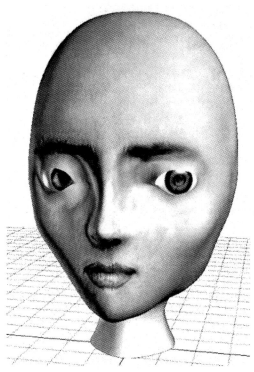

Connect the two surfaces, and then work on a nose and a chin

STEP 3. MIRRORING SURFACE

Once you have made half a face with an eye socket, eyebrow, and a cheek, click on the Freeze button (or Edit→Freeze Operator Stack) to freeze the Push deformer. This is necessary to duplicate correctly.

Choose Edit→Duplicate Single from the main menu bar. Scale the duplicated surface to -1 in the X-axis. This will mirror the surface to the other side.

Connect the two surfaces by selecting the original surface and choosing Create→Surface→Merge from Model tool bar. Select the other half surface, and right-click to finish. In the Merge Surfaces property editor, change Surface1 to "Min V boundary" and Surface 2 to "Min V boundary" (If that looks wrong, it's possible that your U and V boundaries are the reverse of this example. You can either set Surface 1 and 2 to "Min U boundary" instead, or Modify→Surface→Swap UV).

You need the vertical seam to be closed so you don't pull the face apart when you paint the nose and chin. Choose Modify→Surface→Open/Close, and check the U box (or V, if yours is reversed, as mentioned above).

Now both surfaces are merged successfully. Freeze the operator stack of the whole face, and hide or delete the two halves.

You can use GAP to pull out a nose and a chin, but you need to reapply a weight map and Push deformer as you did before, since the merged halves are a new object.

Apply any skin color material to finish the surface. Add eyeballs inside the sockets.

Why does the Paint tool push and pull points? The "generic attribute" painted by the Generic Attribute Painter can be specified. By applying a Push deformation with a weight map selected, the Amplitude of the weight map is connected to the Amplitude of the Push deformation. When you set the weight map Amplitude, Base Value, and Minimum Weight Value, you were modifying the way the weight map affects the Push deformation, as described above in the tutorial.

CONCLUSION

Deformation tools can be extremely useful for modeling and animation, and often provide a very quick and easy method of doing something that would otherwise be very complex. The various deformations, even the malleable ones such as by Lattice and by Weight Map, are fairly specialized; the trick is to know which tool works for your project. It would be a good idea to experiment further with the different deformations, to explore their full capabilities.

QUIZ

1. THE BEND DEFORMATION IS USED TO PULL POINTS OUT FROM A SURFACE.
   a. True
   b. False

2. THE TWIST DEFORMER CAN DEFORM RELATIVE TO THE DISTANCE FROM THE CENTER OF THE OBJECT, USING:
   a. Twister
   b. Vortex
   c. Tsunami

3. PUSH DEFORMATIONS DISPLACE POINTS USING THE GLOBAL AXIS.
   a. True
   b. False

4. DEFORMATION BY CURVE WILL REPLACE AN OBJECT'S Y-AXIS WITH THE _____ PARAMETER OF A CURVE.
   a. V
   b. X
   c. U

5. FREEZING TRANSFORMATIONS IS ABSOLUTELY NECESSARY TO ACHIEVE DEFORMATION.
   a. True
   b. False

6. TO ANIMATE OBJECTS ALONG A CURVE, YOU NEED TO USE THE _____ SLIDER.
   a. Path
   b. Along Curve
   c. Roll

7. WHEN YOU ARE SCALING OR MOVING A DEFORMED OBJECT, TRY NOT TO USE THE SLIDER FOR ____-AXIS TO BEGIN WITH.
   a. X
   b. Z
   c. y

8. THE RESOLUTION OF A LATTICE DEFORMER CAN BE EDITED.
   a. True
   b. False

9. OBJECTS NEED TO BE INSIDE A LATTICE IN ORDER TO BE DEFORMED.
   a. True
   b. False

10. TO REMOVE DEFORMATION OPERATORS FROM AN OBJECT, BUT RETAIN ITS DEFORMED SHAPE, YOU NEED TO FREEZE ITS:
    a. History
    b. Transformations
    c. Operator Stack

11. CLUSTERS ARE GROUPS OF _____.
    a. Galaxies
    b. Components
    c. Objects

THE ANIMATION EDITOR

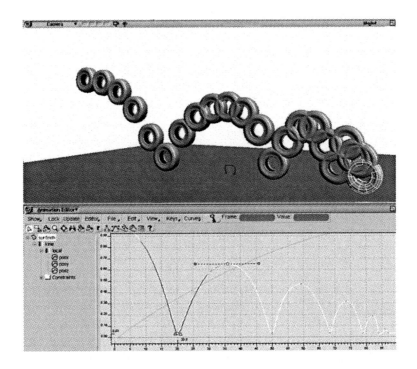

IN THIS CHAPTER YOU WILL LEARN ABOUT:

- A bit about traditional animation: Anticipation, Action, and Follow-through
- The importance of Poses and Pauses between actions
- How to pre-plan the animation process using a Dopesheet
- How to view and understand the graphs of Animation in the Animation Editor.
- How to add more animation, and edit existing work in the Animation Editor
- How to play back your work in several different ways, and evaluate it
- How to refine your animation until it looks good

INTRODUCTION

Softimage|XSI is different from other, less powerful animation tools. Softimage|XSI was built from the start as a tool for artists to communicate visually with other people. The number one goal of good animation is to connect with an audience, to articulate and communicate a story, an emotion, a feeling. Without that emotional connection to the audience, 3D animation is ultimately just unfulfilling eye candy, the visual equivalent of junk food. Softimage|XSI makes it easier for creative professionals to express themselves to other people through animation.

Expressive animation is not just a change in the shape of a mouth, although it might begin there. Expressive animation captures subtlety and nuance through careful timing and precise control over the action. Getting your work to this stage is always the result of much iteration: trying it out, seeing how it looks, correcting the movement and timing, and doing it over until it looks right. This process is called the feedback loop. The more immediately your animation tool can show you how your work will look, the better your revisions can be. The more revisions you can go through, the better the final product.

The Softimage | XSI Animation Editor has accuracy and control over every animated parameter in the environment, and the speedy feedback loop required to edit and perfect great animation.

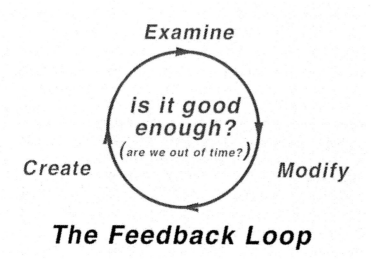

Examine

is it good enough? (are we out of time?)

Create   **Modify**

The Feedback Loop

The feedback cycle is crucial to creating good work

ALL ABOUT TIMING, AND ITS EFFECTS ON ANIMATION

In Softimage | XSI, all time is represented by frames. How long is a frame? However long you want it to be. By themselves, frames do not have any special relation to real-world units of time measurement; they are relative to the speed at which they are played back.

Frame rates from around the world

	Format Name	Details	Frame rate
U.S. Television	NTSC	Interlaced, 2 fields per frame, Odd field dominant	30 frames per second
European Television	PAL	Interlaced, 2 fields per frame, Even field dominant	25 frames per second
Film		Single frame	24 frames per second
HDTV	1080i	Interlaced, 2 fields per frame, Odd field dominant	30 frames per second
HDTV	1080p	single frame	24 frames per second
SDTV	480p	single frame	60 frames per second

You must know your frame rate before you begin

In the United States, television displays 30 frames per second. In Europe, it plays at 25 frames per second. Motion pictures play at 24 frames per second. Some traditional animation is run as slow as 12 or 15 frames per second (so the animators don't have to draw quite so many frames by hand). You need to decide before you start animating how you will be planning to view your animation. Generally, that determines how the Softimage | XSI frames translate into real units of time.

A side effect you need to think about is that running your finished animation at different speeds has the effect of slowing down or speeding up the action in them. This means that the timing that looked perfect when you were previewing your animation onscreen might not look so great on video or on film. Make sure you preview your work and perfect the timing at the same frame rate that you will use for your final output (which is 30 fps most of the time).

After you have the correct timing chosen for your specific work, you need to plan out the timing of the action in your animation. Working out the timing prior to beginning work is an essential component of good workflow. If you wait to figure out how long things will take until you are in front of the computer setting keyframes, you are guaranteed to get it wrong, and your animation will look lousy.

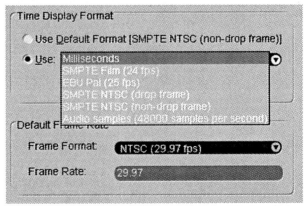

Animation timing is the study of how long each action of a character really takes in real life, and how that real life version can be

Set your frame rate in the User Prefs Time Display dialog

changed to accentuate the effect you are looking for in animation. For instance, If your character is dribbling a basketball, then putting up a shot, it's crucial that the dribbling of the ball be believable. If you make the dribble cycle too slow, it will look like your character is moving underwater. If you make the shot too fast, it won't seem to obey the correct laws of gravity.

The speed with which a character performs an action also determines how the audience will perceive the intent and emotion of the character. The same action, say, a simple walk cycle, will impart a different emotion depending on how long the character takes for each step. If the character walks fast, it's a vigorous happy walk. If the walk takes twice as long, it's a slow, languorous or depressed walk.

There is only one way to determine correct timing for your specific need: act it out with a stopwatch, then convert the time on the stopwatch to frames, and log the timing information you develop on a timing sheet (known as a 'Dopesheet' in traditional character animation).

If your character needs to cross a room and open the window, then stick his head outside, act out the scene yourself, holding the stopwatch. Practice the scene, developing the feel that you want it to have in the finished work. If you aren't acting really silly and dramatic, your finished character won't either. If you can't act out the timing and the action you want with your body, you won't be able to do it onscreen by setting keyframes, which is a million times harder. Collect timing information for each part of the action, broken down. Then convert that stopwatch time to frames by multiplying by the frames per second at which you plan to output your animation. Break repeating motions down into time per cycle.

NOTE You can specify the speed that XSI uses to play back frames when it is keeping timing by going to the File Menu, choosing User Preferences, and going to the Time Display Tab, which shows 30 fps by default.

Your secret weapon - cost: $5-10

Time For action / number of cycles * frames per second

For instance:

Crossing the room in three complete angry strides = 1.65 seconds. 1.65 seconds divided by three strides = 0.55 seconds. 0.55 seconds * 30 fps = 16.5 frames per angry stride.

Throwing the window open = 0.8 seconds = 24 frames.

Sticking head out the window = 1 second, 30 frames

Extending hand, yelling = 2 seconds, 60 frames

Now when you go to set the actual keyframe animation, you'll have a personal, kinesthetic feel for the motion of the character based on your own acting of the event, and you'll have an accurate record of how long each part will actually take. All that is left is to actually pose the character and set the keyframes.

THREE PARTS TO EACH MOTION

When you are performing character animation (or just about any animation at all), it's useful to break each action of the character down into three parts: the introduction, the action, and the result of the action. The proper names for these are Anticipation, Action, and Follow-through. Optimally, you would use the stopwatch to determine the timing of each one.

During the anticipation phase, the character telegraphs to the audience that it is about to do something important. Ren pulls back his hand and holds it for several frames before smacking Stimpy, in a classic example of anticipation. The audience watches the hand, since the animator provided the visual language to tell people what was going to happen next.

These three frames show Anticipation, Action, and Followthrough

In the action, the hand descends rapidly, often in an arc (arc of motion) and contacts Stimpy's fat head. This portion happens very fast, and is barely perceived.

In the follow-through, Ren pushes his hand through to the other side of Stimpy's face (which itself animates as a result of the action), and holds the hand in the fully extended follow-through pose.

Of the three portions of the action, the middle part is the least important because it's the least interesting. The audience holds its breath during the anticipation, and relaxes during the follow-through.

Failure to pay attention to this simple rule of cartoon animation will make your job harder and your work less successful. After you become proficient, after you learn the ropes using the classical methods, you are free to experiment with your own styles, the same way that John Kricfalusi (check out www.spumco.com) did when he adapted standard cartoon timing to create the Ren & Stimpy effects. Just pay attention to the basic rules first...

PAUSES AND HOLDING POSES

Your character does not have to be in motion at each and every frame of your animation. There is, however, an almost irresistible urge when animating with 3D tools to set keyframes so that your character is always doing something - easing into one action or easing out to something else. The effect of this common mistake is that your characters look drunk, or palsied. Powerful animation technique makes use of pauses between actions to focus the attention of the audience on what has just happened, or what's coming next. Pauses can indicate reflection on the part of your character, or decision making, or puzzlement. Try not to have each movement of your character blend into the next needlessly. Changing the amount of pausing between actions and poses can also effect the pacing of the story. Often, the first portion of the script calls for slower, more reflective pacing while characters are developed and motivations are explored. When the earlier portions have used a more measured pace, later sections can occur with more active timing, shorter shots, and quicker editing to enhance the level of excitement during crucial conflict scenes.

Examine the fine work of Nick Park and Aardman Animation (notably, the Wallace and Gromit™ series) for examples of excellent pacing, with effective changes of timing between different scenes.

THE ANIMATION EDITOR: INFINITE CONTROL

Keyframing is only the beginning in Softimage|XSI. To define how a value changes over time, Softimage|XSI generates an equation based on the value of the keyframes you set and at what frame you set them. With this equation, XSI can determine what a value should be at any point in time, not just the points you set explicitly. The equation is a spline and can be seen visually as a graph with the value being changed on the vertical axis and time in frames running along the horizontal axis. The official name in XSI for this kind of graph is an Animation Curve (formerly Function Curve, or Fcurve, in SI3D).

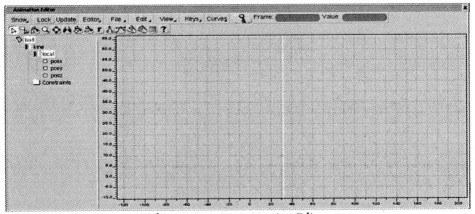

This is an empty Animation Editor

The Animation Curve isn't just to help you visualize animation, however. The Animation Curve is a potent way to create and edit animation. Each object in your scene can have a separate Animation Curve for each animateable parameter, creating hundreds and hundreds of Animation Curves for you to work with. After you set keyframes on an object to change something about an object over time (like it's color, or position, or shape), you can visualize that change over time in a simple graph. The graph is a curve, demonstrating the value that you changed versus time. This graph isn't just a way to see the animation in your scene - you can also change it there!

Using the Animation Editor, you can:

> Add keyframes
> Delete keyframes
> Move keyframes
> Select groups of keyframes and edit them
> Translate and scale the whole Animation Curve
> Remove all animation from one property
> Create and edit animation cycles

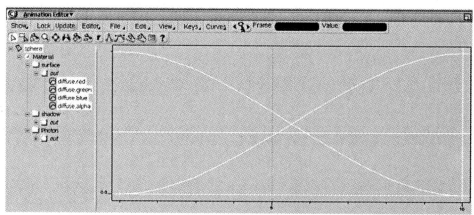

One set of animation curves, for the color of a light changing from green to red

Load the Animation.Tirebounce scene from the Project for this book (downloadable from http://www.mesmer.com/books/) to use as reference material while exploring the Animation Editor.

The Animation Curves for a selected object can be viewed using the Animation Editor. The Animation Editor can be called up in a number of different ways that are convenient for different uses. To see all the animation curves on a selected object (or a number of selected objects all at the same time) go to the bottom of the timeline, click on the Animation button, and choose Animation Editor from the popup menu there. This will replace two of your view windows with the Animation Editor. You can also manually change one of your view windows to show the Animation Editor with the Animation Editor drop-down menu in the title bar of the view.

To see a single parameter represented as a function curve (which is often much more useful than looking at everything), find that parameter in the property page where it lives, and then right-click on the animation divot (the little round button to the left of the parameter name). A drop-down menu just like the one at the bottom of the screen in the timeline will appear. If you choose Animation Editor from the menu, only the curve for that parameter will be shown.

Select the tire object and call up the Animation Editor to examine its Animation Curves using one of the preceding methods. Not much there, huh? Add in some keyframes. Start up in the air on the left side, activate the Translation portion of the MCP, and tap the K key to set a keyframe. Move 15 frames later in the timeline, move the tire forward a bit and down to the floor, and set another key. See the Animation Curves grow in the Animation Editor? Move 13 frames later and translate the tire up, not quite as high as before, and forward a bit more. Set another key. Proceed forward, setting more keys closer together with less tire bounce and forward motion until you get bored, or the tire comes to a halt, whichever happens soonest. Examine the curves you created in the Animation Editor.

Unmark All Parameters	Ctrl+Shift+M
Set Key	K
Remove Key	Shift + K
Set Expression...	
Set Scripted Operator...	
Copy Animation	
Paste Animation	
Remove Animation	Ctrl + Shift + K
Copy All Animation	
Paste All Animation	
Remove All Animation	
Link with...	
Set Relative Values	
First Key	Shift + , (comma)
Last Key	Shift + . (period)
Previous Key	, (comma)
Next Key	. (period)
Sequence Selection	
Sequence All	
Sequence Marked Parameters	
Animation Editor...	0
Expression Editor...	

The Animation Menu from the timeline area at the bottom of the screen

FINDING THE ANIMATION CURVE YOU WANT

If the window contains more than one Animation Curve, how do you know which Animation Curve is which? The left panel of the Animation Editor contains a hierarchical explorer view of all the different animation curves present in the Animation Editor at that time. You may scroll among them to see what parameters have already been animated on the object (or objects) you had selected when you called up the Animation Editor. If a parameter exists but has not been animated, it will show up as a horizontal line in the Animation Editor.

Each and every Animation Curve has a name, made up of the name of the object followed by the name of the property that is being animated. This name is itself a hierarchy which you can read in the left pane of the Animation Editor. At the top is the name of the saved scene, then comes the object name (tire), then under that is how it moves (Kine), then comes whether the movement is relative to the global center or a local center (Global or Local), then comes translation/position (posx, posy, or posz), orientation/rotation (rotx, roty, rotz), or Scale (sclx, scly, sclz). Each part of the name is separated by a period. In this way, some valid names for the animation on the tire would be:

'MyScene.tire.kine.local.posx,' meaning where the tire is on the X-axis

'MyScene.tire.kine.local.roty,' meaning the rotation of the tire around the Y-axis.

These names are represented in the left-hand pane of the Animation Editor as individual words in an Explorer style list, but you can see the actual name in the command line or the Script Editor (both at the bottom of the screen) to see what is really happening.

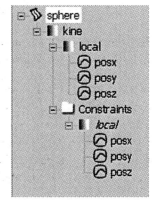

Here are the names of the Animation Curves in the TireBounce scene

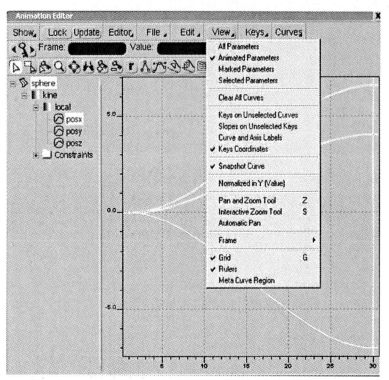

The view menu helps you isolate just the curves you need to see

If you click on the name of the parameter on the left, then the corresponding curve will be activated in the right side of the editor. You may also select curves in the right side, by holding the space bar and either clicking directly on a curve or drawing a selection rectangle that crosses the curve. This will highlight the name of the curve on the left-hand side.

It is often hard to see what you want in the Animation Editor, either because you are looking at the wrong area of the curve or because the scale of the animation makes the curves very short. You can frame curves (or tagged keys) by tapping the F key. The Z hotkey also pans and zooms in the Animation Editor.

If you are looking for the Translate, Scale, or Rotate Animation Curves, you can activate that transformation in the MCP and then toggle on the View→Marked Parameters menu item form the top menu bar of the Animation editor, to view and frame just those curves.

Let's look at a simple example to get started. The tire in the Animation.Tirebounce scene was animated to bounce along the floor using local translation. The Animation Editor below the ball shows the three Animation Curves for local transformation in X, Y and Z. The vertical axis of the Animation Curve shows the value of the parameters in XSI units (set in User Pref→Unit Settings→Length). The horizontal axis shows the time proceeding from left to right. Each Animation Curve tells us exactly where in that axis the object is at each and every frame in the animation (and even between frames).

NOTE XSI has a new feature that solves an old problem. When you want to see two different parameters with different scales (like rotation, which is in degrees, and translation, which in inches, millimeters, or feet) inevitably one parameter is too big and stretches off screen, while the other is too small to see what you are doing. XSI has a feature in the View menu of the Animation Editor called Normalize in Y, which will scale all the selected curves so that they fit on the screen, regardless of the unit scale of the curves.

THE SLOPE OF THE CURVES

Moving through time, the
Animation Curve changes
slope as it passes through the
control points you created by
setting keyframes.
Softimage|XSI uses a Bezier
spline for the curve, which
means that the control handles of the curve modify the
slope (the tangency of the
curve) at every point along
the curve. By default, XSI
eases in from the first point
and eases out to the last
point (you can change this in
File→User Prefs). Using
these Bezier curves avoids
jerky-looking animation,
because the values accelerate
and decelerate at the start
and the finish (Warning: this
can also lead to motion that
looks too fluid).

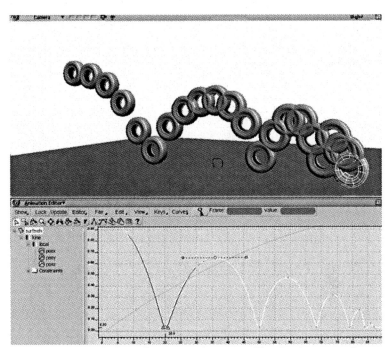

The tire's path through space is determined by the change in the
Animation Curves

Technically speaking, the slope of the curve at any one point is the rate of change in the parameter being animated - think of this as "how fast it's going." The change in that slope over time (say, from the first point to
the second point) is called acceleration, which is easy to think about as "how the animation is speeding up or
slowing down."

EDITING ANIMATION WITH ANIMATION CURVES

If you wish to edit your bouncing ball's behavior - say, to make it bounce higher - you do not have to re-
keyframe the new motion. You can simply edit the location of points in an Animation Curve with the M key,
just as you would edit any curve! By holding the M key and dragging a point on the Animation Curve with the
mouse, you can change the value of the animated parameter and move the point to a different frame in time.

You can add new keys and remove existing
ones without using the keyframe techniques,
by adding or removing keys directly in the
Animation Editor. To add a new key to the
curve, hold down the I hotkey for insert (or
click the insert key button - the one with the
plus sign - at the top of the Animation
Editor), then point to an area of the curve
and click with the Left Mouse Button. If you

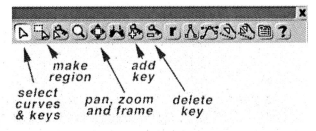

These buttons help you edit the curves

click and hold the mouse you can drag the point to a specific place on the curve before letting go of it.

To delete keys you can simply select them one at a time or by dragging a marquee around them all, then tapping the Delete key on your keyboard. You can also click on the Delete button at the top of the Animation Editor (it has a minus sign) and then click on the keys you want to remove.

The most useful general-purpose button in the top of the Animation Editor is the Edit Key tool - represented as a pointer with a key. With this button you can move points using the Left Mouse Button, add new keys with the Middle Mouse Button, and remove keys with the Right Mouse Button.

Try editing the height of your tire bounces by dragging the top points of the Local Position in Y Animation Curve higher in the Animation Editor and playing back your animation. Later you will also click the Bezier handles to adjust the curve tangency, which changes how the ball accelerates in and out of keyframes, making the bounce more believable.

You may Undo or Redo any of your changes in the Animation editor by typing the standard Ctrl-Z and Ctrl-Y hotkeys, respectively. Try it out: move some points around, then use Undo until you are back where you started.

PLAYING YOUR ANIMATION

The first thing you'll want to do after you animate an object by setting keyframes is see how that object moves and changes over time. Seeing your animation on the computer screen is not only the big payoff for the animator, it's what the client pays for. The only way to make sure that the animation you get is the animation you wanted is to check, check, and recheck the playback. You can play your animation in a number of ways, but they all start with an understanding of the Time Slider and how frames in Softimage|XSI relate to real time.

If you want to see the scene play by itself, you can simply click one of the VCR-style play controls below the Time Slider.

IMPROVE THE PLAYBACK RATE

As your scenes become more and more complex, it will not be possible for XSI to play each frame back at a constant rate of 30 frames per second. However, there are a couple of things you can do to help the playback maintain an appropriate speed.

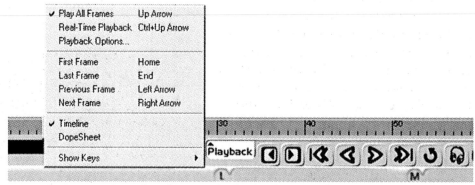

These buttons play back your animation

First, you can reduce the number of View windows that are refreshed each frame by using the Window Lock option. To lock all the windows but one, click directly on the letter in the top-left corner of the window you want to keep active, which will blank out all other views. The fewer windows that have to be refreshed, the more computational power your system can spend on drawing your animation in the window you care about, and the faster it plays.

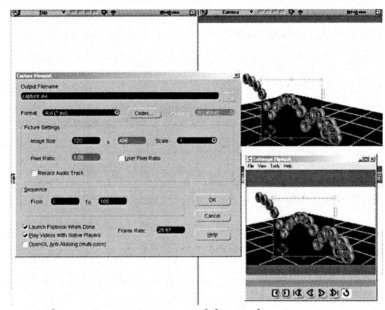

The new Camera Capture capability is a huge improvement

RENDERING TESTS

Seeing a real-time playback of the animation in your scene is critical to good animation during the feedback loop portion of your workflow. If you don't watch it at the speed your consumers will, you can't possibly know what it will look like when they see it. If you don't know what it will look like, it will probably look bad. The solution is to use non-real-time methods of rendering frames, and real-time methods of playing them back.

XSI has a major improvement in how you view your animation work while it's in process. Now, previewing your action is much easier and more flexible than before. You can create a preview of your work in any view window, in any view style, at any time. Just choose a view to capture (usually the camera view) and select Start Capture from the Camera menu in the middle of the title bar of that view window (it has the icon of a camera, not the word "Camera".

A dialog will pop up with options to set the capture size, the picture format and the compression used. To quickly see your capture, change the drop menu labeled Scale to 1/4 size, leave the other defaults and click OK. A new preview window will appear, and XSI will start drawing frames into it, starting from the first frame you have set in the timeline until it reaches the last frame of the timeline. As each frame is drawn it will be written to a cache on disk. When the process is done, the cached files will be loaded into the Flipbook and displayed if you used .pc, .jpeg or other single frame formats. If you used QuickTime, the QuickTime viewer will pop up, and if you chose .AVI the Windows Media Player will pop up. All methods can be used to see your animation play back in real time.

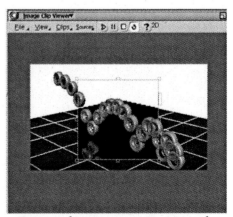

You can play your tests any time in the Image Clip Viewer

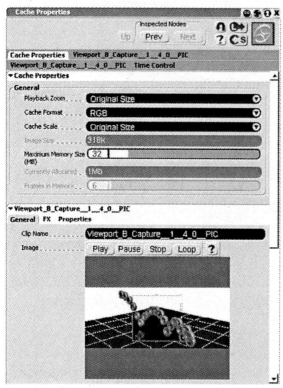

Toggle on the Cache to store frames in RAM during playback

The improvement is that this method writes the image files to disk for later perusal. After closing the Flipbook, which will empty the cache, change another view window to the Image Clip Editor. Now use the File→Load command or drag and drop the frames from a browser into the Clip Editor. This stores the Capture for later in the clip list. (It also makes it available to be used as a texture map on another object.)

If your preview does not play back in the Image Clip Editor at a consistent speed, it may not be possible for your computer to retrieve the frames from the disk rapidly enough (this will happen if you skimped on buying that SCSI drive...). In this situation, XSI must cache the frames in RAM memory, which is much faster than normal PC hard drives. Right-click on the clip and choose Cache Properties, scroll down the clip property page, and toggle on the "Frame Caching" option. This loads the frames into memory on the first round through, then plays them back, keeping the timing you set in the same Clip Property page. You may also increase the amount of RAM allocated to the cache if you have a lot of frames to preview, and a lot of RAM in your computer.

COMMON CAPTURE STYLES

While the Wireframe style is the fastest method for rendering frames into the capture buffer, sometimes it is difficult to make out the action in your scene through all the criss-crossing lines of the Wireframe. One way to make the view easier to comprehend is to use the Hidden Line Removal rendering style. In Hidden Line, only front facing surfaces are rendered, and objects in front obscure those behind them.

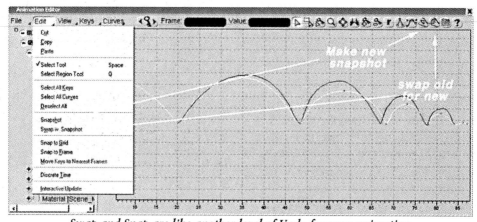

Swap and Snap are like another level of Undo for your animation

Another neat trick is to draw a render region in the view you plan to capture, then initiate a Camera➔Capture session. The mental ray will render just that portion and the view style will be used for the rest of the frame.

Now, back to the Animation Editor:

INTERMEDIATE ANIMATION CURVE EDITING TECHNIQUES

SNAPSHOT AND SWAP WITH SNAPSHOT

Swap and Snapshot enable you to experiment without fear of screwing up your animation. Think of Swap and Snapshot as controllable Undos. If the option named Snapshot Curve is toggled on in the View menu (and it is by default), when you edit an Animation Curve the previous state of the curve is saved into the swap buffer, and a thin black line shows you what the Animation Curve used to look like. This thin black line is called the snapshot. If at any point in your work you decide that the old Animation Curve was better, simply click the Swap with Snapshot button (it looks like one dashed curve and one solid curve with two triangles) to recall the old curve and place the new one in the swap buffer. If, while you are editing, you decide that you wish to save an intermediate Animation Curve before exploring further, click the Snapshot button (it looks like the dashed line and the solid line with just one triangle), which replaces the saved Animation Curve in the buffer with the current Animation Curve, but does not replace the current Animation Curve as the active Animation Curve.

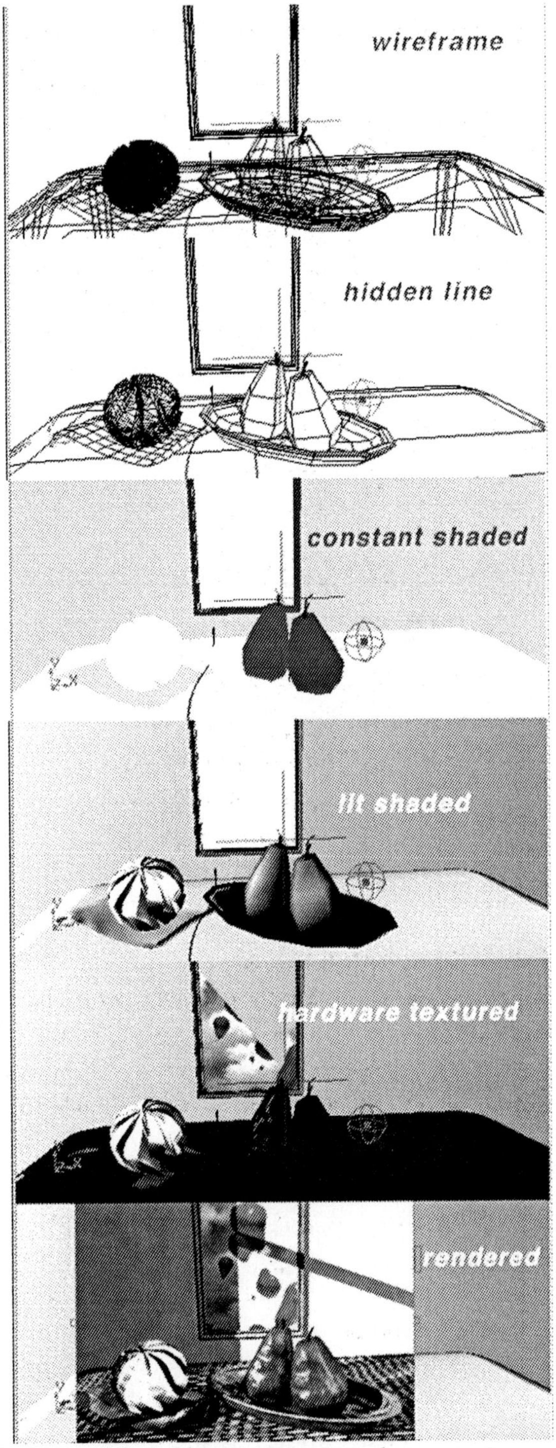

WORKING ON GROUPS OF POINTS: THE REGION EDITOR

XSI has a new method of changing a large number of keyframes, perhaps on many different animation curves, all at the same time. This new feature is the Region Editor. When you have a region defined, it encapsulates all the keyframes within it,

wireframe

hidden line

constant shaded

lit shaded

hardware textured

rendered

Some styles are slower to capture, but easier to see

and the whole group can be scaled either along the value axis or the time axis, or moved in either direction.

the create region button

The region button helps you work with many keys all at once

To use the region, select those curves that you want to work with (you may multi-select curves with Shift-Select), then click on the Region button at the top of the Animation Editor (it has an arrow drawing a box), and drag to define the region. The hotkey for drawing an animation curve region is Q, just like drawing a render region. A box appears as you drag, surrounding the keyframes you will be modifying. Small, square handles on the edges of the region scale it in four different directions. You can move the entire region by clicking in the middle of the region and dragging it around within the Animation Editor.

Translating region of an Animation Curve in the X-axis has the effect of moving the whole animation in time, either earlier or later depending on which way you go. By looking at the frame values on the X-axis, you can easily synchronize action in the Animation Curve with a specific frame.

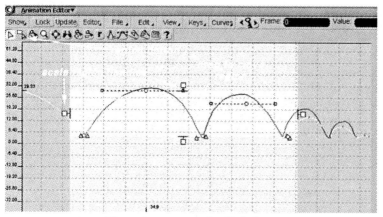

The region surrounds all the keys

Translating the whole Animation Curve in the Y-axis has the effect of changing all the values in that Animation Curve by the same amount.

For instance, in your tire scene you can make the ground plane that the tire bounces on higher or lower by dragging a region over the entire kine.local.posy (the Y position) Animation Curve in the and then moving the region up in the Y direction.

Scaling the region has the effect of making the action of the keyframes more or less pronounced.

You could make all the bounces taller, leaving the floor level where it is by selecting the Local Position in Y Animation Curve and then dragging a marquee around all the highest points (the peaks of the bounces), then dragging the top-middle handle (a small white square) of the region up in Y twice as high as is was. During playback, your ball should now bounce twice as high and hang a little longer before crashing to earth.

DIRECTLY CHANGING KEY VALUES

In XSI, it's fantastically easy to precisely set the values of one or more keyframes. For instance, if you know that a wheel has to rotate exactly 175 degrees at a certain frame, you can select the key by dragging a marquee around it, and then simply type a number in the numeric entry Value box at the top of the Animation Editor, and press Enter. You may also set values on more than one key at a time. To make a number of keys all match the same value, for instance to set the local Y position of a character's feet so they hit the floor at the same level (or to make a tire bounce exactly at the same floor height...), just select all the individual key points in the Animation Editor with a selection marquee and type a number in to the Value box at the top middle of the Animation Editor. That value will be assigned to all the keyframes when you hit the Enter key.

You can also directly enter frame numbers to make sure that a key happens on a specific frame. Again just select the key by dragging a marquee around it with the spacebar, and this time enter a frame number in the Frame numeric entry box at the top of the Animation Editor.

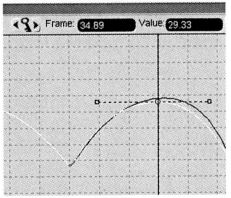

WORKING WITH KEYS AND SLOPES

Slope is a critical tool, because it controls a parameter's rate of change in and out of keyframes. This is a fancy way of saying that it controls the timing of the actions being animated - how quickly things change. Because the normal functions of the Bezier control handles keep the two sides even (with the same tangency), the default Bezier curve is not suited to any motion that changes from acceleration to deceleration (or changes direction entirely) at a single keyframe.

Just select a key and type a value into these boxes to set it precisely at a given frame

A good example of when you might want to use this option is when your tire bounces on the floor. As the tire approaches the floor, it accelerates due to the force of gravity, but at the instant of contact that acceleration should become deceleration as it bounces up against gravity, slowing down. Try breaking the slope of the bouncing

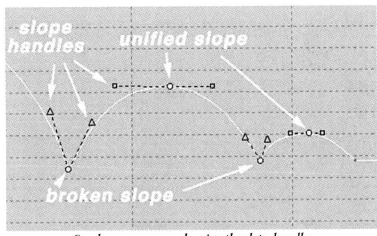

One key on a curve, showing the slope handles

ball Y translation Animation Curve at the point when the ball hits the ground by holding the B hotkey (equivalent to the Break Slope command from the Keys menu) and then clicking the point you want to break with the Left Mouse Button. Then, with the slope of the curve broken at that point, you can adjust each handle of the point separately. The handles should be moved very close to the actual point itself, resulting in a curve that changes abruptly at the keyframe, just like the tire changes direction abruptly when it hits the floor.

You can also Break the slope of many keys at once by selecting them either with a marquee or by Shift-clicking on them, and choosing the Keys→Break command from the top menu bar of the Animation Editor. The Keys→Unify Slope commands allows you to unify the slope, meaning that the control handles are once again connected together in a straight line. Unifying the slope by clicking on the point with the U hotkey makes the Animation Curve interpolate smoothly in and out of that keyframe, preventing any rash, sudden moves.

NOTE If you want all your changes to result in keys that are snapped to exact keyframes in time, there is another clever option hidden in the Edit menu. Toggle on the Discrete Time option to make sure that when you change keys they end up exactly on a keyframe and not in-between. You can also do this after-the-fact by selecting keys and using the Move Keys to Nearest Frames command.

INTERPOLATION: CONSTANT, LINEAR AND SPLINE

The Curves menu Interpolation controls adjust the method of interpolation used between points throughout the entire curve. Because the default Bezier spline curve isn't always the best choice for all kinds of animation, the Animation Editor offers some other types of curves that might better suit your specific needs.

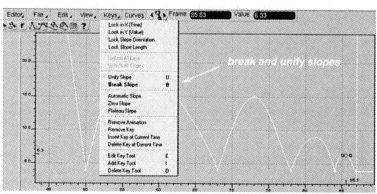

Use these menu items to break and unify the slope on individual keys

Choosing the Curves→Linear Interpolation command causes the interpolation between each point to become a straight line. Linear is an excellent choice for animating lights and colors, where ease-in and ease-out are not so important. Using Linear interpolation on movement creates a mechanical, robotic look.

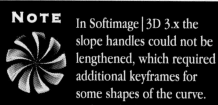

NOTE In Softimage|3D 3.x the slope handles could not be lengthened, which required additional keyframes for some shapes of the curve. You may now adjust the length of the slope handles to make 'fatter' curves.

Curve→Spline Interpolation with Keys→Plateau Slope is very useful for character animation, because it retains the ease-in and ease-out attributes of the Bezier curve, but it uses a linear segment between two points on the curve with the same value. Ordinarily, a Bezier curve going through two points adopts a somewhat serpentine path through the keyframes, which can cause backsliding, foot dragging, and other unwanted behavior in characters. Using Plateau Slope means your characters stay where you put them when they are not supposed to be moving between one keyframe and the next, but still move fluidly when they do move. Curves→Constant Interpolation will make the value stay constant from one key to the next, then jump suddenly to the new value without any interpolation at all. This is not often very useful.

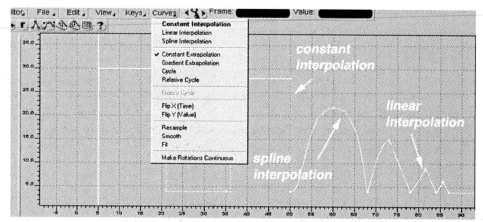

Interpolation changes how the curve works between keys

DELETING ANIMATION CURVES

At this point you should be wondering how to remove animation from an object - you know, make it quit moving. That seems like a tall order in Softimage|XSI, because so much is geared towards adding animation, but it's really quite simple.

If you want to eliminate just one Animation Curve, select the curve scheduled for termination (or mark the parameters you wish to remove animation from) and choose the Keys→Remove Animation menu command from within the Animation Editor. The hotkey for removing animation is CTRL-Shift-K.

Each Animation Divot in the property pages also has an option called Remove Animation located in the menu that cascades down when you right-click on it. This option whacks the entire Animation Curve, as well as any expressions or linked parameters on that property.

On the Animation Menu in the timeline there is also an option to Remove All Animation, which will wipe clean all the Animation Curves on the selected object. This also works for selections of multiple objects.

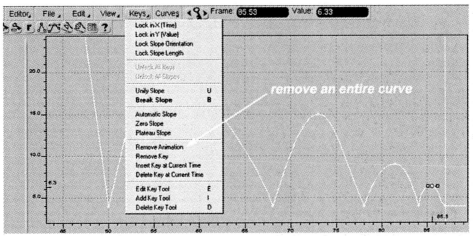

The Remove Animation commands help you clear out unwanted animation, or just start over

CREATING A CYCLE

Sometimes you want an object to have a repetitive motion, such as a wheel spinning or the pendulum of a clock swinging back and forth. In the Curves→Cycle menu, you will find the commands required to accomplish what you need.

When you activate the Cycle or Relative Cycle menu commands, all of the keyframes you have set already will repeat endlessly until the last frame you have set in the bottom-right corner of the timeline. If the first and last points do not have the same value, you may see some jumping in the animation as the object snaps from the last frame back to the first. When making cycles, take care to make them smooth by setting the first and last key to precisely the same value with the numeric entry Value box at the top of the Animation Editor.

GRADIENT EXTRAPOLATION

Curves→Gradient Extrapolation finds the slope of the last two points in the Animation Curve and simply continues on at the same slope indefinitely. This type of motion is great for objects that constantly spin.

PING PONG: AT A GLANCE

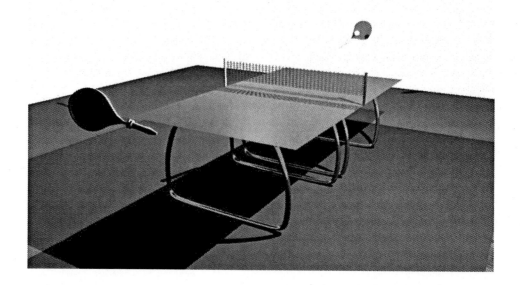

TOPICS COVERED

You'll learn how to:

- Set Keyframes a few different ways
- Edit and fine-tune the animation
- Change timing with the Animation Editor
- Work with the slope of the Animation Curves
- Create Animation Cycles
- Add in anticipation and follow-through to your work

MATERIALS REQUIRED

This tutorial uses the pingpong_start.scn scene file available at www.mesmer.com/books/

TUTORIAL: PING PONG - ANIMATION EDITING

During this tutorial, you will set key frames to create a simple game of table tennis. After setting basic keyframes for the translation of the ping-pong ball back and forth, you'll use the Animation Editor to change the timing and slopes of the ball's translation animation curves so that it seems to bounce correctly. Then after the ball is bouncing right, you'll make a cycle out of the movement so that the ball bounces back and forth endlessly. Next you'll edit some of the translation keys so that the ball bounces to a different part of the table on each bounce, at a different speed, adding some interest to the game. Finally, you'll animate the ping pong paddles to meet the ball at the right place and time, and add in traditional animation anticipation and follow-through so it looks like a human being is swinging the paddles - not a computer.

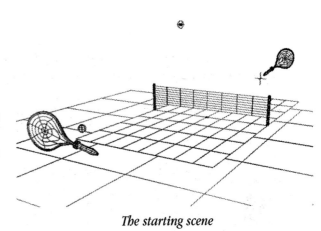

The starting scene

KEEP YOUR EYE ON THE BALL

STEP 1. LOAD UP THE PINGPONG_START.SCN SCENE FILE.

Look into the database for this material (you can download it from www.mesmer.com/books/ if you don't already have it) and load up the pingpong_start.scn scene. It contains a simple pingpong table, with a ball, and two paddles. Nothing is animated yet.

Examine the scene, selecting the ball and the paddles to get the feel of the objects.

STEP 2. SET NINE KEYFRAMES ON THE BALL.

The ball needs to start at one end, at the location of the paddle. In the Right view only, at frame zero, set a key for the local translation of the ball on all axes - X, Y and Z.

Move the timeline ten frames later in time, and set another key for the ball half-way to the net, on the surface of the ping pong table (remember: in ping pong your serve has to bounce once before it clears the net).

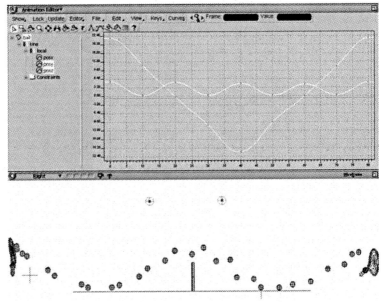

Nine keyframes in the Animation Editor

Since we can't see any change in the X-axis in the Right view, the keys will all have the same X value. That's OK - we want the ping pong ball to travel straight back and forth because we're going to modify that later on with a different technique.

Set another key ten frames later for the ball, directly in the middle of the table, above the net.

Ten frames forward again, set another key for the ball on the table, half way between the net and the far side.

Ten frames later, set another key at the location of the second (far side) ping pong paddle.

Keep going - set keys all the way back to exactly where you started. This should take nine keyframes, so if they start at 0 and are ten frames apart, they should end at frame 80.

STEP 3. TAKE A COLD, HARD LOOK AT YOUR WORK

Play back your animation, making sure that you are seeing it at 30 fps (frames per second), just like your customers would if this were a real job. Click on the small button in the timeline that toggles from All (Frames) to RT, which stands for Real Time. You might also isolate the perspective window so that it is the only window that will refresh, by clicking the letter in the top-left corner (click it again to activate the other windows). You could also set the last frame to 80 and click the loop button to get a good feel for the looping of the animation.

It looks pretty bad, doesn't it? Make a mental list (or a physical one) of all the things that are wrong with the animation. The ball weaves in and out of the floor, instead of bouncing, it just goes back and forth in a fashion that is too regular and boring, and it doesn't hang in the air quite right. In addition, the speed of the ball should vary over each hit, starting fast and then slowing down as it nears the other side. In general, the animation is dull and lifeless. Let's fix it!

STEP 4. OPEN THE ANIMATION EDITOR AND SET A CYCLE.

Change the last frame of the animation to 320 frames, so we can set a cycle and see a few different volleys of the ping pong game.

Open the Animation Editor by selecting the ball and choosing Animation Editor from the Animation menu in the timeline at the bottom of the screen, or by using the 0 hotkey.

Within the Animation Editor window, use the View➔Animated Parameters menu item to show just the animated curves: the local translation in X, Y and Z.

Select the animation curve for local translation in X (the red one). Remember that we never really changed the X value, so it should be pretty flat, even though it has some keyframes on it. We'll want to remove all the middle keyframes on X, leaving the first and last keys (at frames 0 and 80, respectively). That way, when we cycle it, we only have keys for when the ball hits the first ping pong paddle, which we'll edit to make the game more interesting.

 **NOTE** To ensure that the last frame is exactly where the first was, try moving the time slider to zero, then right-clicking and dragging to frame 80, then setting a key. Right-dragging the time slider doesn't update the screen, so it's a quick way to copy values from one key to another.

Drag a marquee rectangle, using the Selection tool (or just hold down the space bar), around all the points on the red X-axis curve except for the first and last point, and then hit the Delete button on your keyboard to remove them.

The Z (blue) curve repre-
sents the travel of the ball
back and forth down the
length of the table. It has
redundant keyframes as
well, but we need to keep
the keys at frames when the
ball strikes either paddle.
Those are keys at frames 0,
40, and 80 (first, last, and
middle). Keep those frames
and delete the others.

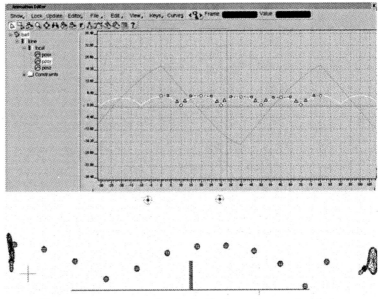

Now we'll make a cycle.
Select all three curves -
local X, Y and Z - and set a
cycle so that they go on
indefinitely into the future
with the Curves→Cycle
menu item.

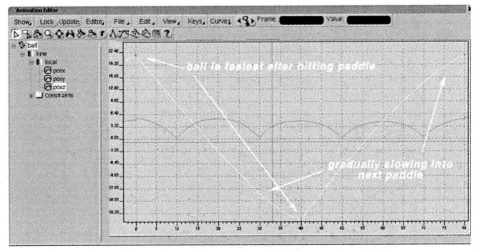

The animation curves for the ball, cleaned up and cycled

Turn off Loop if it's on, and drag back and forth on the timeline, or play back the animation, to see that we now have four complete cycles. If you set the end frame of the animation to be even further out in time, we would get even more cycles, but four is probably enough for us now.

With all the curves selected, look at the menu item Keys→Plateau Slope, and make sure it is unchecked. This menu item would make it tough for us to adjust the tangent handles in the next step.

STEP 5. EDIT THE CYCLES
Now we can fix some of the problems on just one set of keyframes, and see the result on all four cycles - a real time-saver. First we'll change the timing on the ball's travel down the table, which is the local translation in Z.

The ball is moving fastest right after hitting each paddle

When the ball leaves the paddle, it should be moving at its fastest rate (the slope of the animation curve should be the steepest) and the ball should gradually slow down just a bit until it hits the other paddle (the slope should gradually flatten out a little bit - not too much). Then, at that instant the ball should suddenly be going faster again as it comes off the paddle, and repeat the slowing down process due to air resistance all the way back to the paddle at the other side.

To make the slope of the line change so dramatically at the points where the ball hits the paddle, we need to break the tangent handles for the keys in local Z. Start with the first key at frame 0, select it, and use the menu item Keys➜Break Slope. Now you can change the tangent handle after the key independently from the tangent handle before the key. In other words, the ball can now change direction or speed instantly at a keyframe, instead of having to ease-in and ease-out.

Adjust the tangent out key's handle so that the slope of the curve is greatest (steepest) at the instant the ball leaves the paddle, and gently eases into the next keyframe. Then adjust the tangent handle out of the next keyframe so that it is steepest, easing gently back to the next key, the location of the original paddle.

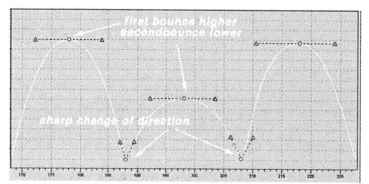

Gravity slams the ball into the table, then slows it down in a gradual arc up in the air, then back down to the table again

Play your animation and fine-tune the effect so that the ball seems to slow down just slightly as it moves across the table, then picks up speed instantly as it changes direction due to the hit from the paddle. Avoid making the changes to the curve too dramatic, or the Z and Y keys won't line up well at the frames when the ball is supposed to go over the net, and it might go through it.

Now we'll fix the bounces off the table. Select the (green) translation in Y curve, and select one of the lowest points in the local Y-axis, which is the ball's height in the air. Look to the top of the Animation Editor and note the value of the Y curve at that key. All the bounces should hit the table at the same level, so now select all the lower points in Y and type the value you noted right back into the same box you read it from and hit enter. All the keys will now be set to the same height.

With only the lower keys still selected, use the Break command again to make the tangent handles independent. We need the handles to come together in a sharp V shape, accelerating into the floor, instantly changing direction, then decelerating out of the floor. Modify each set of handles to look like a V shape, and play back the animation to see the difference. Fine tune-to your liking.

STEP 6. FREEZE THE CYCLES
We need to freeze the cycles now so we can make each one slightly different, adding to the interest of the game. Select all three curves and use the Curves➜Freeze Cycle command. Freezing the curves adds in actual keyframes from your first frame to your last frame, so you can edit them and make the cycles non-uniform.

Currently, the ball travels straight up and down the middle of the table. Let's change that. Keep the Animation Editor up but change one of your other views to be the Top view. At frame 40, use the M hotkey to change the value of the key on the red X animation curve. You must let go of the point to see the change, unless you toggle on Interactive Update at the bottom of the Edit menu.

See that the ball now arrives at a different spot on the table. Also change the other frames where the ball reaches one end of the table, except the first and the last frames, to make a more challenging game for the contestants. We'll leave the first and the last frame so we can still cycle our animation if we wanted to.

Play back your animation using the Real Time playback option, and note how much better it is! Pat yourself on the back.

It's All In the Wrist

Step 1. Move the paddles.

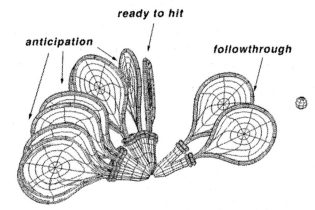

Currently, the ball is moving on its own up and down the table. We need to add the illusion that the paddles are driving the ball back and forth. Start by matching the position of the paddles in X to the position of the ball when it reaches the ends of the tables.

This is pretty easy - just move the paddles in X to meet the ball - but we

The arc of the paddle, showing the three phases of the action

need to throw in a twist. The paddles need to get to their position slightly before the ball does, because that's the way humans do it. Arriving before the ball is a form of anticipation.

There is a quick way to do this. Branch-select the first paddle, and at frame zero set a keyframe for its local translation in X only (by only marking X).

Drag forward in time until the ball bounces across the table and finally comes back to the first paddle (this should be frame 80). Drag the paddle in X to meet the ball, and set a keyframe (use the K hotkey).

Now, right-click and drag the time slider about 8 frames earlier in time, which will change the time without moving the paddle. Set another keyframe in X. The result should be that the paddle moves to take up position 8 frames before the ball gets there.

Follow this pattern for each time the ball gets back to the paddle. Set the key for the moment the ball strikes the paddle, then right-click and drag and set another key a few frames before that (vary the number of frames between keys from 5 to 15 so that the person with the paddle has a harder time getting to some shots).

Repeat for the other paddle, and playback to examine your work.

Step 2. Add Follow-Through and more Anticipation.

The paddles still look like a bad game of Pong - they just don't have any human-ness to their movement. What's missing? Anticipation and Follow-Through. We'll add that in with some simple rotational keyframes.

As the ball approaches, perhaps 15 to 20 frames before the hit, the paddle should swing back, rotating around local Y, to get ready for the wrist action that drives the ball. It should hang in that cocked position until a few frames before the hit, perhaps 2 to 4 frames, and then should swing rapidly through the position of the hit, and fluidly follow-through to a rotation past the original, unrotated pose.

Select the first paddle, and 15 frames before the ball strikes it (about frame 65), rotate the paddle around Y to cock it ready to strike, and save a key.

Right-click and drag the time slider forward to 3 frames before the hit (about frame 77) and set another rotational keyframe, so that it stays cocked for 12 frames before the hit. This waiting in the cocked position is Anticipation.

About 5 to 8 frames after the hit (perhaps frame 88), rotate the paddle through the ball to the other side, as if the weight and inertia of the paddle caused the wrist to over-rotate. Set another keyframe. This over-rotation is called follow-through.

About 30 frames later, return it to the original, unrotated position, and set a keyframe for rotation, so that it is ready to cock again in anticipation and repeat the whole thing over again and again and again.

Since the Rotation curves have spline interpolation active by default, there will be quite a bit of mushy change that you did not intend. Remove the accidental changes in the rotations by selecting the curves and all the points on them and toggling on the Keys→Zero Slope option. This will keep the rotations from changing when you don't want them to.

Repeat this pattern for each strike of the ball. Remember: 15 frames before the hit, rotate the paddle to a cocked position. Keep it there until a few frames before the hit, then unload on the ball, and rotate through smoothly, ending up approximately 8 frames after the hit with another keyframe in the fully rotated follow-through position. One second later, restore the paddle to the unrotated position so it's ready to cock and fire again. You can vary the timing for each one to make it more human and less precise.

After you have all the keys set for anticipation and follow-through, check your handiwork! It should look pretty good.

Extra Credit: Use the Region tool to change the timing of ALL the curves from stroke to stroke, so that some shots are hard (fast) and others are soft (slower).

Whew! What a tutorial. This process of setting lots and lots of keyframes and then adjusting them to fine-tune the results is pretty much what it's like to be a production animator. Also, remember to add the anticipation and follow-through to all your actions, lest they come across as wooden or "computery".

CONCLUSION

Animation is what Softimage|XSI is all about, and the incredible level of control that XSI provides the animator is what makes it such a fantastic tool. Remember that the Animation Editor is often a quicker way of adding in the keys you need, and the only way to change the ease-in and ease-out of the animation. Don't forget to pay attention to the little things: slope, anticipation, and follow-through.

QUIZ

1. WHICH OPTION BELOW DOESN'T BELONG?
   - a. Break
   - b. Unify
   - c. Cycle

2. HOW MANY ANIMATION CURVES CAN YOU CONTROL IN XSI?
   - a. 154
   - b. 379
   - c. Nobody knows

3. YOU CAN MODIFY MORE THAN ONE KEY ON AN ANIMATION CURVE AT A TIME.
   - a. True
   - b. False
   - c. It depends

4. YOU CAN MODIFY MORE THAN ONE ANIMATION CURVE AT A TIME
   - a. True
   - b. False
   - It depends

5. YOU CAN ADD NEW KEYFRAMES WITHOUT SETTING KEYS IN THE ANIMATION EDITOR
   - a. True
   - b. False

6. IN A CYCLE, EVERY CURVE (LIKE LOCAL X, Y, Z) MUST HAVE THE SAME NUMBER OF KEYFRAMES
   - a. True
   - b. False
   - c. It depends

7. WHO ARE THE SMART ONES?
   - a. Ren and Wallace
   - b. Beavis and Stimpy
   - c. Gromit and Ren

8. WHAT FRAME RATE DOES TV RUN AT IN THE U.S.?
   - a. 24 fps
   - b. 25 fps
   - c. 30fps

9. WHICH COMES BEFORE THE MAIN ACTION?
   - a. Follow-through
   - b. Anticipation
   - c. It depends

10. ON AN ANIMATION CURVE, THE SLOPE REPRESENTS:
    - a. rate of change (speed)
    - b. rate of change squared (acceleration)
    - c. movement in space

11. ON AN ANIMATION CURVE, THE CHANGE IN THE SLOPE OVER TIME (CURVING) REPRESENTS
    - a. rate of change (speed)
    - b. rate of change squared (acceleration)
    - c. movement in space

MESMER

Professional Training for
Digital Artists

Seattle, WA | Berkeley, CA

1.800.237.7311

www.mesmer.com

Learn what the pros know!

Mesmer is <u>the</u> premiere high end training facility for 3D animation and effects software on the West Coast. Our clients include Boeing, Microsoft, EA, Psygnosis, Maxis, LucasArts, PDI and a lot of people just like you!

Intensive Training Classes
Mesmer is an Authorized Training Center (ATC) for Softimage, Alias|Wavefront and Discreet products. That means you get concise, accurate instruction from certified instructors, course material available nowhere else, and certificates of achievement to document your accomplishment.

Corporate Services
Need to bring your team up to speed on an animation tool? Mesmer can help. With short term, professional, certified classroom instruction on site or off site, we can tailor a curriculum for your specific needs, your team, your timeline and your budget.

Distance Learning
Can't make it to a Mesmer Lab? You can learn on the internet! We've built www.mesmer.com into an online learning community access ible all over the world. Log on for ebooks, web tutorials, streaming video and distance learning.

C L A S S   L I S T

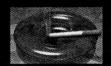

Softimage XSI 101 Essentials

Softimage XSI 201 Animation

Softimage XSI 301 Character Animation

Discreet 3DStudio Max Fundamentals

Discreet 3DStudio Max for Games

Alias|Wavefront Maya Transition

Alias|Wavefront Maya Character Animation

Alias|Wavefront Maya for Games

MESMER

Seattle, WA | Berkeley, CA

1.800.237.7311

www.mesmer.com